# BOY GEORGE
## KARMA

# BOY GEORGE
## KARMA

### MY AUTOBIOGRAPHY

WITH SPENCER BRIGHT

## BLINK
bringing you closer

First published in the UK by Blink Publishing
An imprint of The Zaffre Publishing Group
A Bonnier Books UK company
4th Floor, Victoria House
Bloomsbury Square,
London, WC1B 4DA
England

Owned by Bonnier Books
Sveavägen 56, Stockholm, Sweden

www.facebook.com/blinkpublishing
twitter.com/blinkpublishing

First published in 2023

Hardback ISBN: 978-1-78512-035-0
Signed Hardback ISBN: 978-1-78512-100-5
Trade Paperback ISBN: 978-1-78512-036-7
Ebook ISBN: 978-1-78512-037-4
Audio ISBN: 978-1-78512-038-1

British Library Cataloguing-in-Publication Data:

A catalogue record for this book is available from the British Library.

Printed and bound in Great Britain by Clays Ltd, Elcograf S.p.A.

1 3 5 7 9 10 8 6 4 2

Every reasonable effort has been made to trace copyright-holders of material reproduced in this book, but if any have been inadvertently overlooked the publishers would be glad to hear from them.

Blink Publishing is an imprint of Bonnier Books UK
www.bonnierbooks.co.uk

*To Mum, Dad, Richard, Kevin, Gerald,*
*David and Siobhan x*

# CONTENTS

# PREFACE

I wrote my first book when I was thirty years old. Writing a book in your sixties is quite different from writing one in your thirties. I'm not currently pessimistic but I know this is the latter part of my existence; I'm getting older even though I feel madly young.

What should this book be about? I hope it will be about how I've evolved. I will, of course, throw in some gossip, a handful of dirt, but there won't be any doom dust for anyone that's reading who detests me, Caron, Jon... there are probably more but I've never been good at feuding. I used to be able to hate a little bit, but it never lasted.

I'm not a hateful person. You can keep pushing me to make me hate you but in the end you won't be able to keep it up. The Bette Davis and Joan Crawford feud was fun to watch but who wants to be around that vibration.

Oh, I used to lose my temper at the flick of a tick. Throwing framed pictures and vases down the stairs at my ex-boyfriend, Michael Dunne. Him kicking his foot through my plate-glass front door. Driving my lime-green Cortina into Jon Moss's garage door because he was doing the dirty with a girl in his boudoir. Michael and I remain the best of friends. Jon, well, that's another chapter. Even in the days when I lost my rag a lot, I always got over it quickly. Now I know I don't have to do it. Like you, I am my own centre of control. I am the problem, the solution and every bit between. I am also the vast nothingness that I float in.

I walk down the street talking to myself. I try to reprogram my mind to be more positive. Over the years I've always had these conversations with myself but now I actively direct my mind towards a positive vibration. I chant most days but it's easy to forget. I have to tell myself that ten minutes chanting *Nam Myoho Renge Kyo* is good for my soul. I was once so privy to my internal moods that I spent most of my time overreacting to everything. Now I walk onstage with confidence. I'm light, nervous in a way I never believed I could be. If the sound is bad, I deal with it patiently, but I know it's mostly in my head. Onstage was the place where I always lost my cool. I used to throw mic packs at the monitor guy. I would walk around the stage like I'd been abandoned by Roy and Mikey. I could feel all Jon's mistakes and his negative energy behind me.

It was me against them. With Jon, there has always been unresolved trauma. I think now, though, I could handle him perfectly. He was too late to benefit from my change of mind. My change of heart.

I was told by my friend and teacher, Liliana Bellini, that when something is really important it's best to say less or nothing. It doesn't mean you don't care; it means you are giving yourself space to think something else. How you think often lands harshly as a judgement of yourself or others. Lots of things are not as real as you think. I think having rigid thinking stops you truly enjoying who you are. We are given and then develop a narrative about ourselves that can hold us back or fire us through the roof. Ego can be ugly but also sexy.

I've learned that who you are can change but it should only change for the better. Better is a choice. Meditate and say silently:

*Don't think*
*Don't think*
*Don't think*

You *will* think, of course, but play around with holding silence and try thinking stuff that elevates you. You can only understand your mind if you engage with it. I just stopped writing, closed my eyes and started slowly breathing through my nose. I said 'I am love' a few times. Try doing a mudra with your fingers. Look it up. Slow breathing in and out of the nose is something I started during the pandemic. My friend and sax player James Gardiner-Bateman told me about the Buteyko Method of breathing and I started googling. I watched endless videos by instructor and author Patrick McKeown. The fact that he was Irish seemed important.

I am British but equally Irish. Like that Morrissey song, 'Irish Blood, English Heart'. Irish blood runs through me on both sides and a bit of Welsh too. I grew up in multiracial, eclectic, south-east London in the seventies. It was openly racist, which was accepted by many people. 'Let's all fight for the right to abuse.' Now with the internet we no longer have to accept it and we can tell everyone. Has it changed the world completely? No. I just think we're over-stimulated now. Pop culture is a headless-chicken free-for-all. If you hated me in the eighties and wanted to tell me, you had to write a letter. Now you just tap a keyboard and I know how you feel. Saying that, I don't seem to have trolls. Maybe at times I have been a troll?

> *Who am I today,*
> *Who did I used to be,*
> *Who will I be tomorrow or the next time*
> *that you see me.*

I don't think I was ever horrible, but I'm certainly much nicer than I used to be. I'm nicer to myself and I'm less reactive to behaviour that might have once triggered me. In fact, I think being less reactive has been my life's work for the last ten years. I dip in and out of therapy all the time. People tend to look down at therapy as a self-indulgent pastime. 'Oh, very American,' they say. But I've always said you should get it before you need it. Having someone listening to you impartially and not tell you what you want to hear can be very life-affirming.

The last therapist I worked with, Dr Sarah, was in LA so it *was* very American and we did our sessions over Zoom during the pandemic while I was in London. I inherited Dr Sarah from my manager and friend, Paul Kemsley (PK), and his wife, Dorit. Sharing therapists is very modern.

Dr Sarah told me I was a people-pleaser, which blew my sense of punk. I've always thought of myself as a people-agitator. But when I started to think about it, I realised I don't like arguing as much as I used to. I used to really enjoy arguing and being right, but now I know there is no prize for being right: what's the point?

Growing up, I never really knew that I had the power to change my mind. But being able to change what you think is one of the healthiest things you can do. Right now, you'll know about my war with Jon Moss and, even though I don't like what he's done, I don't hate him or wish him harm.

After all my drug addictions and public car crashes, I started to get a sense of who I really was. My ex-friend, the club promoter (among other things) Philip Sallon said at the time, 'You have all your Irish charm back. You remind me of the boy I met at fifteen.' He said for a long time I'd lost my sense of humour. Sadly, I think the same of him now.

But it's true, I can turn off my anger now in a way I never could before. Though I think I've always been very forgiving because I've been forgiven of many things myself. I sometimes scream out loud when I'm frustrated and Tiffany, my day-to-day manager, might think I'm attacking her but it's never personal. I'm screaming at the universe.

My ability to forgive annoys my family. Especially my sister, Siobhan, but she finds it easy to hate people on my behalf. I don't have a favourite sibling but if I did it would be Siobhan. We are five boys: Richard, Kevin, me, Gerald, David and then Siobhan. All the boys feel protective towards her, she's our baby sister. Mum waited patiently for her and she is a diamond.

David Bowie used to say, 'I'm not a great finger wagger.' And I guess I'm the same. I have morality but it's not overbearing. I joke that I created myself out of cardboard and glitter. And even now I very much think of myself as a work in progress.

Somewhere inside I know hatred is harmful to the self just as kindness is good for one's own soul. I walk down the street and force myself to smile. I google how to be more fun. I want to know everyone's star signs and I judge them accordingly. I have decided that it's a person's moon sign that really tells you the most about them. Morrissey is a Gemini like me, but the Scorpio moon makes him tricky. Like Mick Hucknall, another Gemini with a Scorpio moon.

It's not a condemnation, and I laugh when people ask, 'Is it bad to be a Scorpio?' As a rule, a Scorpio would never ask that question. They are often annoyingly confident. Very attractive. Ask anyone their star sign, wait till they tell you and then roll your eyes. Even those who say they don't believe in it will get flustered. I often get it wrong trying to guess someone's star sign and I'm more willing than ever to accept that most of what I think isn't real. I recently spent twenty minutes at a rave trying to guess a girl's star sign. I was crap. She was a Taurus.

I use star signs as a way of understanding aspects of a person's character. They say that Geminis live in their heads. It's true, I think an awful lot; my mind is a supermodel. I am Gemini sun with a Cancer moon. I also have Taurus and Capricorn. I'm told this configuration stops me from being your typical flighty Gemini. Who would want to be flighty? I've never been the type to look over someone's shoulder to see if anyone more important is in the room. If it's someone handsome, that's another story...

My friend Laura Fireman brought her journalist friend,

Julia Kuttner, to the theatre recently to see the incredible Maureen Lipman as the Holocaust survivor, Rose. I asked Julia, 'What's your star sign?'

She raised her eyebrows and said, 'You tell me, Mystic Meg.'

'You're Cancerian,' I replied, and she was.

I'm surrounded by feisty Cancerian women and her attitude was familiar. Crabs are never shy and their claws are quite sharp. They protect those they love with fierce passion and they carry their home on their backs. They make friends easily but end up with too many friends. They say stuff they don't really mean and then say it again. All hail the double-down queens. It's a good job I love strong women.

I once had a conversation with Professor Brian Cox, the rock and roll physicist, about astrology. It wasn't much of a conversation and his view, without taking a breath, was:'Astrology is utter rubbish, an abomination.' Yet, I see so much truth in it.

I warn you now that star signs will be a recurring theme in this book. PK often tells me I should stop asking everyone's star sign. But it's a fun conversation starter and, in a world where you can no longer ask people where they're from, why not go deeper?

Lots of things happen in our lives and we interpret them based on what we feel about ourselves or the world. Are our lives just one huge projection? I google this stuff a lot, but the internet provides many arguments for and against everything. Only eat cheese. Never eat cheese. The internet is brilliant when it tells you what want to hear. A bit like horoscopes. Everyone loves talking about themselves. Virgo, Capricorn and Taurus are said to be the least inclined to believe in astrology, but Geminis are also meant to be cynical about it. I am deeply cynical, but the windows to optimism are always wide open.

Everything I read about Geminis seems to describe me perfectly. Except the two-faced accusation. No, not two-faced. Only one beautiful face. A Gemini can love or hate you in the same breath. It's why I keep monsters in my life – I can hate that about you but love everything else. If I know why someone is twisted, then I can forgive. But that pain never leaves. It's ingrained in your soul. I think pain always comes from childhood. From what the world told you about yourself.

*Poof*
*Girl*
*Mary*
*Fairy*

At school I was always called a girl. I never considered it an insult. Girls are amazing. I am surrounded by fabulous, gutsy females and I know a feisty woman is a gay's best friend.

I have been accused of being both anti-trans and misogynist. But if I support the trans community, that doesn't mean I don't support women. Geminis don't take sides and I don't need to. I want a safe planet for everyone. I want to get on with my life and let you live yours.

Affirmations are trendy in my life. I use them daily with meditation. Ten minutes when I wake up and ten minutes late at night. People think meditation requires a blank mind. But it's impossible not to think. Try thinking loving stuff instead. Say over and over, 'I am silent,' and follow your breath in and out. Just closing your eyes for a few minutes can be super helpful. A chance to take a break from the relentless thoughts you have about yourself. If the narrative you have about yourself is positive, that's wonderful. If only good thoughts are driving you forward, then God speed.

I've spoken to myself over and over about writing this book. I now have a contract and a deadline.

*I love writing*
*I love writing*
*I love writing*

Walk away from the computer and stretch. Go outside. Think about how amazing and helpful this book could be. What do I want or need to tell you?

Everything and nothing. Let's begin.

# 1

# GLOW UP AND BLOW UP – BEGINNINGS

**G**rowing up, I always felt at war with the world while loving it in the same breath. Being gay in south-east London can make you very defensive. I developed my quick tongue to protect myself and buy time with bullies. They're the thing I hate most in the world. They say bullies are troubled souls but it's hard to care when they're punching you in the face.

At school I sometimes had my brothers to protect me, but they weren't always there at the school gates when I needed them. So I became a quick runner and ended up in the cross-country running team when, really, I was just running home to watch *Junior Showtime*.

I knew I was gay by the time I was about six years old,

and so did everyone else. I said in my first book, *Take It Like a Man*, that other kids have an unnerving ability to poke you where it hurts. At six, you don't fully understand what it means to be gay. At the time, I was called highly-strung and theatrical. I collected broken jewellery and sang show tunes on the doorstep with my gaggle of girlfriends. All my friends were female. Mouthy, tough girls who would punch boys who picked on me and were always getting into trouble at school.

'Would George O'Dowd, Tina Parmenter and Susan Sledge report to the headmaster's office immediately.'

Every day I went to school knowing I was going to get into trouble. I was late, I was rude, I was caned. I spent hours in detention and the only lesson I enjoyed was Art and, weirdly, Religious Education (RE) because we were encouraged to debate and at that time I definitely believed in God – we even had the same initials.

Even though I was bullied for being effeminate and pretty, I never really wished I was straight even at the youngest of ages. Some people have a calling for religion, I had a calling for queerness. Of course, I knew I had to keep it quiet. The worst thing you could be at school was a poofter. And even the teachers were homophobic. My gym teacher, Mr McIntyre, would shout, 'Pick your legs up, lassie.' And every time I walked into a classroom some twat would shout, 'Ooh, shut that door,' which was one of the catchphrases of camp comedian Larry Grayson. I was called John Inman, Dick Emery, Stanley Baxter, Quentin Crisp, Kenny Everett. See, I was already a showbiz legend before the age of eleven years old.

I was eleven and a half when I saw David Bowie as Ziggy Stardust at Lewisham Odeon on May 24th, 1973 and I went to that gig on my own. Even having no one to go with didn't put me off. I borrowed my older brother Richard's clothes: split-knee loons and a scoop-necked T-shirt covered in psychedelic mushrooms topped off with an embroidered Indian jacket. I thought I looked the bee's knees until I came face to face with older Bowie fans dressed immaculately with their very own Angie Bowies on their arms. Proper Bowie fans loved Angie even though she fell out of favour with David. I used to sit outside Bowie's house in Beckenham when I was ten years old and one beautiful Sunday morning Angie opened the window and said, 'Would you all just fuck off.' We were delighted. Back then fans knew their place. When I had dinner with David Bowie and Iman in New York some decades later, he said, 'Tell the story about when Angie told you to fuck off.' I probably padded it out quite a bit and when I finished David said, 'That's probably the most interesting thing Angie ever said.' Bitchy.

Most of the musicians I know had their lights turned on by Ziggy Stardust. Everyone talks about the moment when

Bowie dropped to his knees and gave Mick Ronson's guitar fellatio. Even now, looking back at that Ziggy Stardust concert I still feel the same excitement. Ziggy was so other worldly, it had no time or place. Weeks after I saw Ziggy in Lewisham, Bowie killed him off at the Hammersmith Odeon (it was July 3rd). I heard it on the radio. All the fans were screaming, 'No, David, no.' His words echoing, 'Not only is it the last night of the tour, but it's the last show that we'll ever do.' Not even the band knew, which was terrible. Imagine doing that to Culture Club. I might (LOL).

My Auntie Jan had attempted to give me a Ziggy Stardust haircut but, having thin hair, it just fell flat on my head and I looked like Dave Hill from Slade, which I wasn't actually that upset about because I loved Slade – especially Dave Hill because he was the most outrageous. He had hair like a skinhead girl, a bit pudding bowl and mullet. I went to loads of concerts at Lewisham Odeon and I was indiscriminate. All music was exciting to me. It was the world I wanted to be part of. I saw Chuck Berry, Rod Stewart and the Faces, Medicine Head, Blackfoot Sue, Lieutenant Pigeon and 10cc, and God knows who else. When I went into the local record shop after school, I would listen to records based on the sleeve. Most of the time I had no money to buy anything but I kept going into the listening booths. One of the first albums I bought with my pocket money was T. Rex's, *Tanks*, which had Marc Bolan showing a nipple while seated behind a toy tank. Even to my naive twelve-year-old mind I knew Marc was being suggestive. Mum looked at the sleeve, shook her head and rolled her eyes. It was the seventies and I was growing up queer in the 'spare us the details' culture.

Even when my family finally realised I was a homosexual – such a weirdly technical term – there was a sense that I should get on with my gay business over there in the corner and not talk about it. That was never going to work for me. My brothers brought girls home and they were welcomed into the family, which I thought was unfair. I thought to myself, 'When I do get a boyfriend (optimistic), I will be bringing him home.' The truth is the only person I brought home was a punk straight mate who only wanted to get it on after several snakebites. We were at it one night on the sofa and my mum opened the door and said, 'What's going in here?' as I plummeted off the sofa onto the floor.

'Nothing.'

'Make sure of it.'

I was almost sixteen at the time and, when it came to boys, I had no idea what I was doing. I had a boyfriend called Lenny for a while, but I was too outrageous for him. At that age I wanted everyone to deal with it and accept everything I was.

Being the middle queer child in a London Irish family was less of a big deal than you might think, though. My dad announced my queerness to my brothers in his Bedford van. Turning down the radio he said, 'You know your brother's a bit funny.'

My brother David chipped in, 'Funny peculiar or funny ha ha?'

Richard corrected Dad: 'You mean he's a poofter.'

I think Dad turned the radio back up at that point.

Dad was a bloke's bloke but also a contradiction. Once he realised I *was* actually a poofter, he would try to make me feel better by telling me he wore pink shirts in the sixties. Telling me, 'I knew a gay bloke once. He never said he was gay but everyone knew it. Lovely bloke. I had no problem with him.'

My dad was a boxing fanatic and tried desperately to get me involved to toughen me up. But I preferred going with my dad to the dog track in White City. I loved being in the company of adults rather than kids. While dad was gambling, I would stuff my face with chocolate, chips and crisps, and drink Coca-Cola from a glass bottle (vintage).

My dad could never be alone. He would always ask one of us to ride with him in his builder's van while he visited his various building sites, which always seemed to be the other side of the Blackwall Tunnel. We would stop in various cafés to have cups of tea and bacon sandwiches.

Everyone knew my dad and loved him. Outside of the house he was charm personified. Inside, though, he was a

Jekyll with nothing to hide. He always seemed to be in a bad mood and exploded over the stupidest things.

'I can't find a clean hankie.'

'Get out of my chair.'

'Make me a cup of tea.'

It's too easy to portray my dad as a Paddy thug. He could be brutal but he was also charismatic. He treated my mum very badly, but in a weird way they loved each other. Mum was definitely committed to the idea of marriage and family. A bit of a martyr to the cause. She tried so hard to make it work, to make the house beautiful, but my dad's paint tins, sacks of concrete and jealousy made it impossible. If Mum put on a nice dress, she was having an affair. A dress or a skirt was too short. A jumper too figure hugging. Mum had great style but she never got to fully realise it in Dad's company. She was an incredible seamstress and was always sewing curtains or dresses for everyone, especially my little sister Siobhan who was thrust into puffball ribbon nightmares. Mum couldn't dress up so customised Siobhan into her own personal dolly. It was also because she was so delighted to get a little girl after four boys and doted on Siobhan, who sadly turned out to be a bit of a tomboy.

Mum and Dad were born on the same day, different years, and met on their birthday. Mum was working in a pub in Woolwich with my dad's sister, May. Dad walked in in his army uniform and they got talking. One of Mum's favourite songs was 'Secret Lover' by Doris Day, which is the most romantic, optimistic song you could ever hear. I think about that moment when Mum met Dad and he fell in love with her effervescent charm. That moment must have been so beautiful and full of potential. Dad had the potential to be such an amazing human being, but that temper, that temper. Mum was no pushover, though. Dad's mother would say to Mum every time he hit her, 'Why do you make him angry? Why do you have to answer him back?' Knowing Mum as I do now, she would never have accepted that but still signed up for a life of being devalued.

It's sad to remember those times. When Mum was hurt, she filled the house with sadness. You would come home from school and almost feel the pain through the front door. Mum would be in her dressing gown and the milk would still be on the doorstep. I would say to Mum, 'Why do you let him treat you like that, why don't we leave?' The few times Mum did leave and went to her mother's in Birmingham, she was sent back the following day.

'You can't keep a father away from his children.'

Violence in marriage was accepted back then, it seemed. Unless it was really bad, it was never discussed. I saw some terrible things. I came home from school one day and Mum was under the table screaming up at Dad, who was holding a knife. I went so crazy it startled even him and he backed off. He insisted he was making a sandwich; he wasn't pointing the knife at Mum. But why was she under the table? It's stayed with me all these years. Those rage-filled moments can easily end in tragedy.

Mum took an overdose once and I kept her awake, which was the most terrifying thing I went through as a kid. So traumatic I actually thought I'd made it up, until I read Mum's book, *Cry Salty Tears*, back in 2007 and it was confirmed. I know it was a cry for help. Mum would never have left us. Sadly, even that incident didn't change my father.

I don't want to paint a picture of my father as a horrible, nasty human being because he wasn't. He was handsome and intelligent, had beautiful handwriting and could sing a gorgeous version of 'Danny Boy'. He wasn't racist or bigoted and wouldn't have stolen goods in the house. He helped so many people financially – except Mum – but the rest he gambled. Often on a Friday night, fraught wives would turn up because he hadn't paid their husband. Mum was often in the same boat, having to go to the butcher for scrag ends. When Dad was lucky on the horses or the dogs everyone was smiling – except Mum because she knew she was going to always find betting slips in his trousers.

I had a strong sense of what was going on with Mum and Dad from an early age, though. I listened at doors and took in everything that was said, eventually asking Mum straight out, 'What are the skeletons in the closet?'

'Where'd you hear that?' she said.

'Dad says it all the time. What does he mean?'

After lots of tears Mum told me, 'Richard has a different dad.'

So, Dad had taken on Richard, but kept on reminding Mum whenever he got angry. I, like my brothers, didn't care. King Richard was still our brother. But a lot of things suddenly made sense.

Richard had his own room with a record player, headphones and lots of cool albums. Lots of clothes I coveted too and did wear sometimes without asking. I heard David Bowie, Alice Cooper and Rod Stewart through the wrong side of my brother's bedroom door. My older brother told me, 'This is what you should be into, but you probably won't get it.' I got it all right. I just didn't tell him I fancied all his friends.

I thought my brother was a genius when I heard the haunting strains of Bowie's 'After All' floating through his locked bedroom door. It turns out those songs were meant for me.

Richard embraced early Bowie but passed Ziggy Stardust to me and moved onto Rod Stewart and the Faces and Alice Cooper. When he went out I was straight into his bedroom and I would play his records till he came back and threw me out. Alice Cooper was exciting and dangerous and when he came to Lewisham Odeon there were priests and nuns outside trying to stop people from going in. The press was full of his evil snake-waving, baby-killing guillotine antics. I was gutted I couldn't go. I wasn't even allowed out to wait at the stage door this time. Me and girlfriends loved singing 'Schools Out' in the playground but 'Elected' was my favourite. I remember seeing the video on *Top of The Pops* with Alice in a Rolls-Royce and a white suit, Dad lifting his paper saying, 'Look at the state of that'. Alice was a rock and roll bad boy but Bowie had a special message for boys like me. He was singing about queers and the boys at school had told me that's what I was. I listened intently to every word and learnt each song perfectly so I could sing along at the top of my voice, imagining that I was Bowie and sometimes that I was Rod.

I won't pretend that I only liked cool people because I loved John Denver and could be found whirling around in the dark to 'Those Were The Days' by Mary Hopkin. I liked Abba but not to the extent that some poofs do. I was obsessed with voices and would imitate Bryan Ferry from Roxy Music or try to sing like Marlene Dietrich who uses a similar vibrato to Bryan. I walked the streets with a mini battery-operated transistor radio to my ear and sang along to the Sunday chart rundown. I rummaged through the boxes of records that Dad brought home from houses he had cleared to decorate. Sometimes he brought back mad clothes or a top hat but they were snatched away before I could wear them.

My glamorous and stunning Auntie Josie sent up a box of her old clothes for Mum and Mum said, 'Who does she think I am? I wouldn't wear these.' 'I would,' I thought as a lurex catsuit was pulled from the box. Mum let me try it on but when I went to walk out the front door dad shouted, 'Get back in here now and get that thing off.'

In those boxes of records I found many other sounds that blew my mind. Dirty blues from the thirties with saucy songs like 'My Handy Man' by Ethel Waters or 'Need a Little Sugar in my Bowl' by Bessie Smith. My love of jazz started young and it sat well with Bowie and Bolan. Years later I discovered that Marc Bolan had modelled his vibrato on Bessie Smith. He exaggerated his sound after playing her records at the wrong speed. If you love music you don't take sides. 'Rocky Mountain Way' by Joe Walsh is still one of my favourite headbangers. Music. I love it all.

David and Marc changed the dialogue of pop music in the seventies. Who else but Bolan would write 'I had a car, it was old, it was kind, I gave it my mind and it disappeared.' Who else but Bowie would write a song like 'Moonage Day-dream' by cutting up words and shuffling them to create a narrative. It has taken me years to realise how simple the songwriting process is. You just need some words and a reason to say them.

I got into Bob Dylan after hearing Bowie sing about him on his album *Hunky Dory*. When my schoolfriend

Tracie Carter played me 'Hurricane' from the album *Desire*, I discovered new ideas about songwriting. For me, Bob Dylan is a master of lyrics and and he can wound with a simple line.

The fan in me was mesmerised and I bought into the concept of genius. The music industry tries to convince us that only a handful of artists have the touch. Maybe they need that narrative to maintain control over something that I have now personally transcended.

✳ ✳ ✳

My first kiss was with a girl at my brother's 18th birthday that Mum let him have at the house. There were giant cans of Watneys Party Seven. There might have been vol-au-vents. Who doesn't love a mushroom vol-au-vent? Canapes have got so poncey. What's wrong with a bit of pineapple and cheddar? What about some mincing pies?

But, like I said, I knew I was gay even then. Being gay isn't always a collective experience. When I first went to gay clubs as a teenager, I thought I was going to be embraced and carried on shoulders through the streets but there was so much self-loathing in gay culture at that point. Traditional gay men dressed in checked shirts and Levi's, looking like plumbers and lumberjacks. As far as they were concerned, they had won the right to be normal and people like me were spoiling their bid for assimilation. Drag queens were ridiculed as attention seekers. I heard people say, 'If it wasn't for people like you, we'd be accepted.' For me the drag queens and effeminate gays cut out the small talk.

There are gay men who detest the effeminate, even to this day. I would argue that everything butch or camp is an affectation, and don't get me started on the Queen's English. Of course, some queens overdo it and you wish you could find their off button. Some straight guys try too hard too. That only makes me love them more.

When I saw John Hurt portraying Quentin Crisp in the TV movie *The Naked Civil Servant* in 1975, it was a revelation. I had no idea that people like Quentin Crisp, Oscar Wilde or Alan Turing existed before Bowie and Marc Bolan. OK, they weren't gay, but they were dandies and dandies teeter on the edge of gay. Look at Harry Styles. All those people were part of the daisy chain of change.

Sometimes the most political act is to be yourself and it can take years to really decide who you are. My generation were the beneficiaries of the suffering of these and so many others. It was legal to be queer by the time I was six and, even though we still lived in the 'spare us the details' era, there was less to fear.

Queer people came together in their own spaces, but you could still get beaten up if you were too obvious or mincing down the wrong street. Meeting Philip Sallon was a revelation. He was a mouthy Jewish queer with no off button. He got changed in the back of taxi cabs between nightclubs and apologised for nothing. Even though punk was a straight movement, it had civil disobedience at its roots. It wasn't cool to be uptight. No one cared what you were unless they were morons.

As a kid I went to Sunday School in one of Mum's hats. My friend Michael's mum called my mother and said, 'Do you know what he's wearing?'

'I do,' she said, defiantly.

Mum was talking to a woman in Woolwich market who told her about some sight she'd seen going into the train station.

'It had a green face and hair sticking up on end like it had put its finger in the plug socket.'

'Oh dear,' Mum said, knowing full well it was me.

Some people are born to be weird. People say I was brave to dress the way I did as a kid and it certainly made life more difficult. When you're a teenager you just don't compromise. Like Quentin Crisp, I learnt to walk fast and avoid eye contact. On the bus I would duck down in certain areas like Peckham in case 'Casuals' got on the bus to attack me. Once, I was kicked in the face on the back of a bus. I had blood running down my face and no one helped me. When I left the house Mum would say to Dad, 'Look at him, Jerry, look what he's wearing'. Dad would lower his newspaper and say, 'Up to him if he wants to get beat-up.'

Living in south-east London meant I was always running from thugs. Sometimes even my own brothers would cross the road when they saw me coming. I got pulled over by the police almost daily. I would often walk back to Woolwich from West End nightclubs dressed in punk bondage clothes and studded leather jackets. The police would stop me because I looked weird. Things only got worse when I told them my name. The O'Dowds were legendary. My brother Richard was arrested quite often as a teenager for breaking into local shops and he even stole lead from the local school roof.

I came across idiots at times, but it was casuals, skinheads or Teddy Boys who were the most trouble. In the seventies there was zero political correctness and everyone was abused as standard. The language used on TV and in the media would curdle the culottes of snowflakes. Homophobic and racist language was common and accepted. I knew it was wrong, but I was also a target.

Punk fused with reggae and we came together against racism. Outsider queers joined the punky reggae party, and it was a great time to be a teenager. I wore my 'Bored Teenager' badge with pride. I went on my first Gay Pride march in the late seventies from outside Lewisham Odeon. Two of my brothers were on the other side of the road jeering.

We had the local National Front headquarters in Welling just down the hill from where we lived in Shooters Hill. I detested those Nazis because so many of my musical heroes were black. I would play 'Inglan is a Bitch' by Linton Kwesi Johnson out the bedroom window followed by 'Glad to Be Gay' by Tom Robinson. I played Irish rebel songs too. Being part-Irish played a huge part in feeling an outsider. Having the name O'Dowd in the seventies set you up for IRA bombing jokes. How thrilled I was to discover my uncle Thomas Byrne was an Irish freedom fighter. I think it's safe to assume that we carry the pain and rebellion of our ancestors in our DNA.

I wish people were more tolerant, especially now when it's considered uncool to be intolerant. Sometimes it feels like we're going backwards and I'm hearing the same arguments I heard in the seventies. I guess these days there's more noise in general. If you wanted to be a hater in the past you had to write a letter to the newspapers. Now you can just push a button and hate with speed. The collective sense of humour has changed too. People don't tell jokes anymore, even in bands. I had friends who used to ring me to tell me funny jokes. That never happens now. It feels like people are at each other's throats even though the superficial message is to 'be nice'. I want to say I'm ahead of them because I actually work really hard at being nicer. But there's a new language at play.

Most of the arguments you need to stop are with yourself. I'm not defined by my sexuality but I'm also happy with what I am. For me, sexuality is much more fluid than people admit. Instead of having more words for things, I'd rather have less. You can give what you are a new name, but you are still defining yourself in rigid terms. I recently ran into trouble when I made a joke about pronouns. I said, 'When you come to my house leave your pronouns at the door'. I meant I wouldn't judge you, however you look, however you describe yourself. I call myself Boy George. One of my best friends, Peter Robinson, became Marilyn and I was obsessed with Poly Styrene and Ari Up so I'm not really hung up on identity. As Poly Styrene sang, 'Identity is a crisis, can't you see.'

If I was sixteen years old today, I would totally use the new language. I resisted it briefly because I've always wanted to be the only queer in the world, (LOL). Sometimes in being blindly liberal you end up as a contradiction of yourself by creating another rigid narrative.

I don't want anything too rigid. There's nothing to let go of and nothing to insist on. I practice Nicheren Buddhism now and I chant Nam-myoho-renge-kyo and an eight minute prayer in ancient Japanese which I have memorised. Chanting Nam Myoho Renge Kyo is about emptying your mind and considering what your heart desires. Not thinking is not an option for a human being. We are our thinking.

I started practising The Three Principles a few years ago, which has nothing to do with Buddhism but perhaps everything to do with it. Most of our thinking, even when we are being deeply spiritual, is over complicated.

The Three Principles are mind, thought and consciousness. Life happens through us, not to us. We are able, with practice, to create space in our thinking and communication. Most of what we think is a projection and at this point in my life I look back and think, 'Is that what really happened?' Having already written an autobiography, I do have a totally different perspective on my past. Some things have obviously not changed – the day I was born, June 14th, the same day as Donald Trump, Che Guevara, Paul O'Grady, Alan Carr and Chrissy Iley – but some of the things I wrote in my first book I would never think or even say now.

Being a Gemini doesn't make me two-faced like everyone says, but it does put me in two minds at the same time. Like I said, I love and hate you in the same breath and, in fact, I do (joke). I can dislike certain things about a person but love their music, their sense of humour, their looks, their hat, their tattoos but find them utterly repugnant as a person and yet still hang out with them. I did a painting recently called 'Everyone I've Ever Loved Is Deeply Flawed'. I don't hate people because they are awful if they have some redeeming qualities. Shallow people can be fun on a night out as long as you bring a social ladder. I love kind, intelligent, sweet people too but I don't judge in the way some people do. One of my friends is always telling me she hates people and then I see them having lunch. I don't take sides, and when something or someone is truly awful, I am fully aware of it. Some morality is self-explanatory and a lot of other stuff is completely unnecessary. Get annoyed about things that matter but who am I to say what matters?

*Everyone screaming for attention/*
*But what if your cause barely gets a mention*

One thing I got from my father is the ability to let things go. I'm not against anybody for any reason, even people that hate me, who I frankly don't understand at all. I can safely say there's no one I hate. And some of the people that hate me will be very surprised I say this. The trouble is Dad would throw the table up in the air and no one would eat. Then he'd say, 'Put the kettle on,' and give you a hug. When he was over it, *you* had to be over it. I have been guilty of that myself. Because I'm resilient and forgiving I expect other people to be the same. And I also know nobody has to accept your apology. What you do with your own pain is your business. It doesn't have to be pain, though. Through non-reaction I can stop myself doing things that could have got me sectioned. These stories are endless. But now I want to laugh more. I used to get myself wound up before a gig, about everything. I wasn't loose. I was in control of nothing. I actually tell myself now, 'I'm going to be amazing,' before I go on stage. Not that I am amazing, although I am and so are you. I guess I have that British thing where my ego is raging but I also know I'm a ragbag from Eltham. Seriously though, it's good to have conversations with yourself and do affirmations, tapping in positivity.

I am healthy
I am happy
I am confident
I am strong
I wake up motivated and energised
I love and approve of myself

Your subconscious is running a narrative of who you are, a movie that is running all the time that you never check. So tapping pulse points on your body and telling yourself good things feels like a way of talking to your subconscious mind. The narrative you have of yourself based on what you were taught, how your parents loved, how you were loved, boyfriends, girlfriends, teachers, authority, school hell (Help!) is riddled with misinformation.

The boys in Culture Club have reminded me over the years that I was no one before I met them. And, of course, that's not true. I was born to be who I am. A great big, fabulous queer contradiction. When you lose it, which does happen, and go back to being that person they know, they will tell you, 'See, you haven't changed.' But I think it's about your ability to pull yourself back from those moments. You will always think, you will always be human. Learning what you can do with that thinking and learning that there are always other thoughts within thoughts that you can choose as well, there's a whole lot of space between happy and sad. There will always be people you allow to antagonise you: Joan Moist, Feelip Salome, Empty Kinky (They'll make sense later). There are many. But because I can love and hate people, they can never remain enemies. I focus on what I like about them, even if it's only a pair of shoes or a certain lipstick. It doesn't take much to satisfy me.

dislocated my ankle jumping
ut of the first-floor window.
he police were called and

2

# LIVE AT THE DISCO

**I**'d originally left home to move to Walsall
to live with Martin Degville. I met him in Bournemouth
one Bank Holiday in 1977. Hordes of punks would take
coaches or trains to seaside towns and roam around looking
cool and causing trouble. We were barred from most pubs,
so we walked up and down the promenade and went to the
fairground. Teddy Boys and mods would come too and there
would be endless fights, but I ran with the girls and stayed
away from the fighting. I walked up to Martin and told him
he looked amazing. He was wearing stiletto heels and had a
massive bleached quiff and huge padded shoulders. He gave
me his number and some weeks later when I visited my Auntie
Teresa in Ladywood, I met up with him and his fellow freaks.
They were all so much friendlier than the London equivalent.

In Spring 1979, when I was seventeen years old, I had

what was to become one of many fallouts with Philip. I'd been having an affair with someone who claimed he was straight that nearly ended in violence and I felt threatened. I wanted to leave London and Martin offered me a room and a job working on his clothes stall. We shared a passion for music and dressing up though we both had very different personalities. He was cool and alien and could be a bit snotty. I was bitchy but I would talk to everyone. We both thought we were stars.

Martin didn't pay me much at the stall and we often rowed about money. In Autumn 1979 he opened Degville's Dispensary at Kensington Market in London. We both started to spend more time in London and we drifted apart. I was soon back in with Philip and over my Midlands experience.

I haven't spoken to Martin in years, but I consider him to be an important figure in my life. I once took him to Mum's for Christmas and he opened a box of chocolates from under the tree. Mum said, 'Jaysus, your friend must have been starving.' I reckon he was getting me back for pinching money from his cash box under the floorboards in Walsall. I did help myself to a few pounds now and then but I justified it as topping up my wages working on his concession in the Bull Ring Centre in Birmingham. Martin made bright stretch Lycra tube dresses and I convinced people to buy them.

When I moved back to London I saw him at a party but we weren't friendly. Martin ended up getting a huge record deal with Sigue Sigue Sputnik, the band he formed with Tony James and Neil X. The hype was as big as Martin's mohican. Their first single, 'Love Missile F1-11' was everything and I still play it now. The headline in *Number One* magazine may have sealed his fate though: 'I Hate All Women'. It was controversial, like a line from a John Waters anti-hero, because everyone knows pop music is about girls. Talk about 'Shoot it up.' I know Bowie did a cover of 'Love Missile' though, which Martin must have loved. What a compliment and what a brilliant song.

I wrote to my friend Hilda in London asking if I could live there until I found a squat. I met Hilda at Billy's in 1978. Her real name was Jackie but I called her Hilda because she looked like one. She shared her tiny room with a woman called Myra – whose real name was Sheila – who I knew from Blackheath near where I grew up. Philip named her Myra because she had a bleached beehive that made her resemble sixties murderess Myra Hindley.

It soon became apparent that sharing a tiny room with Hilda and Myra was never going to work, even in the short-term intended. But I was determined not to go back to Mum and Dad.

At first we all got on well. I became close to Hilda too but she and Myra needed more space. Late one night we scoured the streets for vacant properties. Squatting was a viable alternative to renting in the seventies and eighties until the law changed. Many a creative was able to develop their art without the stress of forced labour and rent.

We found a flat in a council block over the road in Kentish Town but it was padlocked like a fortress. So I borrowed a few screwdrivers and a crowbar from Dad's tool kit and we were in. The décor was evil. I claimed the living room and covered the walls with gay porn and cut-up headlines, shoving my mattress in the corner.

While we were out one day, Mum and Dad came by with supplies and left a note:

'Nice wallpaper. Love you, son.'

Mum hated me living rough and wanted me home.

It wasn't long before the allure of a new squat proved irresistible to our friends. Soon Myra's old flatmate Andy Polaris, later a pop star himself, came with his superb record collection and poetry.

Marilyn couldn't keep away either and eventually *wouldn't* keep away, making it known that life in Borehamwood was hideous. Aware there was a spare room she turned up unannounced and broke in with her belongings in plastic bags.

Having Marilyn there was fun until the neighbour smashed a hole in the front door with an axe. He had seen Marilyn prancing up and down the landing in full leopard skin splendour. Marilyn was stunning at the time and most straight men 'thought he was a bird'. Unlike me, he was muscular and taut. He didn't wear false breasts but he wore dresses that hugged every inch of him.

The butch guy next door would chat to Marilyn all the time when she was in drag. But one fateful day he saw her as a boy. That night, inebriated, he came to attack us with an axe. We had to jump out the window. He had kids and apparently wanted to protect them by trying to kill us. I dislocated my ankle jumping out of the first floor window. But when the police were called they were totally unsympathetic.

'If you stay here, we can't protect you.'

That night we had to find somewhere else to live. Luckily, I had stored some of my dad's tools for that very purpose. We had a crowbar and a screwdriver; very useful when you're squatting. We had already scouted a new location in a block of flats a couple of streets away. We broke in and took up residence, much to the horror of the elderly residents. On the staircase you could smell over-cooked mince and murdered vegetables. At least we were safe.

After living there for a few months, we moved to Great Titchfield Street off Warren Street on the edge of the West End. The squats in Warren Street were legendary and we needed to be part of that scene; characters like Stephen Linard, Kim Bowen, Leslie and Jane Chilkes, Lee Sheldrick, David Holah and the emerging milliner Stephen Jones. The squat spread out from Warren Street to Euston Road and Barry the Rat lived in a shopfront. Barry slept with everyone, except me. I don't know what I did wrong because I was well up for it. He was also seeing a young Tracey Emin who I only knew then as Tracey from Margate.

There were massive parties at the Warren Street squat with lots of speed and acid. There was heroin, too. I didn't really do drugs at the time but one beautiful Japanese girl called Mitsu overdosed and died there. Her mother used to stand in the shop doorway on Euston Road and cry out her name. They say that Iggy Pop wrote 'China Girl' about Mitsu. I knew her very well and loved her – she definitely deserved a song. The morning we found out she died we all met in the café across the road. Everyone was devastated and it wasn't long before the squat imploded.

Stephen Jones had his workshop there and Kim Bowen was his muse. Kim was a fashion student and wannabe stylist and would ooze around in Stephen's creations. He made me a few amazing hats, like my Boudicca helmet made of silver leather and dashing white plumes. I didn't like Kim to start with; I thought she looked down her nose at us, but I soon realised she was just trying to live up to Stephen's hats. When our friend Jeremy Healy started sleeping with her, I was furious. But it was because of their love affair that we were no longer outcasts at the Warren Street squat.

The first time I heard Nina Simone was in Kim's bedroom. She had white muslin drapes hanging in the windows and around the bed like she was Mata Hari. Hearing Nina

Simone sing 'Everything Must Change' while Kim's drapes floated in the breeze is a moment I'll never forget.

Jeremy Healy and Kim Bowen fell madly in love. They held a dinner in the PX shop that both myself and Philip weren't invited to. I accepted my rebuff with grace but Philip pushed his way in and kept shouting at Jeremy, 'Why are you ignoring me, you fucking upstart.' Jeremy said it was really embarrassing, but that was clearly Philip's intention.

There were times when I was ostracised from fabulous events but being friends with Philip meant we weren't going to take it. You had to make even more effort with your outfit and eclipse the fuckers at their own game but it was very rare that you got turned away from anything if you looked fabulous. If the cameras started flashing when you arrived, no one would dare turn you away but it did happen from time to time. We were delighted if we got mentioned in a society column. Steve Strange got the most mentions because, as Philip said, 'He would turn up to the opening of my legs.'

It was a world of emerging everything: parties on the tube, clubs closing before they opened, pub crawls, and fashion shows. Steve Strange was wearing outfits made in shot taffeta by Judith Frankland. It was Judith who got my job in the cloakrooms at Hell and Blitz after I got fired for stealing. So I went back the next week and stole all her takings, running off with a massive handbag full of change.

I hid it wrapped in bin liners in the toilet cistern. A lynch mob of clubbers arrived at the squat.

'We know it was you. Give it back.'

I was in a kimono and had already removed my make-up for bed. I acted dumb. No one believed me but I got away with it. But I was banned from Hell and a few other clubs. I felt so guilty that the next morning I took the entire squat for breakfast at Sam's caff. It's amazing how people lose their conscience for a bacon sandwich. I bought make-up with the leftover money and even gave some change to beggars. I justified my behaviour by sharing the spoils.

The Warren Street squat was a disused Georgian town-house with wooden floors and no electricity. After Mitsu's tragic death people started moving out. Some people got council flats and some went home to mother. A bunch of us stayed in the squat in Great Titchfield Street and a new set of dreamers moved in around us. Photographer Mark Lebon lived at the end of the street and would invite us in for glamorous photo sessions. His brother James was a celebrated hairdresser with his own shop, CUTS in Soho. He worked on fashion shoots and with emerging bands, and would go on to cut everyone's hair from David Bowie to Alexander McQueen. Fashion was everywhere. One day one of the squats caught fire and we were all outside being photographed.

I moved from Great Titchfield Street round the corner to Carburton Street and a bunch of new people occupied the shop on the corner. Artist Grayson Perry lived there with his then-girlfriend Jennifer Binnie. My friend Christine and Jennifer Binnie would perform cabaret shows in the disused squatted shop. There was an old typewriter and I used to bash out bitchy poems about everyone, possibly honing my future lyrical skills. One day Grayson was climbing into a pair of tights. Marilyn said, 'You look like you've done that before' and Grayson blushed. It was a long time before he became his alter-ego, Claire. I would never have known it was the same person had Grayson not told me himself. I love his art.

I was living in Carburton Street when Steve Strange turned up at the squat one night in a black taxi with his girlfriend, Scottish Jenny and Kirk Brandon. Steve looked amazing, dressed head to toe in Melissa Caplan with completely black contact lenses. I know for a fact he turned up to show off his new look. I had to quickly pull an outfit together and join them in the pub over the road. After the pub we ended up at the Blitz. Steve got us a table, free food and free drinks, and we spent the night talking. A week later Kirk turned up at the Blitz on his own and hung out with me in the cloakroom. Kirk became a big part of my life but he sued me about comments I made about our relationship in my first book. He lost, by the way, but I'm not out for revenge so won't comment further here. You can go and read about it elsewhere if you want to.

I was dressed as a nun that night. It was a costume

from a show I was rehearsing with Marilyn. We had been recruited by a wannabe producer for a cabaret in the South of France and were rehearsing in Heaven nightclub during the day. Marilyn appeared from a coffin dressed as Marilyn Monroe singing 'Diamonds Are a Girl's Best Friend'. I did a performance as Marc Bolan and another as Boudicca, which is why Stephen Jones made me the headdress. I thought this was going to be my big break. We were going to France and were going to make some money and possibly become massive superstars. Marilyn was iffy about the whole thing. He had met a man called John, a posh boy whose family had a stately home in Scotland. This was an easier gig for Marilyn and on a whim he said, 'I'm not going to France,' and moved into John's flat in Knightsbridge – much to the horror of John's mother. I was furious that Marilyn didn't want to go to France and without him there was no show. After I found out we weren't going, I shoved all my costumes into a suitcase and took them back to the squat. The producer turned up one afternoon to see if he could get them back and, again I played innocent. A few days later I wore the nun's outfit to the Blitz. I took the view that who else was going to wear them? I had earned those clothes, rehearsing for weeks and I hadn't been paid. The good news is I had upgraded my wardrobe in one fell swoop.

Eventually the council took action to get us out of the squats. I went to the High Court with a green face for my eviction hearing. The court lawyer told me, 'If you go into court like that, you'll be chucked out of the flat today. Leave it with me and I'll get you six months.'

I have so many fun memories of living in Carburton Street and it was sad to leave. For a while Marilyn lived in the basement with John after his mother banned them from Knightsbridge. I already knew we were being evicted by that point but the basement was a no-go area full of rubbish so I said to Marilyn, 'You clear it, you can have it.' It was John who did the clearing and in they moved. John had a sports car which Marilyn would drive and park outside the squat. It was comical that Marilyn had lured a blue blood into the catacombs of Carburton Street.

Marilyn was like a cat. He would disappear with a bunch of cool friends that he didn't want me to know, characters like make-up artists Stevie Hughes and photographer Johnny Rozsa. He's always kept his friends separate. And he was obsessed with John. The fights were endless. I was always called to mop up the tears. One afternoon Marilyn invited me to Johnny Rozsa's flat in Belsize Park and a young Susan Sarandon was there. Johnny took photos of me topless with a bunch of net wrapped around my shoulders. Even on a boring Sunday I was in full war paint with my hair backcombed and hairsprayed to look like I was hanging upside down. The shots were incredible. There's one of Marilyn from that shoot in the National Portrait Gallery collection.

It seemed like everyone in fashion or the arts was connected at the time. There were obvious cliques and some people looked down on you if you hadn't been to fashion or art college. But if you spent long enough getting spruced up you could easily eclipse the lot of them – and on a shoestring. My imagination and belligerence took over. I sometimes spent an entire day getting ready to go out. I had no money except for a few quid I made doing the windows for a funky shop called Street Theatre in Old Compton Street, Soho. I also got dole money from the Government, which was a life saver for any freak. It wasn't much and they constantly tried to get you to work as a pot washer or shelf stacker. Looking how I did I would only ever get sent to places where I wouldn't be seen. Kitchens or warehouses were ideal. Every now and then you had to take work or risk not getting your dole money. My parents helped me loads too though. Especially Dad. And especially if you got him on the right day after a win on the horses. When I was living in the squats, I was constantly going home to Shooters Hill to eat and get my washing done. I wasn't living the nightmare like everyone else. I took outrageous friends home and Mum always made room at the table. Dad would ask, 'How d'ya get hair like that? Plug yourself in?' I went to Clare Thom's parents' place in Esher. It was fun to discover that my mates, however outrageous, came from ordinary families. Probably hoping at some point they would grow out of it. Some did. Not me.

For years I convinced myself
I was a creature of habit,
unchangeable, immovable.

3

# SEX, MUSIC AND DRAMA – CULTURE CLUB FORMATION

*C*ulture *Club never really split up, but I* officially left in 1986. It's always going to be one of those lovers I go back to. I've railed against it and that stupid Boy George character I created. For years I convinced myself I was a creature of habit, unchangeable, immovable. But eventually you have to look in the mirror. Not looking for spots, but for something deeper. Why the hell am I here? I would say life is the point of life.

Culture Club is a mythical dinosaur. A kick up the arse, a slap in the eye. Why did I start the band? The idea that I could be in a band was planted when I attended Spear of Destiny rehearsals with Kirk Brandon when I was nineteen.

I thought, 'Ah, this is excitement.' I'd never thought of being a musician before then, but I was loving it.

My first opportunity came when I was recruited by my friend, the guitarist Matthew Ashman, to be an additional singer in the band Bow Wow Wow. Matthew was the boyfriend of my friend Gabrielle Palmano who was part of Philip Sallon's gang. Matthew used to hear me sing with Philip and say, 'Your voice is amazing. You should sing for Bow Wow Wow.'

Matthew said Malcolm McLaren, the notorious pop Svengali, wanted me to replace Annabella Lwin who was only fourteen years old and a bit non-compliant. Who wants to be told what to do at fourteen, and Malcolm had unusual ideas.

Apparently Malcolm's talent scout, Dave Fishell found Annabella singing along to Abba in the local dry cleaners. It could all be a lie, but it sounds good and Malcolm would never let the truth get in the way of a good story. I know Annabella a little better now and she is a firecracker Scorpio with a Taurus moon. She can't stand the rest of Bow Wow Wow now, which is a shame.

One twisted afternoon Matthew brought Malcolm to meet me. As afternoon turned to evening, Malcolm invited Matthew and me over to his flat in Bayswater. We arrived to chaos. All the staff from the Turkish restaurant below were in the street. Vivienne Westwood had arrived on a bicycle in full pirate garb and thrown a brick through Malcolm's window. Vivienne thought Malcolm was sleeping with one of the young girls that were always hanging around the shop. He probably was. It was all very exciting. Malcolm fed me steak and wrote lyrics in front of me. His approach was very surrealistic. Without rules. He had the words before he had the melody.

Malcolm had his finger in every aspect of the band: how they sounded, how they dressed, how they walked. He was very persuasive but it didn't work with me. His attempts to get me to sign a contract were thwarted when I told him my dad wouldn't let me sign anything. Truthfully, I could have signed it but I didn't want to. After that, any time I refused to obey Malcolm he would taunt me: 'Yeah, your dad says no.'

But Malcolm found a way to use whatever talent he thought I had for his own nefarious ends, throwing me into a brief but thrilling stint with Bow Wow Wow. They had a massive gig at the Rainbow Theatre in Finsbury Park in February 1981 where the seats were ripped out and replaced with fairground attractions. Vivienne Westwood tried to put me in her clothes but I rebelled and wore my own drag. The theatre was packed and, at the end of Bow Wow Wow's main set, I was pushed on stage during the encore instead of Annabella and sang the Peanuts Wilson rockabilly song 'Cast Iron Arm'. The crowd were clearly miffed and I could hear Malcolm's wicked laugh in the wings.

My next gig was two weeks later at the University of Manchester where I was given a couple of songs: 'Sex Gang Children' and 'Biological Phenomenon', about an imaginary horse race where all the jockeys were gay historical figures. It was very Malcolm. The crowd in Manchester were caught between punk and the future. It was chaos. They were spitting, no, gobbing at me, and I grabbed the mic stand and swung it over their heads. I went verbal with a few 'Fuck offs' and 'You cunts' and left the stage invigorated. I think Leigh Gorman on bass and Dave Barbarossa on drums had already had enough of me. I was outrageous in the car on the way up the motorway, waving at lorry drivers and exposing my chest. I think Dave and Leigh put their foot down but Malcolm had fired a warning shot to Annabella. My work was done.

Malcom was an imposing figure. At the time, it was claimed that Malcolm McLaren had designed the look for Adam Ant's band for a small fee. The look was based on the fashion that Vivienne Westwood was creating, which was quasi-historical pirate drag with a modern, sexy twist. I don't know the real story but allegedly Malcolm screwed Adam over and stole his musicians to create Bow Wow Wow. Maybe Adam had too many opinions for Malcolm who liked to be the loudest opinion in any room. But it's true that Matthew Ashman was originally the guitarist in Adam's band and left to be in Malcolm's new band, so who knows? When Malcolm was bored of you that was it. He lacked the vision to spot what a star Adam Ant was and he missed a trick with me, admitting later that my success 'baffled' him.

Both Jon and Mikey from Culture Club had tried to get into Adam and The Ants. A shop assistant who worked for Vivienne and Malcolm had told Mikey Craig that the bass player had been sacked. Jon also auditioned but didn't get the job and later told me how Adam had two drummers and dressed a bit like me. Jon was clearly excited by the colour and theatrics of Adam: 'Punk is sunk, we need colour.'

None of us had met at this point but destiny was putting us in the same place at the same time. Adam and The Ants were the big pop sensation before Culture Club, and we knew we had something similar. I loved Adam Ant from when he he was a leather clad punk. He always had a strong melodic edge. Tracks like 'Physical' and 'Young Parisians' are cool pop. He was and is still beautiful. A total star. I went on stage with him at the Jazz Café and he was like Marc Bolan. I felt it. I saw his magic and electricity. Adam Ant went more pop, and he was the biggest pop star ever. He owned the eighties and set a new pop standard.

I met Adam Ant once in a flat in Earls Court. Chrissie Hynde was there. She was friendly with Phillip Sallon, who got her a job in Vivienne's shop, Sex, on the King's Road, and Philip had taken me to the flat to impress me. It was when Adam was more punk and wearing lots of tight black leather. He was gorgeous. I still find him gorgeous. There were other famous punks there but I only remember Chrissie and Adam. They were very unfriendly because that was the currency of punk at the time. Attitude and hostility. I was a kid and only fit for a sneer.

I didn't speak to or see Malcolm McLaren until years later when I was walking round Soho with a journalist for an article in *Out* magazine. We saw Malcolm in a café and I went to speak to him. He made some bitchy comment about me, which tickled the journo and ended up in the piece. I was upset and vowed to get revenge... Years later my guitarist John Themis was working with Malcolm on a project called Junk, a Chinese version of the Spice Girls. In hindsight, it was probably a genius idea. But at the time, I was writing a column for the *Sunday Express* and using any leftover column inches to wield an axe. I wrote about how embarrassing Malcolm's project was, from punk to predictable. He read it, traumatised, in front of John Themis.

'What have I ever done to George?'

John related my story but Malcolm said he didn't remember doing anything like that. In the spirit of hindsight, I *was* a touchy queen in those days. Do I regret what I did? Well, I definitely read into things that weren't being said. I was tearful when Malcolm passed away from cancer in 2010. He was an important figure in my life. He didn't believe in me but he gave me some much needed attention – I would walk round telling anyone who would listen that he was my manager and how famous I was going to be.

And I really did crave attention at that time. Long before his superstar DJ days, I deejayed with Jeremy Healy at Philip's club, held in the little underground nightclub Planets in Piccadilly. Jeremy and me were the only people Philip knew who had records and would work for drinks and all the attention we could crave – and the DJ booth was the best place to be seen. It was high enough to stand out and have your outfit appreciated. The club was so popular, sending Philip into an instant power trip. He loved dictating what people could wear into the club. If a guy was cute, Philip would get them to strip on the pavement and turn their clothes inside out.

It was 1980 and I'd just found out via *Melody Maker* that I had been sacked from Bow Wow Wow after only two gigs. The picture of me and Annabella that they used was amazing and the caption went something like, 'Lieutenant Lush's flirtation with fame is over.' That's what *they* thought.

It was Mikey Craig who first approached me about forming a band. He had seen my picture in *Melody Maker* and read about my sacking. So he got a friend who worked for Vivienne Westwood to dress him and get him into Philip's club. He approached me in the DJ booth asking if I could sing. I said I'd go and see him at his mum's house in Hammersmith. A few days later I went over with my fashion-designer friend, Clare Thom – also known as 'Clare with the hair' because she had gravity-defying punk spikes. She wore Siouxsie eyes and was as gorgeous as Liz Taylor. She was friendly with Michele Clapton – who went on to win an Emmy for her *Game of Thrones* costumes. Back in the early eighties, Michele's look already had a *Game of Thrones* edge: she shaved her head and wore floor-length smocks with a crucifix halo.

Clare was the first white girl with dreadlocks and influenced my early Culture Club style, throwing in a hint of Ari Up from The Slits. Fierce girls were my flavour and Clare was the queen of cool. Cool enough to come with me to Mikey's house and tell me whether he was any good at playing bass. I had no musical qualifications except my obsession with Bowie and Bolan. I heard music through my older brother Richard's bedroom door and kept my ear to the radio.

But Mikey could obviously play and he'd searched me out, which was impressive. Lots of great bands were forming around that time. Punk had morphed into new wave and the New Romantics were becoming fully-fledged pop stars. I had seen Annie Lennox and Eurythmics in

Birmingham when they were a bit candy-pop new wave. All hail androgyny. The story gets more nuts. Me and Martin Degville had climbed in through the window to get into their dressing room. When you are seventeen, being in a dressing room is Mecca. But Annie and Dave were really nice and we actually became friends. In fact, I bumped into Annie a few months later crying in Soho Square. I took her to the Krishna Café off Soho Square and we put the world to rights. Is it a coincidence that a few years later in 1984, Annie married Radha Raman, a Hare Krishna with commercial aspirations? He actually turned up in my hotel room in New York soon after he split with Annie a year later. He thought I knew more about Annie than I did and I didn't know him well enough to discuss what I did know. He was flirty, he was handsome, he was charismatic and religiously repressed. What's not to like?

Anyways... I was the only person allowed in Mikey's family home with dreadlocks. I was maybe seen as a confused white boy. Dreadlocks were like punk spikes to conservative Jamaicans and Mikey's mum was lovely but very proper. The day Clare and I went to see Mikey, we were sitting in his bedroom as he played bass when a fourteen-year-old white boy with real dreadlocks burst into the room on roller skates. His tracksuit was red, gold and green, and an oversized beaver hat was cocked on his head to one side. Oh my God, he was cool and speaking in complete Jamaican patois, which sounded absolutely real. My mind was going: 'I want him in the band, I want him in the band.'

Amos Pizzey was the younger brother of Mikey's then girlfriend, Cleo, daughter of Erin Pizzey, renowned writer and the first person to set up a Domestic Abuse refuge for women in the UK. Mikey was living on and off in Erin's house with Cleo and Amos and a bunch of other kids Erin had informally adopted. There was a big reggae sound system with speakers in the lounge. And that was that, I agreed to play with Mikey and Amos joined us too.

Jon Moss had been pointed out to me by Kirk Brandon on the King's Road.

'He's that drummer from the band London. They think they're The Clash'.

Musicians are always dismissive of other musicians and punk was all about attitude and hostility. In Kirk's opinion, London were New Wave and not punk. A couple of years later, when Kirk changed the band's name to Spear of Destiny, Jon called them 'Spear of Mid-European Angst'.

Jon Moss was wearing a black full-length leather coat with black everything. His hair was in that half state between a seventies mullet and a fully committed punk. Like a punk who still lived at home. [Anyone with an eye on fashion can see the connection between Bowie and Johnny Rotten. Ziggy was the mother of punk. It was Suzi Fussey, a local hairdresser on Beckenham High Street who gave Bowie his famous haircut, but the mullet was first coiffured by a French hairdresser called Henri Mollet.]

I had started to think about starting my own band, but I was yet to meet Mikey Craig at this point. Jon was a drummer, and he was cute. I had a feeling I would see him again.

One of my first jobs was for a print firm near Hanover Square off Regent Street. I mostly stuffed envelopes and licked stamps – I licked them rather than using the nasty sponge. Sometimes I was sent out to hand deliver parcels or big bags of letters to the post office. I loved being out of the office and they allowed me to wear mostly what I wanted to wear. London was my catwalk and I worked it. One day I was asked to remove the strap on my bondage trousers for safety reasons. I agreed to take it off in the office but never outside. People were always tapping me on the shoulder and saying, 'Your belts dropped'.

I met Les Daly, a Scottish journalist who edited *My Guy* magazine. I had met him at a gay club in Swiss Cottage and he gave me his number. I went to meet him after work at the *My Guy* offices. On the wall was a picture of Jon Moss.

'What do you think about our pin-up of the week?' Les asked me.

I knew who he was. By then, London had released an EP and one of the songs was called 'Siouxsie Sue' (sic). I loved

Siouxsie and dressed quite similarly a lot of the time. She wore men's shirts with ridiculously long sleeves or a tuxedo with ripped tights. That was her, not me. I never had long enough legs to show off.

Fate was conspiring; spotting Jon Moss on the King's Road; Les showing me his pin-up; and then out of nowhere Jon tried to interview me at celebrity boxer John Conteh's supposedly posh club in Mayfair. Jon was working for an entertainment-news film crew and thought I was Siouxsie. He approached me and I laughed: 'I'm not her. I'm him.' It must have been seeing him again that night that prompted me to get his phone number.

I met Diana Dors, her husband Alan Lake, and Mohammed Ali the same night. I wrestled through his security and got in front of him.

'Sorry. My dad loves you. We've got your picture in our hallway.'

He stared at me and asked, 'Are you a boy or a girl?'

'Boy,' I said.

'You're a very pretty boy,' he told me.

When I told Dad he said, 'Oh, you showed me right up.' But he was excited that I met his hero.

Les had a boyfriend. A very jealous boyfriend called Scottish John who was less relaxed. A few times he let himself into the flat when I was there so I left Les to deal with him. I would call Les after a night out with Marilyn and Philip and go over to his flat in West End Lane, West Hampstead. The sex was amazing and affectionate, and he pretty much taught me everything while playing Nico's album *Chelsea Girls*.

When I hear 'Somewhere There's a Feather' I think of Les. He was probably the most uncomplicated lover I ever had. There was an unspoken understanding. I knew Les for a few years, even when I got famous, and he was an editor at *The Sunday Times* Magazine. He was a beautiful person, and I was devastated when I lost him to the Aids epidemic

It was around this time that I moved into my friend Jean Sell's flat in Goodge Street when the squatting community in Warren Street, Great Titchfield Street and Carburton Street disintegrated. It felt like the end of an era. Jean was a friend from the Blitz. She offered me the room when she was drunk, but I think she regretted it.

Jean was a seamstress and I stayed in her sewing room, which had no windows. I had a single bed pushed up against the wall amongst huge reels of fabric and leather cuts. My walls were covered in pictures of fifties beefcake pin-ups, Bowie, Marc Bolan, geisha girls and my favourite movie stars like Bette Davis and Elizabeth Taylor. There was a picture of Klaus Nomi and a bunch of fashion postcards shot by photographer Richard Avedon (who would shoot Culture Club for the cover of *Rolling Stone* magazine only three years later).

Jean's flat belonged to her ex-fiance, but he called it off

just before the wedding and then let Jean stay in the flat out of pity. Through Jean I was hired to do make-up at the Royal Shakespeare Company. Trudie Styler told me she was there, but it was long before anyone knew who either of us were. I love Trudie and Sting. He plays with her feet. They are too cute.

Living with Jean was amazing, and I was a perfect flat guest. I kept the place clean and we got along brilliantly.

I don't know why I fell out with Jean, but they say if you want to lose a friend move in with them or take them on holiday. She got two gay friends to send me a fake legal letter ordering me to leave her flat in thirty days. I showed it to Dad, and he laughed. 'This is not from a lawyer.' But I left as soon as I could, vowing never to speak to her again. So I arranged to rent Philip's flat with a boy called Richard Habberley, who was pretending to be straight and failing miserably. George Michael was just getting big at this time and we 'fought' over a girl called Pat Fernandez, or Black Pat. She had been my best friend and she had a car, and now she was ferrying George Michael everywhere. She dumped me for George. Everybody loves up and coming.

But before I moved, I made my first phone call to Jon from Jean's flat phone.

That phone conversation was as dumb as it could possibly be. I was nervous, talking fast and asking silly questions but luckily it didn't put him off.

'Have you got a drum kit?'

'Obviously,' he said, 'I'm a drummer.'

I remember that day of our first rehearsal like a scene from a movie. He was handsome and smelled lovely. He was wearing a plaid shirt, with tight blue jeans and Westwood pirate boots. He had a diamond earring in one ear and was driving a VW Golf convertible. I looked lovely too. I must have spent a fair time getting ready because I wanted to make a good impression. He pretty much took over from that rehearsal and that was the theme of Culture Club from that moment. Jon had been in bands; he was older and came from money. Compared to the rest of us he was sophisticated. He took holidays in the South of France and told me he had sex with his nanny when he was a teenager. He caught on quite quickly that there was something unique about me. But if I said I knew that about myself I'd be lying.

It was an awkward first rehearsal but we played around with ideas and afterwards Jon said that our guitarist, a guy called Suede, wasn't cutting it. He liked Mikey on bass but thought we needed a better lead guitarist. He also thought the music was too goth, which didn't offend me because I was into every type of music. Typical Gemini, I wanted to be Siouxsie with a bit of Bow Wow Wow, with that pulsating Burundi beat that was also being used by Adam Ant. We chucked in a bit of Gladys Knight and The Pips, and of course Bowie and Bolan. I didn't plan for Culture Club to be an insane hybrid of everything I loved but that's what it became. To start with I knew very little about music and because Jon had experience I knew it was smart to keep him around. Truthfully, I also fancied him and I wanted a good-looking band.

Jon and I hit it off instantly. He had auditioned for Adam and The Ants and told me that Adam had two drummers, which he thought was pointless, but he was blown away by Adam's look.

'He's colourful like you, wearing all this mad pirate stuff and a white stripe across his nose.'

I'm not sure what Jon thought of my look but he would accompany me to Le Beat Route and other clubs, where I was virtually in drag. I liked people thinking Jon was my boyfriend, even if he wasn't yet. At the time, he was engaged to a girl called Caroline, a pretty blonde Jewish girl who worked in Endell Street, Covent Garden, near PX, the premier New Romantic boutique. I never bought anything from PX, I couldn't afford it, but it was just as important to be seen in there considering a purchase.

'Will you hold it for me?'

We cassette-taped our rehearsals and listened back to them. It was primitive but hopeful. Jon would suggest classic soul songs, like 'Private Number' by Judy Clay and William Bell. We did a version of 'Taxi' by J. Blackfoot and we tried to write. I was using my friend Myra's poetry and nicking lines from Andy Polaris, who wrote incredible poems and was in the band Animal Nightlife and had been part of our squatting family.

Back then in 1981, I already had a degree of notoriety as a club face. There were constant mentions of me in the music papers, mostly bitchy and derogatory. I was still in Jean's fabric room waiting to move.

Eventually I became quite obsessed with Jon. It was a while before I slept with him but I confided in him about all aspects of my previous relationships, so you could argue that he knew what he was taking on. Jon paid for every dinner and drove me to clubs in his fancy car. He was spending more time with me than he was with his fiancé.

At that time, I'd called our band Sex Gang Children, a reference to the song Malcolm McLaren had written for me for Bow Wow Wow. It was about animals escaping from the hold in an airplane and having sex with the passengers, it was nothing like 'Leaving on a Jet Plane'. The name of the band bore no relationship to the sound, I just wanted to shock.

Jon went on holiday to Los Angeles and took our rough demo tapes with him. He sent me postcards saying that his friends loved the music but hated the name. I agreed that our name had to change so I gave the name to Andi Sex Gang, who I knew from the punk scene. I was probably taking a dig at Malcolm. Andi was already called Andi Sex Gang so it made sense for him to have the name. We played around with all sorts of new names – Caravan Club, Can't Wait Club – and ended up with Culture Club. Once Roy Hay had become a member it dawned on me how culturally diverse we were. We had an Anglo-Saxon guitarist, a gay Irish singer, a Jamaican bass player and a Jewish drummer. We *were* the culture club.

After briefly working as a window dresser for Street Theatre, the owner Peter Small decided to give me my own shop, The Foundry, round the corner off Carnaby Street. He was working with a designer called Sue Clowes and we collaborated on ideas. Sue was doing her own prints using hobo symbols used by travellers to let each other know where they could get food, shelter or were warned to keep away.

I was running The Foundry as I waited for fame. Culture Club were attracting more and more fans and tons of media from all over the world. We had a lot of support from Peter Small who paid for some of our early rehearsals. Jon would pay for stuff too because he was the only one with a job, copying soft porn videos in some dark office off Heath Street in Hampstead.

In the early days of my romance with Jon, who was actively bisexual, he bumped into an ex-girlfriend, Sam, and offered her a lift home leaving me at the club promising to come back. When he didn't I was in tears and Tasty Tim comforted me, telling me, 'All men are cowards.' God knows what that made us?

The first time I saw Tim on the King's Road I spotted his red eyebrows and wanted to kill. A bunch of us saw him from the bus outside the punk boutique, Boy. We got off the bus, got on another bus and went a few stops back so we could walk past him and sneer – I was the only person in London allowed to have red eyebrows. When we got up close and I saw how pretty he was I abandoned my assault. How ironic that a few months later he came to my rescue?

It was Alison Green who delivered her boyfriend Roy to us. She had come into the shop with her friend Keith who worked with Roy in the City. Keith modelled Sue Clowes clothes for photoshoots, and we asked other friends to join, like Annie Ruddock from the pop group Amazulu who knew Mikey and Amos. We also used Mikey's kids, Amber and Keita and his partner Cleo. We wanted to create the feeling of a tribe or a family – a multicultural family.

Most of the shoots were done by Mark Lebon from the squat down the street.

When Roy joined the band, we started setting up our own gigs to try and get a record deal. We did our first performance near where Roy grew up in Grays, Essex at a club called Crocs. I'm told we were awful but two of Depeche Mode turned up to see us. We got dressed in Roy's parents house and walked out in our stage clothes like aliens in suburbia. I remember that Roy gave Jon and Mikey a quick haircut before we went on stage. Roy was going to be a hairdresser after doing insurance in the city but decided being worshipped worldwide was a better option (LOL).

It was an exciting time for music. Depeche Mode were at the forefront of electro pop alongside The Human League. There were others like Fad Gadget, who is the unsung king of electro. Kraftwerk led the way for all these artists and went on to influence Hip Hop and House music. Bowie was quick to embrace the electronic sound and made some of his best albums. *Heroes and Low* took us all by surprise at the time: *Low*, with its long intros and instrumental tracks. At first, like many fans I felt cheated but then completely got it.

Jon wanted nothing to do with the plinky plonky electronic sound. Coming from the punk scene, he was more traditional but also loved soul and classic song writing. I loved any kind of music from Elvis to Bowie to Kraftwerk and a shedload of reggae thrown in. I know for sure now that I only really care about great songwriting and great storytelling.

⚡ ⚡ ⚡

We could not get a record deal. I say this because every slightly weird-looking person in London was being signed.

I was considered too much. No one actually said, 'Wear less make-up,' but we did a photoshoot with Mark Lebon for promo photos and I was toned down. A make-up artist called Kitty was hired and she softened my look. I became a bit more Brooke Shields. I was weird about letting anyone touch my face – I did it better than anyone – but that day I was well-behaved.

We carried on rehearsing and waiting for our big break. So that meant more time with Jon. The first time we kissed was in my windowless room in Goodge Street. He turned up with scratches on his face after having a row with his fiancé, Caroline, at a friend's party. He had just returned from a trip to LA and it turned out that he had only sent postcards to me and not her. I'd gone into the shop where Caroline worked in Covent Garden and showed her one of the post-cards without realising.

I wasn't trying to be bitchy, I was just excited about the band, but she was livid. That night, Caroline had been making jibes at a friend's party about me being Jon's 'boyfriend'. When Jon said he had to leave to see me, she screamed, 'Just fuck off to your boyfriend,' and scratched his face.

'You fancy him, don't you?' she said in front of everyone.

'What did you say to that?' I asked Jon when I saw him later that night.

'I told her I did,' he replied, and then he grabbed me and we kissed for the first time. I only have vague memories of that night, but I remember he was wearing corduroy trousers.

After that night there was a few months of absolute bliss and I moved to Alma Square in St John's Wood. Being with Jon made everything about the band more exciting. He started to take our demos to record companies and, when he showed them Mark Lebon's pictures, they asked, 'Who's the girl?' That's when I decided to call myself 'Boy George', which added a bit of humour to the gender confusion.

We wear all wearing Sue Clowes designs from The Foundry and, once we had the name Culture Club, Sue started to add more cultural references. One of my favourites was a huge red cross with tiny black fighter jets and roses. For me it was about Catholic guilt, inner turmoil, self-destruction and war. We did one T-shirt that caused a scandal with the word 'God' written in Hebrew. But we took it out of the window when an old Jewish lady came in wagging her finger saying, 'It is forbidden.'

The Foundry was a hive of cultural appropriation but we were celebrating cultural differences. Mixing Jewish culture with Catholic symbolism, punk and the Rasta movement. Sue and I worked well together: we traded ideas and she found ways to create them. She had a workshop in Old Street where she printed everything by hand.

A young kid called Johnny Melton came into the shop looking for a job. I already had Roy's girlfriend, Alison, working a few days a week, so I said, 'Go and see Sue Clowes at her studio.' Johnny ended up working for Sue for years and I forgot all about him until he became Jonny Slut from the goth band The Specimen. My friend Ollie had started the band and I knew Ollie from New Cross. Talk about six degrees of goth punk separation.

I had a sign made for the shop of a rabbi painted by my friend Mark Wardell. It hung from chains like a pub sign. Jon's influence was everywhere – we added Jewish stars to everything, including underwear. Jewish mums would buy them for their son's bar mitzvahs. The shop became a meeting point for fans and fashion freaks.

We never really made any money because we didn't have the infrastructure for mass production – Peter, who owned the shop, was an ideas man and had more passion than business sense, and because Sue made everything by hand, it was a labour of love.

So we were all working in the day and gigging at night, trying to get heard. Danny Goodwin, an American working for music publishers Virgin Music, happened to be down in Southend and decided to come and see our gig. He thought we were raw but he could see the kids in the crowd liked us. He turned up at my shop and we chatted career moves. He was good looking too, which helped, so I gave him Jon's details. Jon was running the band even though there was nothing to run.

Through his dad's accountant we met a music manager and publisher called Tony Gordon. We went to his basement office in Mayfair, and I was impressed by the fact that he managed punk bands The Angelic Upstarts and Sham 69. He had also published a song I knew called 'Hello, This Is Joannie'.

I was clueless about everything to do with business and record deals, so I let Jon take control. Suddenly things started happening and my head was spinning. I had told Tony I worked in Carnaby Street and the next day he came and found me. The way I looked, it wasn't hard to spot me but I was impressed he had made the effort and he bought me a sandwich.

We were in discussion with Tony about a management deal when Jon decided to sign our publishing with Danny at Virgin Publishing. Tony was offended when he found out and said the deal was rubbish and, luckily, later it was renegotiated. Tony had contacts at EMI and he got us some studio time to record demos. We finally had a publishing deal but still no interest from any record companies.

Those demos were exciting to record but we were still trying to find our sound. I had been influenced by my short stint in Bow Wow Wow but my songwriting had a way to go. Those demos formed the basis of our first album, *Kissing to Be Clever*, which, if you'd heard it, you'll know was everything thrown into a big eclectic pot.

There was starting to be a buzz about us but there was no bidding war. I know I was the problem. Malcolm had called me a drag queen and I was a very unlikely pop star. Little girls bought pop records and, even though we had already had Bowie, Bolan and Adam Ant, there was something about me that troubled the music business. All my glam predecessors had worn make-up and feather boas, but they were still men. My androgyny was a new threat, and I was queer. I have been dumbed down by history but it's because I was and still am a contradiction.

The world can understand you better if it can put you in the right box. I was one of the first 'geezer gays', a working-class poof with a swift right hook. It was TV that really made me – my personality and ordinariness coupled with my appearance was disarming. I wasn't aware at the time; I was just winging it and didn't really understand the fuss. As a gay kid in the seventies my reference points were camp characters like Danny La Rue, Larry Grayson and Dick Emery, who wasn't gay but helped out at weekends. TV was littered with gay comedians dripping inuendo into our living rooms. I knew they were gay, they knew they were gay, but Mum just called us all 'theatrical'.

Many gay men resented what they saw as gay stereotypes on TV, but I loved those queers. These men and women had lived in fear of prosecution and trial by media. We should carry them through the streets, not condemn them for hiding in plain sight. I didn't model myself on them, but I found them hilarious, and I still do. I was free, perhaps because of them, to shape myself in a new way.

I didn't set out to change anything but my own circumstances. I wanted to live in the Bohemian world that my musical heroes lived in. I wanted to be free. I wanted to be a grown-up. I wanted everyone to know I existed. I must have wanted to be famous for something.

I wasn't motivated politically like Jimmy Somerville, who I saw dancing in the late seventies in a gay club on Sunday night in Soho where they gave out free sausages and chips. He was in white jeans and a tight T-shirt showing off the figure. He was a great little mover. Queer but in a different way to me.

We were something else entirely, drag but not Dockyard Doris drag. We got turned away from lots of gay clubs because we were too outrageous or just not gay 'in the right way', whatever that means. Even The Black Cap in Camden, which was famous for its drag, said, 'Sorry.' The older drag queens hated us because we were breaking the rules. We removed the comedy but kept the sarcasm.

Marilyn turned up at the annual Porchester Hall drag ball – a legendary event and queens spent the entire year preparing their outfits – and won without wearing any tights. He had just been in a movie called *Stepping Out* with Steve Strange and Princess Julia, and a drag queen walked over and said, 'Oh, I saw your B-movie.' Marilyn looked like a girl with virtually no effort. He never worse false titties but he contoured his cleavage. I was there that night dressed as Boudica. There's footage.

We finally had our publishing deal with Virgin Music but we wanted a proper record deal and they weren't sure, so the publishing deal was seen as a starting point.

I only cared about Jon, and the music was my very personal diary. Business wasn't on my radar. There are so many things that I was unaware of at this time, but we'll get to that later.

When the band started to take off, things soured because Jon wanted to run around town with his mates being 'Jon the pop star'. I was by now being kept away from his Jewish circle but he was happy to be seen with me in magazines. He cheated on me with girls but got very jealous if I was seen with another guy.

By now, Jon had dumped his fiancé, Caroline for me and for Culture Club. Jon says he genuinely fell in love with me, and he may be telling the truth, but sometimes I don't know how to feel.

I believed I was creating a democratic utopia with Jon, Roy and Mikey. When we agreed to a four-way split on everything, I expected things to be completely transparent. It was Jon who said let's share everything equally and I agreed without flinching.

Looking back, I think it would have made sense to have separate legal representation from Tony Gordon so that no suggestion of possible conflict of interest could have arisen.

I was immature and blinkered by love. But I'd do it all again. I'd just look out for myself a bit more.

We released two singles 'White Boy', on 10 May 1982, and 'I'm Afraid of Me' on 7 June 1982, and created a buzz but did not receive much radio play. Only what's called 'specialist plays' which is hilarious but that was radio then and now. I would never regard those first releases as 'flops', which was the term used back then. I don't know how many copies we sold but I just couldn't believe anyone had bought our records. When 'White Boy' was released, I heard it being played by the DJ at the Camden Palace and saw the crowd dancing. I watched from the balcony so proud.

Steve Strange had opened the Camden Palace in April 1982 and it became his biggest success. It was around the time that Spandau Ballet and Duran Duran were breaking into the pop charts. You would see everyone there from Sade to Phil Lynott from Thin Lizzy. I saw him go into a cubical with Steve Strange and Pete Townshend from The Who. They were probably praying.

This is where Madonna alleges she met me, and I was bitchy. She describes me as head to toe in Westwood. Hmm, I was wearing Sue Clowes's clothes religiously, so I assume it was Pete Burns who was rude in Westwood. He was certainly rude to me when we met on the stairs at Camden Palace. Pete, his wife Lynne Burns and drummer Steve Coy appeared and Pete said, 'Why are you copying my look?'

'I look nothing like you, love and I know everyone in this club so don't fucking try to intimidate me,' I replied.

I shouted 'Fuck off' again as I walked away.

That encounter set us up as enemies for some years, but we never came to blows. It was just bitchy quips in the press or on TV. On *The Tube* TV show Pete was asked about me and said, 'I am at least eight stone lighter than receding George'. In return, I called him 'Severe Burns' or 'Third Degree Burns'.

I saw a TV interview with Pete before he had all the plastic surgery, and he predicted a future where people will have head transplants. He did make himself look amazing but he just didn't know when to stop. I remember he had a Cher obsession and a story about him digging up Sinead O'Connor's front garden with a spoon.

When Pete got to Number 1 with 'You Spin Me Round' in March 1985 I was reluctantly pleased for him. When Culture Club failed to enter the top thirty with 'The Medal Song' a few months earlier, Pete said, 'I'm sending Boy George a wreath'. I am chuckling as I write because it was all so childish. It's a fact of life that drag queens bitch and we were a pair of bitchy drag queens. We should have collaborated, and I would jump at it now.

Pete Burns was bloody amazing, iconic even. But Mum thought he was a 'nasty piece of work'.

'I'd smack him right in the mouth,' she said.

Imagine mum swinging for Pete and his lips exploding! But it was all a shame because we had so much in common. I admired his fearlessness. Me and Pete were a pair of hard-core attention seekers from rough beginnings. I loved him though. Love is thicker than filler!

*We just argued all the time and over nothing and every-thing.*

# 4
# NUMBER 1 – CULTURE CLUB'S RISE

**A** stroke of luck meant that Culture Club were offered a spot on *Top of The Pops*. We were going to be on TV. I had lived for that show every Thursday so it was a massive moment. There are two conflicting stories about why or how: Shakin' Stevens, who was our British Elvis, was unwell or Elton John wanted his latest video shown and refused to perform in the studio. Thanks to one them you have all of me.

We got the news the night before filming and I was awake all night trying on clothes. I ended up choosing a Sue Clowes printed smock with a red cross and fighter planes and red roses all around it, and a matching red fedora hat.

I went barefoot as a tribute to Sandie Shaw because I saw her do it on *Ready Steady Go*. Years later, I met Sandie when I was exploring Nichiren Buddhism. Sandie and her psychologist husband, Tony Bedford have practiced and taught it for years. Sandie was every bit as fun as I hoped. Both Sandie and Tony are off the wall. Very human. Very real. Very Buddhist.

Culture Club on *Top of The Pops* felt like a dream but the nation gasped, *'What is it?'* The next day the press was full of homophobic pearl-clutching, and I was dismantled as a bad influence on young kids. Sound familiar? We were cancelled from a bunch of kids TV shows, but I was mobbed in the street. The public loved me – or were at least curious – even if the music business was unsure.

These days the pearl-clutching is about drag queens reading stories to kids. I knew I was gay at six. No kid turns gay because a drag queen reads them a story. No kid turned gay because they saw me in concert or played 'Do You Really Want to Hurt Me?' backwards. You are gay because nature decides it, and if you believe in God you must believe it's God's work. If you don't then what do you have to fear but your own twisted imagination? As Quentin Crisp said, 'He, she, made me'.

Journalist Nina Myskow called me 'Wally of The Week' in *The Sunday People* and the bitching continued in the tabloids. I was the talk of every playground. I've been told by many straight blokes, 'I thought you was a bird.' I lapped up all the attention.

Before Culture Club hit the Number 1 spot with 'Do You Really...' it all felt like a dream. We crept up to Number 2 and after a brief chat with Noel Edmonds on his show we got to Number 1. I swear it was me talking that made the difference. As soon I spoke, we went to Number 1. Was it the shock of 'It's speaking!' or just my camp working class tone? Either way, I remember saying something quippy and funny.

We were touring when we heard the chart rundown. The night before I'd had to cancel the show in Glasgow because I lost my voice. I went on stage and started the show, but my throat seized up. I panicked and ran off and Jon followed, and an argument ensued. It was a shit-show.

We left the gig and went back to a miserable hotel room with an orange candlewick bedspread and no lampshade above the bed. Jon and I continued our discussion in that bright ugly room and things got uglier. I was upset that Jon hadn't supported me and we got physical, which happened often. He stormed out of the room and went to the bar. I sat on the bed and cried. We all knew there was a chance that we would be Number 1 that next morning, but I remember just wanting to run. I had screamed at Jon that I was leaving, and he said, 'Good. Fucking leave.' I was the Boy George who called wolf all the time.

After sleeping off my tears, we had breakfast, loaded the coach and waited for the chart rundown. We were Number 1! But it felt weird after having to cancel a gig and the row with Jon. Everyone was smiling, even me, though I wondered if things between myself and Jon would ever be peaceful. But we drove to the next gig and the tour exploded and my lost voice was forgotten.

I always struggled vocally in the early days because I had no regime and didn't warm up my voice. Everything was a problem: air conditioning dried out my throat or the room was too hot. Now I see how psychological it was because I rarely have any problems now. The anxiety day in, day out must have contributed to it. I had grown up around screaming and now it was me losing it constantly.

The tour we were on was small but, with being Number 1, places were packed and there were more fans dressed up. I had been running around with a ton of make-up and my plaited hair full of ribbons for a couple of years. It was the beginning of what became the classic Boy George image.

At our second ever gig at the Regency Suite, Chadwell Heath, near Romford, in January 1982, we saw the first wave of lookalikes, dozens of young girls at the front with ribboned hair and hats. Boys too. After that night we saw the army of lookalikes grow and grow until the crowds were full of them. What had I started?

Before being in the official chart our audience was cool

girls and boys dressed in Westwood or New Romantic drag. There were a few groups of trendies that followed us to the handful of gigs we did before making it to the top. They soon disappeared, and we were thrust into the arms and hearts of teenyboppers. We had become The Bay City Rollers. Of course, we thought we were much cooler: we had a message.

The songs were really all about me and Jon and his struggle to be his own man. He had the pressure of expectation from his parents who wanted him to settle down with a nice Jewish girl, but he was shagging a volatile drag queen thing. I was at him all the time not really knowing what I wanted, and he was now famous. All the girls and boys fancied him, which just added to my paranoia. Imagine if he ran off with a fan? The opportunity for him to cheat was constant and there were wider pickings. I was very clear about not abusing our position with fans and there were some gorgeous boys too. But I just wouldn't do it.

By the time we appeared on TV, I was fully loved up with Jon. I feel now like fame was the reason everything went wrong. Before, I would hold Jon's arm as we walked into clubs, and he didn't flinch. We did a photo shoot for a pop magazine where we were openly affectionate and touchy and Jon would always kiss me in public. Suddenly any type of public affection was out of the question. He would say, 'The press will ruin everything for us'. Turns out, we didn't need their help.

The fans on the doorstep knew about us though and the press speculated. Only closeted interviewers ever asked about my sexuality.

It's hilarious when people say I was closeted in 1982. I had been out since I was fifteen and was as gay as the gayest day in May. When we started to do press and radio interviews my presence clearly unnerved people. They could see I wasn't some glam rock chancer dressed up for the stage.

However uptight Jon became in public, in private it was another story. The more I knew him the less I knew him. He would go out with his friends being 'Jon Moss. the pop star' and visit me late at night. He went from being my best friend and confidante to being someone that just wanted a late-night shag. So many nights I waited for him to arrive. Looking out the window. Waiting for the sound of his car. Listening to 'Car on a Hill' by Joni Mitchell.

I must hold up my hands because I was difficult too. I always had one foot ready to run. Jon could never have loved me in the way I wanted. I was impossible to make happy. Even now I don't know why I do what I do. It's not the glory, the sound of the crowd, the smell of the greasepaint. I fell into music in the same way I fell into Jon's arms. But it seems like the universe played a part because he kept popping up.

✳ ✳ ✳

Our first album, *Kissing to Be Clever* was full of songs damning our relationship but with echoes of my violent father. 'I'm Afraid of Me' was our second single and I was singing about betrayal, dishonesty, and sexual confusion. All the songs were about what was going on in my head, but also social attitudes and bullies. 'White Boy' was a diss on the straight boys who would heckle me from cars and objected to my presence on the planet; the boys at school that called me 'Larry Grayson' and tried to trip me up. We had 'White Boys Can't Control It', which was about Jon who was really a white boy despite his olive skin. White boy. Uptight boy.

> *When you're a white boy*
> *Your life is lust*
> *You kiss and run*
> *And you mistrust*
> *You hold out*
> *With the nowhere men*
> *You dance your dance*
> *And try again*

It wasn't just white boys that objected to me, and I was talking more about the lack of colour in their souls. White was a metaphor for strait laced and boring.

Plenty of black-skinned boys wanted to punch me as I walked around with dreadlocks and make-up. A dreadlocked

Rasta spat in my face in Notting Hill Gate on my way to an interview once. I was getting out of a black taxi and the window was open and *'splat'*, right in my painted face. Unsurprisingly, I arrived rattled for my interview.

Lots of Rastas gave me the thumbs up too though and enjoyed the fact that we were embracing reggae. It was white journalists who really objected. They didn't call it cultural appropriation in those days but that was what they were implying. But living in London I had grown up around Jamaican culture. My friend at school had a Jamaican Dad and an Irish mum and there was nothing weird about it. Black culture and music provided the essential cool in the seventies even if the mainstream had yet to catch up.

I can't tell you how important it was to me as an emotional being and a writer to hear every Stevie Wonder album. *Innvervisions* was released in 1973 when I was twelve. I would play it over and over. To hear Nina Simone for the first time or Millie Jackson, Gladys Knight, The Stylistics, Barry White, Chairmen of The Board, Tina Turner, Smokey Robinson, Marvin Gaye, Sly and The Family Stone. Then mixing it with glam rock, punk and electronic music. The seventies was the decade that kept fucking with your senses.

Culture Club didn't really understand that we were one of the first racially diverse bands because we didn't think about it. I had seen so many bands with black and white musicians, and it was normal. It was hip. It was cool. It was right. It was life in London. I had seen UB40 play a pub gig in Edgbaston in Birmingham and Sade sing on the back of a lorry in Greek Street. No one judged you for being a white or black-only band, but it was no longer a big deal.

The reviews for 'Do You Really...' were hateful. I can still recite one of them perfectly and it was written in 1982: 'The only thing Culture Club have got going for them is the hideously unphotogenic Boy George, ignore the airbrushed sleeve.' We cared, well, I cared and wanted to get revenge on every vile journalist who wrote an unkind word. Journalists were desperate to be stars and they tended to show off and be cruel to make their presence felt.

I was barely a year into my relationship with Jon, but I could see where it was going and I wrote about it in every song. I don't think the other three ever commented on the lyrics if there was a strong chorus and, in Roy's case, space for a guitar solo or strings. Because I couldn't play an instrument, I was aggressive in controlling the lyrics and melodies. I felt it was my only musical role but, in the end, it didn't matter because we shared everything. I can listen to melodic suggestions these days, but lyrics are still my domain. I push myself to not repeat old ideas and I listen more to things on the radio or what's considered the latest sound.

I repeat that everything has been done. It's why I write down every thought or anything I read or hear. I scroll through my notes and find hooks and abstract lines that paint a new landscape. Things don't have to make sense and I can change subject mid song. Always looking for that melody, tone and lyric that stands out. It's laughable, like when very recently my friend Laura was banging on about new techno. It's just old techno from the nineties with better quality sound. It's crisper, bangs better but the elements are the same. I'm tired of hearing, 'Listen to this it's amazing', when it's not.

'Do You Really...' was the heartbreak song that was never meant to be. I wrote part of the lyrics and melody over a random reggae dub track at Jon's friend's flat. It was Mikey's bassline that pulled it together, but I always thought it was too slow, too long and too personal to be a hit record. At the time it was like nothing else though and it stood out on the radio. The more I heard it the more it made sense but to start with I thought it was the end of us.

Sharing my pain in an abstract way was a winning formula but I laugh at some of the dramatic song titles. It was all very 'woe is me': 'Church of the Poisoned Mind', which was announced on the radio by Simon Bates with the words 'Alistair Crowley eat your heart out.' It was about Jon being Jewish and me being Catholic. I mean, it was never going to work:

*Watch me clinging to that beat,*
*I had to fight to make it mine,*

*That religion you could sink it neat,*
*Just move your feet and you'll feel fine.*

The success of 'Do You Really...' opened up Europe for us and we had hits everywhere and started travelling more. I feel like we talked more than we sang. Most music shows required you to mime to your hits and I was happy and great at miming. There was a ritual for *Top of the Pops* where you were supposed to sing live or re-record your vocal under the supervision of someone from the Musicians Union. It was always faked and we always used the original mix, but it was a song and pointless dance. Our producer, Steve Levine would prepare tapes and then swap them. Who cares if you mime, I had already spent ages getting the vocal right and Steve Levine had dedicated himself to the production. Why should we allow some TV show to ruin all our hard work?

There were some hilarious moments during those promotional trips around Europe. We arrived in Holland, and they had created a set that looked like a hospital. There were brains in jars that were pumping. It was cheesy and very uncool. I said no right away, and I always refused to have dancers swirling around us. I know that I was considered difficult, but I had to protect something about us. I think of those kick-offs as my Shirley Temple moments.

I had a habit of going mental and refusing to do something but then doing it anyway. I've never been one to cut off my nose to spite my career. I have done many things I didn't want to do but only because in the end it was easier. I'm not ruthless and I don't walk over people to get what I want. But if I get turned away from anywhere you won't see me for dust. Chase me down the road if you want, but I won't come back. Looking the way I did in the eighties I was always welcome but out of drag I experienced some proper rejection.

Of course, I got fussed over more than the boys and at times it caused friction. I was the mouthpiece for the band, and I didn't always say the right things, but in the end I got sick of talking. I don't really enjoy the sound of my speaking voice. I think I sound like Bernard Bresslaw from the *Carry On* movies. These trips were exhausting and always ended with a record company dinner and that's when I started to put on weight. I am an emotional eater and tend to eat more when I'm feeling anxious. Those restaurants were getting more fancy as we got more famous. It's one of the reasons I wore such loose designs to create powerful lines and hide my love handles. Everything was a distraction from who I was. The hats added height and distraction, the plaits framed my round face, and I pulled my bandana so tight it gave me a face lift and a constant headache. I really tried to avoid being seen out of my Boy George drag. Only Jon was privy to the real me and he seemed to like it, but even he preferred me when I was dressed up.

I realise now after so many years of heartache, longing and

outright madness that Jon and I had zero chance from the start. It was never, ever going to work but it was happening, and we couldn't stop it. I'm sure the reason we didn't tour much was because Jon wanted to avoid being on the road with me. Short promo trips were one thing, but big tours meant more time together and more drama. If it wasn't me and Jon fighting it was Roy and his wife, Alison. They would throw their wedding rings at each other, and the hotel walls would rattle. Mikey seemed to escape these dramas and while he had girlfriends, he was more private about it. He was so relaxed he even missed the video shoot for 'Do You Really...' and his brother Greg played him in the video. It blew my mind at the time, but we hadn't had a hit so maybe he needed to be convinced. It seems every big star or band in the eighties struggled to get their careers going. Maybe every artist throughout time. Even Bach or Beethoven.

For Culture Club, it wasn't overnight but it kind of was. I was ready to leave the band every five minutes and I had no faith in the future. Jon, to his credit, was more of a believer and would tell me not to be negative.

Once it happened it happened quick and everything I did was news. On the cover of the *Daily Mail,* which was my second home, an article appeared describing my entire outfit in detail. It was suggesting that I was nothing more than a clothes horse but, and it may sound surprising, I really didn't care about clothes. Clothes have always served a purpose, but you won't find a wardrobe full of designer clobber in my house. I went through a shopping addiction once I had money, but it was just my ego shopping. I would buy five of the same shirts in different colours but never wear them. I threw some amazing things away which I regret now, but I do have a few treasures. I'm not talking because they were expensive, I'm talking about items like the cheap kimono I wore in 1979 – it's full of moth holes but brings back memories – or my acid house waistcoat covered in smiley badges and safety pins. When I did wear Gaultier – which I, admittedly, loved – it was gifted to me. I've been given tons of free designer clothes, but you always run the risk of looking killed to dress. Designer looks have got to be broken up with thrift store chic or you look too done. If I'm wearing head to toe Gucci or Versace, I'd prefer to be paid. I consider myself outside the music and fashion industry in this way. I might be looking through the window, perhaps.

I knew underneath all the flowing smocks and ribbons that I was just George O'Dowd from Eltham. My upbringing, as rough as it was, set me up for insanity and redemption. I had madness and common sense running through my veins and it pulled me back from the edge so many times. I have this weird ability to forget the worst things that happen because you can't live in your mistakes. I was probably heading towards addiction from the day I was born.

'Do You Really...' was shoved on *Kissing to Be Clever* at

the last hour. The album title was me wondering whether Jon's tongue in my mouth was just a cynical act or if it was real. As the band got bigger and bigger, our friendship got smaller. I should have broken up with him, I should have walked away from every relationship I have ever been in, but I never leave. I'm a martyr, just like Mum.

We all had our own struggles with fame. We had the world at our feet but the emotional capacity of sea sponges. I had fun, lots of fun but there was so much more fun to be had. I think Jon, Roy and Mikey wanted to be eligible bachelors of rock and roll. I was supposed to be the radical one, fearless and, in many ways I was but with an underlying need for the white picket fence. Looking back, I could have had my cake and worn it. I had guys throwing themselves at me, but it always felt creepy. I wanted Jon and I wanted him all to myself. He always said, 'I love you' and wrote me amazing notes when we fell out. A couple of years back I took all those very personal letters from Jon and burnt them.

I had no idea what love was, and I had terrible examples in my mother and father. Now I know that you can't own anyone. I guess you can't help whose arms you fall into.

✳ ✳ ✳

At this time I was still renting a flat from Philip, and at a reduced rate.

It was just two bedrooms and a living room with a galley kitchen to one side – Philip didn't actually live there because he refused to leave home. 'I love home comforts', he'd say, and he couldn't leave his mum. She screamed at him constantly but there was such a bond between them.

I shared the flat for a while with Gary Crowley's girlfriend, Niamh Fahey whose sister Siobhan was in Fun Boy Three then Bananarama. I famously styled Bananarama in Sue Clowes stuff from The Foundry. They said I made them look like shot-putters! Siobhan, Sarah and Keren had a brilliant look anyway, so they didn't need me. I watched them on an old *Top of The Pops* recently and they looked amazing.

Very quickly my doorstep was littered with teenage girls and gay boys.

We were on rise and flew to New York in November 1982. Steve Dagger, Spandau Ballet's manager, had told me that we were getting played in America, but I couldn't believe it. Every British artist dreamed of breaking America, but I was quite nonchalant. 'Why wouldn't Americans love me?', I thought.

I was excited to be in America because I loved American music and John Waters. I thought I might meet Divine swishing down the street, but instead we saw artist David Hockney at breakfast at the Waldof-Astoria. We did a small but packed show at The Ritz Theatre and I met my first superfan, Bonnie Lippel. Bonnie had taken photos at the gig and waited outside with a bunch of lavender roses so I invited her to breakfast the following morning and she brought contact sheets and photos that she'd had printed overnight.

But despite that, there was no fuss in New York like there was in the UK. No fans outside the hotel, or people following us. We just weren't important enough, yet. But when I met Bonnie, I liked her instantly. She was heavy-set with bedraggled hippie hair and big open eyes. Her voice was hardcore New York and she was loud. I probably wouldn't have invited her if she'd been more conventional, but she felt like a fellow outsider. Some friendships are instant and that's what it was.

Bonnie's schtick was to take photos at live shows and she said she was friends with a bunch of singers like Linda Ronstadt and Dolly Parton. I didn't check and I didn't really care. When we toured the East Coast she followed us in her VW Beetle and took photos. Half-way through the tour she broke down and I invited her on to the tour bus, much to the horror of the other guys.

It was cold in New York, and we did photos in Central Park and a bunch of press. I was treated very much like a visiting alien, but I charmed the media. I talked about Liberace and said surely I was nothing outrageous compared to him.

'What about the Pope?' I said, 'He wears dresses.'

I found myself talking about lots of things I had no

interest in and I was asked ridiculous questions. I found an old magazine recently where I'm talking about Gary Glitter and the Pope and predicted that Iron Maiden were going to be massive. Luckily, I was right but I don't know on which authority I was pontificating. It was obvious that journalists wanted to trip me up but I gave good quotes.

I was poked continually about my sexuality. And while it was no big deal to me it was clearly a big deal to everyone else. I'm not sure if anyone said, 'Don't say gay', but I'd lived in the world long enough to know it wasn't the best calling card. Ambiguous sexuality is more exciting than actually admitting you dance backwards and live with your mother. Every time I spoke, I felt like saying, 'I'm shagging the drummer.' But I had to remember who I was entertaining.

Of course we all have our sell by date, but as soon as I started being more political about my sexuality I was accused of going on about it.

Could I have been as successful in America had I been bold enough to say, 'Yeah, I'm queer'? I enjoyed the ambiguity and mystery, and I was protecting my relationship with Jon. I was doing quite enough with what I was wearing. And when Jimmy Somerville appeared on *Top of the Pops* his father wouldn't watch in case he was dressed like me. For some I was the benchmark poof and for others I wasn't doing enough. It's one thing to tell your parents you're queer, and quite another to tell the universe.

I believe Bowie's career was marginalised in America because of his bold statements.

Why did I become so huge in America? Why did they love me? Well, it all turned a bit sour when we got our Grammy from Cyndi Lauper and Rodney Dangerfield. I said 'Thank you, America. You've got style and taste and you know a good drag queen when you see one.' Turns out that statement was as bold as Bowie's 'I'm gay'. Country singers fell off their seats and my then-publicist, Susan Blond was apoplectic. Little queer kids all over America felt the lights get brighter but the dimmer switch was turned down on me. There were morality protesters outside the gigs with signs like, 'If sex is a sin what is Boy George?' A musician, actually.

But in the eighties, America was ours for the taking. There were certain parts we weren't invited to like Texas and down South, but we were received with love everywhere we went. Just like at home, kids were turning up in full Boy George regalia and competitions for the best lookalike popped up in bars and clubs all over the country.

Duran Duran had cracked America just ahead of us but we were hot on their padded shoulders. They were portraying a much more rock and roll dream and they were straight boys. I think Roy thought he was in the wrong band and wanted to swan around like John Taylor. He wore the jackets with the rolled-up sleeves and would have preferred limos to the functional vans we drove around in.

I must admit I was a bit of a killjoy when it came to the rock and roll dream. Duran did videos on yachts in Antigua and we filmed by the Thames on a rainy day. But I was really conscious of not wanting to be like Duran. They were our competition and fans were divided. Of course, I like their records but I never would have admitted it then. But yes, I'm officially a Durannie.

Our debut album, *Kissing to Be Clever* reached Number 14 in America and 'Do You Really Want to Hurt Me' got to Number 2. The record label has to really believe in you to invest the kind of money it takes to get a hit in America. Obviously lots of people bought it because they loved it, but it takes more than love in America. We could have nudged those records to Number 1 had we toured more. That's where Duran Duran were smart. We no longer sell records in America but our live tours are hugely successful. I feel like America is getting to know me all over again now. And why not? I'm an entirely different person.

I think my popularity really soared in America when I appeared on the *Johnny Carson Tonight* show. Joan Rivers was sitting in for Johnny Carson and I was terrified of meeting her. Joan Collins was also a guest and I had a fabulous photo taken between them both. I love Joan Collins. Meeting her was so Hollywood. At that point I remember thinking, 'my life is completely glamorous.' I was a little bit spikey during my interview with Joan Rivers which I didn't need to be because she was so warm and seemed to genuinely like me – I did it for the attention. Someone like Joan Rivers can see through bullshit a mile away. She took the piss out of everyone but God help you if you had no sense of humour. Like the time she interviewed Bridget Nielsen. Watch that if you want to be uncomfortable.

It was Culture Club's first trip to LA and it was like being in the movies. Everything seemed iconic. We were riding in a stretch limousine up Sunset Boulevard and when we pulled up at the lights Kojak was in the next car. I shouted, 'Look, it's Kojak,' and he gave me a smile. I have no idea if he knew who we were but I certainly knew who he was. I wrote the song, 'It's a Miracle' about that trip to LA. It was originally called 'It's America' but we thought that was too cheesy. Lots of British artists were making their videos to be more American, adding school buses and yellow taxis. I didn't want to do anything that made us look like we were trying to ingratiate ourselves.

'We're British,' I would say. 'That's the point. God save the Queen.'

It wasn't all easy. I found LA difficult because you couldn't walk anywhere. We stayed in a hotel called the Beverly Comstock Hotel on Wilshire Boulevard. I went walking one night and got pulled over by the police, which was really intimidating. Our manager Tony loved a frilly hotel, with lots of cushions and a chandelier. He loved his cup of English tea and would sit by the pool in his salmon shorts taking phone calls. Tony was like a manager out of the showbiz era and he enjoyed our success so much. He actually reminded me of my dad, albeit a very posh version, who sounded ridiculous when he swore. 'Fuck orf,' he would say. When I was upset with Jon he would say, 'Jon's a potz.' He probably said the same about me. He probably didn't realise it was Yiddish for penis.

I returned to London and after Christmas with the family I started to look for my own home. I didn't have to look far. I could see my new house from the window of Philip's flat, a two-storey mews house around the corner in Abercorn Mews. I loved that house and it was exciting to have my own home that I could decorate any way I wanted. It was the first time I'd really owned anything. I painted the walls regency green and avoided leather sofas. I was happy there even though I became more accessible. The neighbours shooed fans away but they'd gather at the end of the road. There were fans from all over the world. They travelled from Italy, France and Japan. There were even fans that moved here and got jobs as chamber-maids just so they could see me. They were wild times.

In early 1983, we flew out to Hong Kong and did a gig before touring Japan. I was excited about being in Asia, especially Japan because I'd seen pictures of Bowie on an escalator in Tokyo. I'd seen him wearing Kansai Yamamoto clothes when he was Ziggy Stardust and I was desperate to see a kabuki performance. In Hong Kong we played to a largely expat crowd but we had many Chinese fans. Japan was another level with young girls following us everywhere. They would throw gifts at us everywhere we went: ornate fans, dolls, kimonos, you name it, I got everything. As crazy as the kids were, they were super polite and they kept shouting, 'Boy-ee'. In the hotels there were some older Japanese girls who had their eye on the three boys. I kept my eye on them when Jon was around.

The concert reviews were factual and unemotional. They simply listed what songs you sang and gave a description but no opinion. We were used to getting slaughtered in the sneering British press so I much preferred the Japanese approach. I also loved the food. I loved the energy. I learnt that Japanese people never say no even when they say yes, and they are never going to do what you ask. Politeness and reputation are everything, as I was to find out later on. A very famous journalist refused to speak to me for years because I was late for an interview.

I went to a kabuki show and was invited backstage to watch Tamasaburo – who was called the Japanese Boy George – do his make-up. In kabuki all the women are played by men. It was so exciting to watch how quickly it was done and to watch him transform himself into a female for the performance.

I felt comfortable in Japan dressed up as me. Even though Japan is a conservative culture they seemed to accept me as a foreign oddity.

Back at home we had our second hit with 'Time', which was the final single release from *Kissing to Be Clever* but was a taste of our maturing sound. *Kissing to Be Clever* was a splurge of youthful anxiety but *Colour By Numbers*, our second album, soon to be released in October 1983 was in every way the perfect pop album. It was produced by Steve Levine, who guided us towards a more soulful sound. Helen Terry arranged and sang most of the backing vocals and we had guests like Colin Blunstone, from sixties band the Zombies and comic actor Derek Guyle, who played washboard on 'It's a Miracle'. I love having guests in the studio and Steve was like an excited teenager about sound, production and gadgetry. Sometimes we couldn't move in the studio for new keyboards and life-changing sound equipment. I will never forget the sunny morning when Steve picked me up in his Aston Martin which had the first car CD player. He was playing 'Why' by Carly Simon and Chic and it sounded so crisp.

We were writing songs for our second album, and it was heavily influenced by American soul and had jazzy pockets. We always had pop in our music, and we added Motown with 'Church of The Poisoned Mind', which was kind of Motown meets The Addams Family, a traditional Motown groove with dark twisted lyrics about supressed queer love and fear. I hate to break it to Roy, but 'Miss Me Blind' is about queer sex and hypocrisy. *Bet you got a good gun.* Loaded or what? Of course, the listener can make the song about anything they want.

'Karma Chameleon' was just a rough demo at the time but it went with me and Marilyn to Egypt on holiday. We decided to take a two-week break in Egypt, and we went with our dreads and make-up. From the moment we landed the men were shouting 'pretty ladies, pretty ladies' and we got lots of attention everywhere. I had a version of 'Karma Chameleon' on a cassette tape which I played all the time. Marilyn hated it but I insisted it would go to Number 1. It's funny how quickly you become an expert.

I loved Egypt because no one had a clue who I was, and it was like being an old fashion weirdo. Fame comes with so many complications and explanations but in Egypt I was a Blitz Kid again. We stayed at The Holiday Inn right next to the pyramids, which was full of American soldiers who obviously knew who I was but, for the most part, I was just a foreign bloke dressed up as Nefertiti. I've never been one to sit by the pool and at that point everything was about publicity so I got Andre Csillag to fly out with his camera to document me and Marilyn dancing up the Nile. I took a plastic rubbish bin from the hotel and cut it so it fitted perfectly on my head. I wrapped black silk around it and used the rest to make a flowing robe. I wore a tabard and some jewellery I bought in a local souk and turned myself into Cleopatra. I remember walking into the lobby with Marilyn and there was a round of applause. We went to the pyramids, and I rode on a camel. Everyone was taking photos.

Egypt was a break from being Boy George. I had a copy of *Kissing to Be Clever* on cassette and showed it to people when they asked what I did. No one was that impressed. But back home, things were about to really kick off.

⚡ ⚡ ⚡

Culture Club arrived in Sydney to mob scenes. It was described as Beatlemania and we had to be smuggled out of a side door. My dreadlocks were even ripped out of my head and my clothes were pulled everywhere. It was exciting the first time and maybe a few times after but I soon got to dread those airport arrivals, especially after a long flight. I couldn't fly in my sweatpants because I hated being photographed out of make-up so I would fly as Boy George. Sometimes I applied my make-up in the toilet, inventing the mile high drag club.

By now, we were already huge in the rest of the world. We had won a Grammy for Best New Act and I had dropped my drag bomb. We arrived in Australia with so much notoriety. The Australian press were direct and asked blunt questions. Looking at old Lou Reed interviews from Australia I realised it was nothing new. Lou was asked by a journalist, 'Are you a homosexual or a transvestite?' To which he replied, 'Sometimes.' The journalist insisted, 'Which?' Lou said, 'What difference does it make?' He was clearly on another planet when he was answering questions and being a little bit Andy Warhol but the Australian journalists kept poking. I did some hilarious interviews in Australia and was asked stupidly, 'Do you like football?' I replied, 'I've got better things to do with my balls.'

But instead of living the life I was punching Jon and crying in my hotel room. Behind my back they were all snorting coke. They passed the coke around on flights while I sat there oblivious. I had used drugs prior to being in the band, mostly speed and a bit of acid. I had drank heavily in my late teens but was actually pretty straitlaced by the time we started Culture Club. I would go mad if I smelt weed or knew the others were high.

Something changed in me then. I started smoking a bit of weed. At first it was just a toke of somebody else's joint. I started having the odd cigarette too, menthol ones because I thought they were less harmful. At first, people were more shocked by me smoking the cigarettes than the weed but eventually the weed became more useful. Suddenly I realised what I'd been missing. The boys had been taking drugs for ages and I had been on Mikey's case a number of times when I caught him smoking a joint. But once I started smoking weed, I got over myself.

Drugs are everywhere in music and I had managed for a while to avoid the cliches, but weed really takes the edge off things. I didn't need it until I started using it and it soon became essential. We were in Holland a lot where attitudes to smoking weed were completely relaxed. They considered it a vitamin and I looked cool which was helpful. I sneered at coke in much the same way but within a couple of years I'd tried that too.

It was very rock and roll to do drugs. It was mostly hidden from me but eventually I found my own sources. There is no one to blame for my drug use but myself. They say tragedy always seeks a hostage and you find people to accompany you on your way to hell. I can't even say the schedule drove me to drugs but it didn't help. Weed in particular allowed me to expand my thinking and it improved my lyrics and, at times, enhanced my innate cynicism. It helps you to see and laugh at the bullshit more clearly. It sounds crazy to say that I hate fuss because I cause so much of it. I guess I like fuss on my own terms but not the fuss that's inflicted on me by fame or other people's ideas of fame.

From Australia we went to Germany. There were times when I had to walk into a press conference after a fight with Jon, or sing on a German pop show in a Hansel and

Gretel castle. When Jeremy and Haysi Fantayzee appeared on *Musikladen* they were surrounded by shitting and copulating rabbits. Germany can be quite surreal but I was amazed at how popular we were there. When you perform a new song on German TV it is a known fact that if everyone claps along you will have a hit. On our first visit to do a small live show our coach was bottled and bricked by skinheads. Poor Tony was horrified and Jon wasn't exactly pleased but thought we must be doing something right if Nazis hated us.

I was using my newfound insight to write. I was still hooked on 'Karma Chameleon' being a hit. When I first discovered the word 'karma' I understood it as a punishment for bad deeds. Of course, the word karma simply means action. Some people believe that you get bad karma in your next life if you've been a shit in this one. It's a little bit optimistic to think you get another chance to mess things up but it's a nice idea.

I often start a song with a title because it can provoke the imagination. I would smoke weed and think about Jon.

The lyrics are really simple but they tell the story.

*If I listen to your lies would you say*
*I'm a man without conviction*
*I'm a man who doesn't know*
*How to sell a contradiction*
*You come and go, you come and go*

Jon certainly did come and go, quite literally. It wasn't meant to be innuendo but if the cap fits. I sang it *a cappella* in Roy's kitchen and had to fight with them to get it on the album. They hated it so much that Steve Levine brought in Phil Pickett from seventies band Sailor and he helped us write the middle eight:

> *Every day is like survival*
> *You're my lover not my rival*

Phil ended up working on a few other songs and became our live keyboard player. I was a massive fan of Sailor – they were one of those anachronistic bands who made a sound from another era – and Phil brought their pop sensibility to Culture Club.

However much the boys hated 'Karma' it was the last track added to the album, almost over their dead bodies. Was it country? Was it camp? Was it camp country? I didn't care about those details and I still don't. One morning I'll wake up wanting to be Dolly Parton and the next I want to be in Bauhaus.

When 'Karma Chameleon' was released in September 1983 it was an instant hit on radio and with the public. The reviews were predictably scathing. But it stayed at Number 1 for six weeks and it became that albatross song. Everyone has one, if they're lucky. I think we have a few but no song fires up a gig like 'Karma Chameleon'. It's like it belongs to the people.

The video was shot on a paddle steamer on the side of the Thames. The day of the shoot it was overcast and we had to get on with it. Looking back, it looks like an episode of *Bridgerton* with black extras in Victorian period costume. Mikey is dressed like a suave Bill Sykes and there I am in the middle of it dressed like Boy George. I think video directors had a field day with Culture Club. Some of their ideas were terrible and I hated every single video we made. The worst being 'Victims' where I'm on a wobbling crane and Helen Terry looks like she's about to appear in *Up Pompeii* with Frankie Howerd. In the video for 'Time', Helen looks like Hilda Ogden. She hated it. Her best look was in 'Church of the Poison Mind', which is probably my favourite Culture Club video because it wasn't trying to tell a stupid narrative. I hated storyboards and narratives that had nothing to do with the song.

Once you have a hit record you have to be careful not to be swallowed by media duties. Just because everybody wants to talk to you doesn't mean you can't shut up for five minutes. I started to enjoy and need the attention too much. Roy talks about the cult of Boy George's personality and he has a point. We never took breaks or time to breathe because we feared it could all end tomorrow. Of course, if Roy, Mikey or Jon had been the centre of attention it might have gone the same way. It's easy for other people to tell you what you are doing wrong when it's too late. Everyone's a genius after you've been arrested.

Roy ended up with a massive cocaine problem. We're talking helicopters and FBI agents and Roy hiding in the rafters of a house. I don't know all the stories but there are hundreds. One afternoon my friend, Amanda Ghost bumped into him at the St. James Club in Los Angeles and thought he was Dee Snyder from Twisted Sister. Roy was rake thin with a full perm and guyliner and was very animated. Roy's only daughter, Sunny, who is my goddaughter, ended up on drugs too. I hope one day she writes her own book because the Roy Hay story makes me look like Mother Theresa. Sunny has been through hell but she loves her Dad and has become a beautiful young woman. She has a young son called Lion who has made Roy a proud grandfather.

✻ ✻ ✻

The lights got even brighter and the attention was more extreme after 'Karma Chameleon'. Such was the Culture Club schedule, we were touring in America when 'Karma' was released in the UK. We were lucky we were famous enough for the records to survive without us: Karma was at Number 1 for two weeks when *Colour by Numbers* went to Number 1 in the album chart.

The worst thing about fame was me and Jon. Instead of being fully present at the Grand Canyon or at the top of the Empire State Building I was distracted by us. I missed so much because of my petty obsession. That doesn't mean there wasn't laughter and fun because there was, but it was all too quickly dulled down by our drama. I could write about all the good times but that was always in between the sheets or up against the wall. Laconic platonic.

I got so good at covering up for the both of us I started making comments like, 'Sex? I'd rather have a cup of tea.' A cup of tea would have been more reliable and I was being deeply sarcastic. They took me literally because I was the face of a sanitised queerness. At the back of Heaven nightclub there were some arches that served as a dark room, not the kind you process photos in, I mean sex clubs where there was little conversation or discretion. If somebody puts their penis through a glory hole you don't get to know their star sign. I never went into those rooms because I was always dressed up and I'm a little bit of a romantic. The way I looked made me feel so alien towards other gay men. Carmen Miranda meets Colin the carpenter and they don't get on. That hyper sexualised side of gay culture was going on while I represented the slightly more acceptable poofter.

Meanwhile on the border of America and Canada one of the band was discovered to have a tiny amount of disco weed in his luggage. They wanted to strip search us all but I started crying. I was so emotional. We were starting a tour after weeks of promotion and almost anything was making me cry. I was such a good boy at that time. Virtually a nun when it came to narcotics. I'd had the odd joint but was not so invested that I needed to carry it round with me.

On that tour we went through America and dipped our toes in the south. Suddenly they couldn't resist us. We were in everyone's living rooms via MTV and I was as familiar as Big Bird. Japan was next and we rode on the bullet train and were followed by even bigger hoards of girls throwing Japanese dolls and cuddly toys at our toes. Jools Holland greeted us at Tokyo airport and followed us to film a Culture Club special for *The Tube* – it showed just how big we were. We went back to Australia and the crowds were even bigger and even more intense. We were surrounding by moats of fans at every hotel. You couldn't go out and if you did it was for a photoshoot. We would go restaurants and there would always be fans peering in through the windows.

I wanted it as much as I didn't. You can't prepare for what shape fame will take. It changes too, depending on which country you are in. There were a few countries like Argentina where my quirkiness might have been misunderstood. My bad moods were untranslatable to any reasonable person. I hate fuss. I keep saying this. I don't want it but I sometimes expect it. You get thrown into situations without warning and no one tells you anything, and if they do you don't listen.

I am much better if I breathe, and I find as I get older I can pause before reacting. When I can't control myself, I come back from it more quickly.

I wish I could have done that when I spoke about Princess Margaret on Australian TV. I cannot emphasise how glamorous it is to be using my name in the same sentence as one of the royals. I'm not a royalist unless it suits me and in this instance it does. I shook hands with Princess Margaret at the Sony Music Radio Awards at the London Hilton. Afterwards she was heard to say, 'Who's that Boy George? He looks like an over made-up tart.' I snapped back in the press and had T-shirts made of Princess Margaret's face on my body with my hat and ribbons with the words, 'I'm not a tart.'

Later, I ran into her son, Lord Linley in Knightsbridge while having lunch with Marilyn.

'Can I have a word?', he said.

'Of course.'

'I just wanted to say my mother never called you a tart. She had loads of gay friends and knew exactly who you were.'

'It must have been Carol Decker,' I said. 'Although I don't think she wears as much make-up as me.'

I actually loved Princess Margaret. She was my type of royal, very glamorous, full of it and excited. She did all the things the Queen could never do.

Aside from being insulted by Princess Margaret, my royal credentials are rubbish. I did some work for the Prince's

Trust and became an ambassador; I went to Clarence House with Mark Ronson and hung out with Charles and Camilla. Tom Hardy was there and Eric Clapton. Neither seemed pleased to see me. I met Princess Diana twice. The first was at the Hippodrome at a charity event attended by Diana. I had just gotten over a very public heroin addiction and my reputation was ragged. I wasn't in the official line-up of guests but nightclub owner Peter Stringfellow whispered in my ear, 'Princess Diana wants to meet you.' I was with Mum and she said, 'Go on, meet her.' I went upstairs and stood in line with the other guests but a palace official shooed me away.

'You're not on the list. Stand aside.'

So I went over to the bar and ordered a drink. After shaking hands with everyone, Diana broke protocol and approached me. She was very sweet and complimented my outfit, which was a Judy Blame coat and hat covered in silver safety pins.

'Wow, that must have taken forever.'

'I didn't do it myself, love.'

I asked her if she would meet Mum and she said, 'Where is she?' So I walked her to the balcony and pointed out Mum who was wearing a gold sequin top. Later she sent for Mum and they spent ten minutes chatting. She told Mum I was a true survivor.

I met Diana again at a Capital Radio charity lunch and

she sat facing me and had the vegetarian option because I was vegetarian. Morrissey would have loved her. Wayne Sleep was animated and falling on her shoulder. She looked at me, smiled and shrugged her shoulders. I think Wayne was later led away. My boyfriend Michael Dunne met Diana and she asked him what job he had.

'I'm on the dole,' he said.

'That's nice,' she said.

He was so embarrassed and kept saying, 'I told her I was on the dole.'

'Don't worry. So is she.'

This queen flew to Miami after touring Australia and bleached my hair in the hotel bathroom.

It was like I was going into my own witness protection scheme. I thought going blond would annoy Marilyn, who I was due to meet, and give me a disguise. We went to Jamaica on holiday thinking I could escape Culture Club and recognition. Turns out 'Karma Chameleon' was a massive hit in Jamaica too and I landed to, 'Boy George has just landed in Jamaica,' on the taxi radio.

Walking around with Marilyn people would say, 'Which one of you is Boy George?' Followed by, 'Whitey, whitey.' Marilyn was trying to get noticed and I was trying to hide. We went to Dunn's River Falls and Marilyn was wearing a negligee and had his nylon dreads pulled up in a pineapple. People were shouting, 'Boy George, look look.' I just walked behind, furious that he was bringing so much attention to us. Marilyn was born in Jamaica because his Dad was in the Army. Someone tell Buju Banton that Marilyn is a sista.

We were waited on hand and foot in Jamaica. The food was amazing. But I got sunburnt on the first day and had to stay in for a week so we extended the holiday. I was relaxed for the first time in ages and spending freely. I felt like I deserved it. We smoked weed and spent the day at Keith Richards' house. Marilyn got his phone number from a cab driver, such is security in Jamaica. When I rang and said it was me there was a pause followed by laughter. Keith said, 'Is this really the bag lady?' I put the phone down.

Somehow a message was sent telling us to come to the house and we went. We didn't discuss the phone call and there were lots of chemical distractions. I had taken cocaine already in New York with Marilyn but it didn't leave a massive impression. The first time I had ever seen cocaine was in a bowl in Freddie Mercury's hotel room in San Remo. Culture Club were beckoned to meet Freddie and we went down fully dressed on our way to the TV show. At first, I thought it was sugar but the boys knew what it was and I glared at them. Freddie was checking me out and it was exciting to be in his presence. I could tell he was nice. All the times I met Freddie after that he was charming and friendly. We had a mad chat on the doorstep of the Townhouse studios and discussed everyone from Elton to George Michael and a bit of Bowie.

He always used to say, 'Oh yes, dear, completely.' He talked about me in an interview once and said, 'I don't think Boy George is going to come and go. I think he's here to stay.' This was when Freddie was more straitlaced and perhaps he wouldn't have become quite so iconic had he stayed Killer Queen. Ironically, he turned into the archetypal gay clone and I took the mantle of wearing Zandra Rhodes's blouses. The interview was suggesting I was a wannabe, nothing more than my clothes. Freddie put him right. If I was just a clothes horse I would be completely out of fashion.

Jamaica was bliss. We drove up at night to Fern Gully and ate food from flaming pots in the darkness; jerk chicken, fried plantain, rice and sweetcorn. That Jamaican weed makes the food taste even more pornographic. In the house we were served sandwiches all day and one of the cooks knocked up a marijuana milk shake which sent me doolally for days. I went to sleep thinking I'd sleep it off and woke up even more stoned. We were by the pool listening to Luther Vandross's 'Never Too Much' and reggae, which goes well with Jamaica.

We even met and befriended the Prime Minister's wife, Mitzi Seaga and went to her house for dinner. I shook the Prime Minster's hand and went up to Blue Mountain Studios. That trip was super friendly. Only one nasty guy said to me, 'Which one of you is fucking Boy George.' He meant fucking, literally. We ignored him. We hung out with some Rastas up in the hills and we were embraced. I could have stayed there forever.

Andre Csillag, my friend and photographer, came for a few days and we posed around the island. We set up certain pictures for the press because Andre could get them directly to a newspaper: I wanted to control the pictures in the pool rather than be at the mercy of a snapper over the fence. I was successfully shot in the pool and looked like Ursula Andress. By then, I was getting comfortable with the idea of shattering my public persona. I casually but quickly became a regular drug user despite having been quite sanctimonious in the other direction. Like a convent girl who suddenly gets exposed to boys. I was young, I could handle it.

It was in Paris that I first tried heroin. I wanted coke but the guy said what about this.

'Heroin? Oh.'

Maybe I wanted to look cool. I bought it. I snorted it in the hotel and was instantly over the toilet bowl throwing up the lining of my stomach. It was hideous and then *boom* – I felt such peace. It was like time stood still. I think taking heroin was the most dangerous thing I ever did, and I was lucky to survive it. It took a few of my friends but I thought I was safer because I never injected it. I was too fearful of doing that. I stuck to snorting and smoking it. I don't know how Marilyn started taking it or how we started using it together but I remember taking heroin with Steve Strange, and I found others who were in the same dark hole. Before I took heroin, I thought it was a disgusting drug taken by low-life addicts, but I soon found it completely normal. After that first time in Paris, it was a while before I used it again, but I guess it had left some cellular imprint.

I let my guard down in Jamacia and freebased cocaine for the first time and it was euphoric. Cocaine is a bit of a one-night stand because it's only powerful the first time you take it. Whether you snort it or smoke it, you are always chasing a one time high. Like many people, I thought I could control my drug use and even when people were dying around me, I still didn't get the message.

Culture Club was starting to fall apart, and our records were failing to impact the charts. Maybe it was my energy or my relationship with Jon or maybe it's just what happens to all artists or bands. I know the boys and our manager Tony could see the changes in me but what could they do? Especially when everyone except Tony was using drugs. Like me, I guess they all thought they were in control and I don't know how they dealt with it. But I had the pressure of being under media scrutiny and I know there was talk on Fleet Street about my partying.

I had a massive birthday party in New York, which started with a small select dinner party and went on to the Palladium nightclub and then to Area. The dinner was thrown at the apartment of Publicist Couri Hay who was friends with Cornelia Guest, my socialite new best friend. Couri had worked with Andy Warhol and was one of those classic 'move that building' types. Nabila Kashoggi was at dinner dripping in so many diamonds she had security standing behind her. I hardly knew anyone there but Couri, Marilyn and Cornelia. The drug taking started at the hotel, and I hardly touched the food at dinner. By the time we got to The Palladium I was high on ecstasy and coke and the cameras were flashing.

Those nightclub moments are always a blur and I spent the night avoiding cameras and people who just had to tell me something. Everyone was high or very drunk. The mix of booze, coke and ecstasy made people very touchy and talkative. I could write a book on nightclub moments alone but, in the end, they all dissolve into one big nightmare. Was I having fun? I thought I was.

The night continued at Area with Breakfast in Bed. Well, that's what it said on the invite but who was eating? I had been getting birthday snogs from strangers all night, but I was agitated and suddenly had the worst asthma attack. Someone had to rush to a pharmacy and beg them to give me an asthma spray. I was saved and carried on partying with the likes of Jean Michelle Basquiat and Matt Dillon who was nervously seated next to me on a bed. I had said in an interview that I wanted to be reincarnated as his underwear. Classy. I don't think there was a man more beautiful in the world at that moment. Warhol was there taking pictures and staring into the void. The party was the talk of Manhattan and I slept for days after.

I was going back and forth to New York alot on Concorde, sometimes jumping on at the very last minute with Marilyn or Fat Tony. Those flights were a fortune, but by now I had money and I didn't care. I was having a Marilyn moment and living like a glitzy star like he always told me to. Marilyn wasn't famous in America, but most fans or trendies knew we were associated and Marilyn in those days could own a room. I covered up with layers of clothing and Marilyn went for 'give her an inch and she'll wear it'. Her look was a big Kate Garner from Haysi Fantayzee but less Vivienne Westwood and more like the cheap part of Hollywood Boulevard.

Now everyone was noticing me, it wasn't quite what I thought it would be and even when I tried to hide, the spotlight would just get brighter. I never thought of myself as 'cuddly' but it was said about me. The cup of tea thing. I said it on the Russell Harty Show and it followed me like Lynx deodorant. I wanted to be bad. Like Marilyn's inner Rolling Stone.

New York is a city that indulges you, and even more if you're famous. I was very famous by now, but doesn't that just mean I am everywhere all of the time? I was. I was always in the press and without trying. Even now I get so much press but mostly the negative variety.

During this time in New York, Marilyn wanted to write and make some music. He met producer Man 2 Man in a club, and we worked with him in Jersey. He knew musician Michael Rudetsky and we all went into the studio. I loved Michael and we became super close. He was one of those musicians who just got me. Very talented and funny as funny can get; a true unforgettable character. We created music for Marilyn, but we were all taking too many drugs and going around in circles.

We managed to finish a version of Norman Greenbaum's classic 'Spirit in The Sky', which we mixed with Nina Simone's 'Oh, Sinner Man'. I had met a powerhouse singer called Diva Gray and she came back with Jocelyn Brown and a tall white chick. The white girl did all the falsetto, but the power came from Diva and Jocelyn. Marilyn sounded great on it, but it never came out.

Michael ended up coming to London after a stint in rehab and we used drugs together. It's shocking to look back on this time because he died in my house after a session. He had just come out of treatment and was vulnerable. I wasn't there as I was still partly living in St John's Wood, but it was the saddest and most brutal news and I remember watching him being carried out by the coroner. I was questioned by police and his family tried to sue. I understood how much they hated me, and I hated myself. I still think of Michael all the time and even talk to him. I loved him. He was my friend.

It was around this time that I was found with a tiny bit of hash and my world was crumbling. It wasn't my first or last arrest though. I had been arrested at fourteen years old for going with the intention to steal. I used a bunch of wire hangers bent together to create a claw and put it through the letter box of a local boutique. I say local, it was close to my then-girlfriend's house in New Eltham. I ran when I saw the police and a ginger one tried to catch me and fell over ripping his trousers. They put me in the back of a police car and punched me in the face. Like, smack in the face, full force. I screamed that my Dad would murder them, and they just hit me more. At Eltham police station they strip searched me and then realised I was underage and needed a parent present. I remember sitting in the cell scratching and pinching my face so the bruises wouldn't go down – I have a skin disorder that makes me react to even subtle touching and they battered me.

Dad and mum arrived and when Dad saw my face he yelled, 'Which cunt did this?'. I was quick: 'the ginger one' and Dad almost jumped over the counter swinging at the two coppers. Mum was screaming, 'No Jerry, no'.

At home, I got a bit of sympathy but not too much as I *had* broken the law. I remember that Dad wanted to act against the police, but I was warned by a visiting officer that it would not be wise. I had to live in Woolwich, and I was already constantly being stopped by cops. The O'Dowd's, well, Richard had a reputation. I stood out like a sore thumb with my dyed hair and bondage kegs.

Despite my second run-in with the law, there was still a lot of partying and flying back and forth. I went to a fashion show in Austria, fully intending to stay sober for the aristocrats in attendance. I think I remember a Prince and a Princess someone, but that might have been somewhere else. I was unpacking my luggage and found a gram of heroin in my trousers. Like an idiot I took it before my performance and I was as to be expected. We were heading to Switzerland to work with producer legend Arif Mardin. To say I was distracted is the least of it. The first three days I slept under the console. Arif was such a beautiful man but he worked with Aretha and Chaka Khan so he knew about temperament and tripping.

In Montreux I shared a private chalet by Lake Geneva with Jon which we called the bunker. The recording was chaos and mostly held down by Roy. I was smoking pot relentlessly and invited Philip Sallon and a car-load of misfits to visit. Philip brought Linda Queenie, who was a trans dominatrix who had once worked in the mines. She kept running around screaming, 'Innit camp, Switzerland.' She would show her tits to everyone and say, 'I got these on the NHS. God Save the Queen.'

Me and my siblings as children.

**Below Left:** Stephen Linard's St. Martin's degree show. c.1980.

© Shutterstock

**Below right:** Culture Club sequin horror show!

© Andre Rela

CC decked out in Sue Clowes. © Andre Rela

Do you know who I am? © Shutterstock

Hanging out on
my namesake street!

© Shutterstock

Pinball Wizard on tour
in Japan.

© Shutterstock

Our platonic affair.

© Andre Rela

Brit Awards 1984
with Frankie Howerd.

*© Shutterstock*

The pinnacle of our
excess. *© Andre Rela*

Punking it up
backstage with
Grace Jones.

*© Shutterstock*

Reach out and touch. © *Getty Images*

Friends of Freddie Mercury and Judas Priest! © *Shutterstock*

*Anti-clockwise from top:* Stevie Wonder, Debbie Harry, Little Richard Alison Moyet. © *Shutterstock*

Filming a Suntory whisky commercial in Death Valley that never got aired.

© Shutterstock

The A-Team and the Gay Team. © Shutterstock

With Mum and Dad. Look what we created! © *Shutterstock*

Kissing my Queen. © *Shutterstock*

My friend Paul, who we called Tranny Paul – in fact he called himself that – was wearing a one piece swimming costume with stilettos and a huge Priscilla Presley wig swapping use of the real fur coat that belonged to Linda. I can hear her coarse voice: 'Fucking animal rights. Bollocks.' Linda was terrifying unless you knew her but she was basically terrifying. Linda had full transitional surgery and considered herself to be a woman. She taunted anyone who was pre-op, especially if they took themselves too seriously. 'You're not a woman. You're a man in a dress.' Spreading her legs, 'This is a pussy.' You could never have cancelled Linda because she cancelled herself. Philip said she used to stand in a doorway in Soho and say, 'Help me. Help me.' And then when anyone did she would holler, 'Git away.'

But despite all this, recording continued, and this time I was in a hotel. Me and Jon had the fight of all fights which threw itself into the corridor and Tony and Avi Gordon's room. I belittled Jon in front a group of debutantes he was trying to impress and as I put my key in the door he jumped out of the lift and lunged at me. Veteran journalist David Wigg popped his head out of the door hoping for an exclusive. He got one and wrote it up in the *Daily Express*. Liz and Richard were at it again.

Jon broke a finger and a wrist after he punched a lift door after I had run into the lift. A sympathetic picture was given to the press along with a dishonest explanation.

I was invited to the opening of a new club, Palladium, in New York by Steve Rubell who founded Studio 54 and owned Morgans with Ian Schrager. The opening of the Palladium was wild and everyone was there. Madonna arrived with Sean Penn and pretended she didn't see me. I saw John F. Kennedy Jr at the bar and somebody gave me a box of quaaludes. I didn't even know what they were but I took one. Keith Haring was there, Grace Jones, Warhol of course and his lover Benjamin Liu, known as Ming Vase. Compared to Andy, Ming was effervescent, which took very little effort. Of course, I didn't know what Andy was going through. He'd lost his lover to the Aids pandemic, and he was very fragile. I kicked myself about not being nicer. Okay, he slagged me off in his diary three times, which was a badge of honour. We were mean to him, but only because we were mean to everyone. Meanness was polite conversation at times. We could get scathing, one notch up from meanness.

I gave Jean-Michel Basquiat, his alleged protégé, $300 cash in a nightclub. He literally asked me if I had any money on me and in those days I carried wads in my handbag. I was old school, I thought I was Aretha Franklin. I don't know what he used it for, but I hope he had fun. In return, he told me to come to the studio and choose something. Marilyn reminded me of that constantly, but I never felt comfortable doing it. I would have kept anything he gave me because I was such a fan and still am.

I flew Philip to New York a few weeks later and he hated it. He kept saying it was 'dry' and everyone was pretentious. We did have fun in New York but Philip doesn't take drugs, so he had less fun. He knew what I was up to though and made comments:

'Marilyn's bad news for you, dear. I warned you.'

When I invited Philip to join me in Jamaica he asked, 'Are there any gay clubs there? If not, we'll start one.' So Marilyn, Philip, Cornelia, Dencil and me flew in. I paid for everything but I was going anyway and I rented a big house. Philip hated Jamaica more than New York and did nothing but moan. I suppose it was unsurprising because we just stayed in the house getting off our nuts round the pool while Philip wanted to explore the island.

After a few blazing rows, Philip flew back to London needing another holiday and we flew back to New York. We checked into the American Stanhope and planned to do some recording work for Marilyn.

I remember we stole two straight boys from a restaurant and took them to see Madonna at Radio City Music Hall. They were having dinner with their girlfriends when Marilyn walked up to the table and said, 'Do you want to be our dates?' Such is the audacity of fame and the desire to be around it, they dumped their girlfriends and came to the gig. Marilyn and I spent the entire night slagging off Madonna's vocals but as I've said, I actually like her music.

In those days drugs were still scandalous even though you saw people openly snorting cocaine in restaurants, clubs and bars. There was a looseness under Mayor Koch and clubs were hedonistic and brazen.

Back in London I had acquired a new house guest in Alison Hay. She said she wanted to spend some time with me but she'd actually just been sent by the band to make sure I got on the flight to Holland where we rehearsing for our upcoming tour to Israel, Greece, Japan, LA, Puerto Rico and New York. Alison was a rubbish detective. I gave her the slip and went to Heaven, arriving back at 4am. They had trouble getting me on the flight but they managed it.

We had a lacklustre rehearsal but we were playing our hits so we weren't worried. Things were awkward with Jon but I was mostly over it anyway, clinging on for dear life but feeling less enchanted. We returned to London in July 1985 on the day Live Aid was broadcast live from Wembley Stadium. The boys were furious that we weren't taking part but I knew I wasn't in a good enough state to do it. I knew it would cause damage rather than be a moment like it was for Queen.

We flew out to Israel and I stashed a gram of heroin in my underwear and took it on the flight. I arrived incoherent behind dark glasses.

I wanted to get to the hotel and sleep it off while Jon went to visit family friends.

We played our show to 35,000 people, that was one per cent of the population. It went well even if it could have been much better. It was a tired performance and the reviews complained there was a lack of style. I wasn't dressed like traditional Boy George but I thought I was moving on. I'm always moving on.

When Culture Club got bottled off stage in Athens, Robert Smith told the press we deserved it for making crap records. Athens was bad timing because the anarchists were coming for us all. It was a huge government-sponsored festival in an amphitheatre with the weirdest line up of century: The Stranglers, The Cure, Culture Club and The Clash. The troublemakers demanded free entry and broke into the stadium just as we took the stage. We were bottled, stoned and jeered. A brick hit our keyboard player Phil Pickett and I heard an 'ouch'. I enjoyed the animosity, which I completely misinterpreted as homophobia. I told the crowd, 'You Greeks invented homosexuality.' Obviously, I know it's not an invention but sometimes I feel like one.

It got worse. In Japan I invited Billy McKenzie from The Associates to sing 'That's The Way' with my backing singer Jocelyn Brown and me. Culture Club were on tour with The Associates and Paul Weller's Style Council. Billy went off on a vocal tangent and Jocelyn looked at me with that Jocelyn face. Of course, I loved Billy and that never changed but it was an awkward moment.

It was the end of Culture Club for a while. We did our last tour date on Long Island and went our separate ways for a time. I spent some time decorating my New York apartment. I brought over some friends from London, like Fat Tony.

I've mentioned Tony in passing throughout this book but he probably deserves a bigger mention. We met on the King's Road when I first got famous, and he made a bitchy remark about my 'weave'. He called my dreadlocks 'shitlocks'. These days, and for some time, Tony has not been fat but he keeps the name because it holds a certain legend. His Instagram page has become a go-to for those who cannot bear to be too politically correct and it reflects Tony's twisted and dark sense of humour. Like the time we were in a limo in Manhattan with our friends and he adapted the classic, 'The Twelve Days of Christmas' to torture me: 'On the first day of Christmas, Boy George ate in front of me...' It went on and on.

'Five doughnut rings, four calling birds and a partridge in a pear tree.' It was funny for about the first ten minutes but I stopped the car and hid in a shop doorway until he stopped. If Tony found it funny almost everyone else did until it was their turn to be tortured.

In those days, Tony was well known on the club scene and even when he got skinny he was able to throw his weight around. No one messed with Tony, and I didn't need to because I was part of the circus. At times I envied Tony's ability to dodge the public bullets I got hit with.

## NUMBER 1 – CULTURE CLUB'S RISE

One time, when I relapsed at The Wag Club, he said, 'Welcome back to the dark side'. He was there for most of my tragedies, and I witnessed and often experienced his. He could go further with everything and would get his new sneakers dirty in the pursuit of debauchery. I have never seen his one-eyed trouser snake, but I hear it has its own postcode. He had more stamina for excess, but I had a cut-off point. Or so I believed.

I really got to know Tony when he got sober because he lived with me for five years with his dogs, Reggie and Tailor. Our lives became all about banter. We've always liked to trade bitchy comments. He likes to call me Gina. He says, 'Gina I love. Boy George I can't stand.'

Alice was another friend I brought over from London. She was like a boy so we decided to have an affair. We were doing loads of drugs, Ecstasy and Quaaludes, heroin and cocaine, and I hardly remember what we got up to. There were always new clubs opening and parties to go to.

I think I was a safe middle ground for Alice who is now gay and sleeps exclusively with women. With all the drug taking I wanted to break some other rules. Rigid ones about my sexuality. Turns out, just like Alice, I am homosexual.

5

# EXPOSED

The term 'heroin chic' wasn't coined for me, but I used it often in the eighties. Lots of fashion people were taking heroin. After all, I got my first wrap of smack at a Paris fashion show so it was rife: models wanting to be thin or throw up their last meal; talented people who I knew were dying, like John Moore who made shoes and ran the 'House of Beauty and Culture' shop and design studio, which sold designs by Judy Blame and the ground-breaking clothes of Chris Nemeth who I was obsessed with. The artist Trojan died aged just twenty-two, which while hideously sad was not a surprise. At that point it could have been any of us – we were all out of control.

Culture Club were at the height of our fame and I was doing regular photoshoots during that period, and I got some amazing images. I was skinny and could wear almost anything, which I loved. Looking back, I probably looked awful. The photos had to be airbrushed before they were seen.

I went through a badge obsession and bought a machine to create my own badges. Judy Blame had got me hooked on badges at a photoshoot with photographer and make-up artist Paul Gobel. They carried messages like 'I hate Jon' and pictures of Nick Kamen, who I loved.

Culture Club's last album, *From Luxury To Heartache*, which summed up the situation well, was released on April 1st, 1986. Maybe being April Fools Day was apposite. It spent a week at Number 10 then dropped to 25. In America it only got to Number 32 and Australia Number 25. It was a comedown from selling millions so we were delighted when 'Move Away', a single from the album, reached Number 7 in the charts after its release in July.

But by now the Fleet Street sniffer hounds were after me and it was only a matter of time before they caught their prey. There was a rumoured £50,000 bounty on my head.

The first stories about band battles appeared early in the year. The *News of the World* quoted Jon saying, 'George isn't quite himself at the moment.' The first story mentioning drugs appeared in the *Daily Mirror* with the headline 'What's the trouble with Boy?' It talked about my dramatic mood swings and erratic behaviour in shops. Laughably, Marilyn told the *Mirror*, 'I'm going out to LA to help a friend who has a problem. I think I can help him.'

We were booked onto *Top of the Pops* to perform 'Move Away', which almost ended in disaster when I refused to leave my dressing room. The band had hoped that having a hit would be like showbiz smelling salts. But we nearly lost the slot and risked being banned for life.

The *News of the World* tracked down Alice who said I had taken her virginity. If I had, I had no memory of it. Journalist Jonathan Ashby – who had smoked copious amounts of weed with me when he tracked me down in Holland – attempted to befriend me and set up an interview with Alice for the *Daily Mirror* under the ruse it would be about our romance, though in reality he was after the drugs story. He didn't get what he wanted.

Even journalist Fiona Russell Powell, who I regarded as a vague friend though I kept my distance from her, interviewed me for *The Face*. She attempted to get the drugs story out of me too. What about her own story? We both auditioned to host *The Tube* TV show on the same day in 1982. Obviously neither of us got the gig. She looked amazing, though, and they were obviously looking for a quirky blonde, but this one was maybe too quirky.

*From Luxury's* brief stint in the charts was not going to recoup the £500,000 recording costs. The boys met with our manager, Tony and agreed to shelve plans for a forthcoming tour and put the band on hold until after I'd received treatment.

On April 9th, 1986, a story by Jonathan Ashby appeared in the *Evening Standard* with the headline 'Worried About The Boy'. It didn't explicitly mention drugs and relied on gossip about me appearing to drift off to sleep during a TV interview, spending days in the bath and looking grey without make-up. As soon as the paper appeared, a *News of the World* journalist was on my doorstep. I was a mess and furious about the article so accepted her lift to go to Fleet Street so I could hit someone. My co-writer on this book, Spencer Bright, was the stooge sent out to deal with me. His advice was to go back home before I embarrassed myself further. Thank God he was there, and he was right.

It was around this time that Marilyn had one of his comeback shows at the Hippodrome. He was delighted to have pocketed £5,000 and said, 'Let's get the first plane to Jamaica. We're a mess.' He thought the tropics would help us kick the habit. I knew it wouldn't be that easy, and didn't want to stop, but agreed to go. I informed my drug dealer we were going, and she said she and her boyfriend had planned a visit to Jamaica themselves to visit his relatives, and wouldn't it be great if we were all there together.

For the first three days, Marilyn and I sat by the pool. Paradise, apparently. I had my DF118 painkillers but was restless and couldn't wait for the dealer to arrive. I hadn't told Marilyn, who was unsurprisingly disappointed when they turned up. Predictably, drug-fuelled mayhem ensued.

While there, I received a letter from Richard Branson, which said it was becoming plain to everyone I had a problem and pleaded to let them help me do something about it. I just thought Branson was interfering and tossed the letter in the bin. I couldn't see it for the genuine offer it was. I was too far gone.

But when we were home we became even more reckless, taking huge amounts of drugs; freebasing cocaine and then using heroin to bring us down. Marilyn realised it could be the death of us and said we needed another holiday to get over Jamaica. I felt like shit so my travel agent in LA booked us onto a ten-day cruise round the Caribbean from Puerto Rico. On the ship I had a stash of some prescription drugs from a dodgy doctor in London to help with my planned detox, but I soon ran out. We befriended the nurse in the hope that she would prescribe some tranquilisers, but she couldn't help us. After mostly sleeping and throwing up for a few days, we decided after just four stops to get off at Guadeloupe. We left with only hand luggage, arranging for our cases to be sent on to New York.

As we walked through a colourful food market, people pointed and laughed at us while we searched for a quick way back to New York. We must have looked nuts as we asked strangers where the airport was. But when we finally found it, there were only flights to Paris. I phoned a dealer friend in New York, pressuring them to get on a plane with heroin and to meet me there. Wandering around the airport we eventually found out there was a private airfield nearby where we could get a plane to Antigua, which had direct flights to New York. In the spiteful heat, Marilyn and I dragged ourselves the half-mile to the airfield and an hour later – and $300 lighter – we were triumphantly on our way to Antigua in a tiny plane. As we landed, I spotted an American Airlines jet about to take off. We jumped over a barrier and ran towards the plane waving and shouting 'STOP!' as they pulled away the stairs. Armed guards shouted at us to stop. We could have been shot but we were so desperate to get back to New York to get heroin. We were escorted back into the terminal to get our tickets while they agreed to hold up the plane. Looking back, it's utter madness.

I tried to ring my friend heading to Paris from the plane's credit-card phone but it didn't work. As soon as we reached JFK I ran to the information desk and found out an Air France plane was due to leave for Paris from another terminal. So, sweating and panting, Marilyn and I ran there and found my friend at the gate just as she was about to board. She was incredulous, wondering what the hell was going on after expecting to meet us in Paris. We didn't care – all we cared about was getting our hit. Minutes later, Marilyn and I were in the men's toilets. A wave of relief came over me as I took a huge line of smack. Suddenly nothing in the world mattered and we were laughing about our adventure and wondering if we would ever see our luggage again.

The dealer followed me to New York, where she was staying with friends, and charged me $500 for a gram of heroin. I don't remember much about those few weeks except that there were massive fights and arguments. I was wasting away and would just wander the streets of New York late at night, drifting till daylight as New York came alive and I withered away.

One morning, I tried to get out of bed and was involuntarily thrown across the room from a convulsion. It was twenty minutes before I realised where I was. I knew that it was time to head back to London.

At Heathrow, the press were there to greet me. How they knew I'd be there, I'm not sure. I told the reporter for the *Daily Mail* I'd had amoebic dysentery and this was the reason I'd lost two stone. I denied being a heroin addict.

'I'm not guilty... I've always tried to tell kids to stay off drugs. I've never taken them myself but people think I've been going round taking everything in sight. It's not true and it never will be true.'

The next morning, I went to my dealer and a few days later was back in America promoting *From Luxury To Heartache*, convincing myself everything was normal and I was fine. Once back in London, Mum turned up at the house and tried to reason with me and we cried together. I talked her round and said I had it under control. Even if she didn't believe me, what could she do?

'Why do you need that stuff?' she kept asking. 'I thought you had your head screwed on.'

She blamed all the people around me, but it was down to me. I had money and I was paying for the drugs. I had methadone from the doctor to deal with any withdrawals and I chose to use it to balance myself if I ran out of heroin. Using methadone and various pills, I managed to appear normal for days, but I was always drawn back to the dealer to get more heroin. If I wasn't using with Marilyn, I went to find Steve Strange and spent a few days at his flat. One day, he pinched my credit card and tried to go shopping. I was furious when I found out because the shop confiscated my Amex card and he ran off. He denied it. So I had badges made that read: 'American Express, Steve Strange never leaves my house without it.'

Mikey and Roy apparently even discussed a kidnap plan for me with Dad, who wanted to tie me up and take me to the Irish countryside. All sorts of mad plots were being discussed. Friends joked with me about spilling my story and splitting the takings and, in the end, it was someone I regarded as a friend who became my Judas.

Photographer David Levine had shot the cover for 'Karma Chameleon' and was the brother of our producer, Steve

Levine (who was mortified by his brother's betrayal). David had been booked for a session with us for American music magazine *Spin*. I forgot to turn up to a few sessions, and when I did, I was out of it and belligerent.

He kept asking my make-up artist to ask me to get him cocaine as he was tired and needed a pick-me-up. I can only presume he was too nervous to ask himself but it was clearly becoming annoying so I finally agreed and got a friend to deliver two packets of cocaine to the studio, one for him and one that I kept for myself.

I went out clubbing that evening and at 7am was listening to music with my friend Hippie Richard in my house in St John's Wood when the doorbell rang. I thought it was a neighbour complaining, and shouted through the door, 'Who is it?'

'We're reporters from the *Daily Mirror*. Can we speak to you about some allegations that have been made against you?'

They said David Levine told them I sold him cocaine. I laughed and shook my head and said, 'I don't believe it.'

The phone didn't stop ringing, with calls from Tony Gordon and my press officer, Elly Smith at Virgin, among a lot of hacks too. That night I went out, defying impending disaster, and picked up the first early-morning edition of the *Daily Mirror* at the newspaper stand in Leicester Square. The headline was 'Drugs and Boy George'.

David presented himself as a concerned friend, worried I was destroying myself with drugs. I ran home and was besieged by press all day but hid behind closed blinds.

Stupidly, on reflection, I couldn't resist calling Levine a few days later. He didn't pick up so I left a message saying he was going to be dead if I got my hands on him. Naturally enough, the *Daily Mirror* then printed a story with the headline: 'You're Gonna Be Dead.'

It didn't stop me, though. I was brazen, only changing how I carried my drugs, making sure I could throw them away if I had to. I carried on clubbing, smoking a joint as I went into the Wag and grabbing it back from a security guard who nabbed it off me.

The worst public catastrophe was my appearance at an anti-apartheid rally on Clapham Common. I was off my nut long before I arrived and channelling Bob Dylan, with a big red, gold and green Rasta hat and my face plastered with a quick-drying face mask. I forgot my usual make-up and hid behind John Lennon-esque-mirrored sunglasses. My grubby white jean jacket read 'Heroin Free Zone' and 'Suck My Nob'. I was dishevelled and all over the place, mumbling and not making any sense. I don't know how I sang 'Black Money' and 'Melting Pot' with Helen on backing but I did, and the audience gasped. I was rake-thin and clearly smacked out of my brains.

Backstage the other artists tried to avoid me as I scratched my face and smoked one cigarette after another. Sting, Sade and Peter Gabriel were there. There was no hiding my problem, which had been discussed on Fleet Street for the past few months. After the gig I was smuggled out and went back to St John's Wood to hide and take more drugs. My appearance even made *News at Ten*, apparently.

My family were at their wits end and Dad started playing detective, surveilling St John's Wood round the clock. He and Mum were convinced Hippie Richard was the villain, but no one was forcing me to take drugs. He cornered Richard at my house in Hampstead and got him to hand over my keys.

When I heard Dad's voice, I locked myself in the bathroom and ordered him out of the house. He said I was killing myself.

'If I want to kill myself, it has fuck all to do with you,' I replied.

He said he was going to set fire to the house and we could die together. When I opened the bathroom door, I could smell smoke. I ran downstairs to see he'd set fire to a pile of clothes on the living-room floor. I screamed at him to get out.

In my panic I phoned Jon. He arrived to find the police there too. Dad had called them saying I had set fire to the flat. Two policemen came into the house and saw the smouldering clothes. Dad was hoping they would arrest me but no crime had been committed. Jon and I hugged. None of us understood what was happening. When Jon left he nearly came to blows with Dad, who accused him of supplying me with drugs. It was a messy scene.

Mum was furious with Dad. Despite his protestations to the contrary, she knew what he had done. She came with Bonnie to clear up the mess while Dad sat outside in the car. I told her to keep him away from me.

On the way back to Shooters Hill, Dad was raving people were trying to kill me. Mum went to bed exhausted while he was up all night. My brother, David, found him in the morning huddled up on the settee, crying like a baby. My other brother, David, was a freelance photographer supplying Fleet Street and the pop mags with pictures and had good contacts. Dad pleaded with him to go to the newspapers and tell them everything. He resisted but Dad was hysterical and said I'd tried to set fire to the house and was a danger to myself.

So, back at his studio, David called Nick Ferrarri, his contact on the *Sun*. Ferrari screeched down to David's studio in Greenwich and asked how much he wanted but David didn't want to be paid. He just wanted to help.

On July 3rd, 1986, the story appeared: 'Junkie George Has 8 Weeks To Live.' I had an £800-a-day habit, which would have meant I had just seconds to live.

I'd been trying to make sense of the last few hours and

was listening to 'Morning Has Broken' by Cat Stevens when the door went.

'Who is it?'

'Boy George. I'm from the Associated Press. Would you like to comment on the story in today's paper?'

Obviously, I told them to fuck off and turned up the music. I peeked out the window and saw a massive media army outside, which I did my best to ignore.

I sent Hippie Richard to get the paper. I felt betrayed, what else could I feel? Angrily, I rang my brother. 'You cunt, I knew one day you'd take the pay-off, arsehole, selfish cunt.'

Just then, Philip rang with the news a friend of ours was in a coma after a drugs overdose. Perfect timing. On hearing what was happening, he advised me that if I was going to talk to the press I should dress up. I took his bad advice and foolishly denied the story to ITN.

During all the heroin madness, I had started seeing an Irish boy called Michael Dunne. He was living with my friend, Tony Vickers, close by in Hampstead and we started dating. It was probably the worst time to start a relationship, but he was gorgeous, with huge lips and Irish eyes. He was a beautiful distraction. He was a pot smoker when we met but eventually got involved in it all. He is still handsome these days and we are great friends. Better friends then we were lovers, for sure.

It was Michael who got the surprise call from Richard

Branson, who said he was home with David Bowie and that I should come over. Branson knew what was going on; he'd tried to help all those months earlier when I was in Jamaica. He obviously thought the lure of Bowie would help get an audience. I was tempted – I knew David had used drugs – but I didn't fancy a lecture from my hero so I agreed to visit Richard at his office on a barge the following day.

In the morning, we met Richard and he suggested I try a 'Black Box' treatment pioneered by Dr Meg Patterson and drove me over to see her in Willesden. The invention looked like the Jewish tefillin placed on the arm and forehead in prayer, and was about as useful to me. It was based on acupuncture but, instead of needles, sent an electric current to electrodes on pressure points. It was supposed to make withdrawal from heroin easier. So, from Meg's office we went to Mill End House, Richard's home in Oxfordshire, and started the treatment. But it was ineffective. I went through all the usual symptoms of withdrawal over the days I was there, and tossed and turned in sweaty agony. I agreed to just use this contraption without medicine, but it was a mistake.

It was while I was there that the press coverage became hysterical. The *Daily Mirror* asked, 'Boy George is a junkie. What are the police doing about it?' Politicians waded in and the Home Office put pressure on the police.

On Tuesday, July 8th, at 7am, Operation Culture went into action. The police raided my home in St John's Wood –

where my American friend, Bonnie, was sleeping – and my new home in Hampstead, where they arrested my brother, Kevin. They also picked up my dealer and her boyfriend, two other friends and Jon Moss.

They wrongly thought Jon was part of my drug circle but that didn't stop them charging him when they found cocaine at his home. Everyone was put in separate cells. The police wanted to know where I was.

I watched it all on TV, weeping and feeling helpless. The police said they wanted to talk to me. Richard and Dr Meg conferred and agreed it would be best to speak to the police. He told them I was undergoing treatment, refusing to say where, and asked that I be allowed to complete a month's treatment before any interviews took place.

Branson issued a statement at the request of the police. But once the press knew of his involvement, they started stalking his properties. Tony was furious that he'd not been kept informed and, after his repeated insistence on knowing where I was, Branson gave in. Tony's gold Rolls-Royce parked outside Mill End House gave the press a fresh scent. I could sense their presence. The papers were full of my fall from grace. I scribbled a message on a piece of card:

'Moral Majority. Have you come to return my grace?'

I sellotaped it to a window near the front of the house in the hope it would be seen alongside deeper stuff like 'Fuck off' and 'Thanks for caring'.

Tony decided it would be best to move me to a safer place and one evening we all crept out the back of Branson's house, walking across the fields into a nearby church graveyard. Branson piggybacked Meg through the long grass. It was all very surreal. A car was waiting to drive us to Roy and Alison's house in Billericay, Essex.

The police reneged on their promise to leave me alone while I got treatment. Branson was threatened with arrest if he didn't comply, despite his and Meg's protestations that they were setting an appalling precedent and no addict would put themselves forward for treatment if they knew they might be arrested. My solicitor, John Cohen, met with the police and told them I was not fit to be questioned but they said they had no choice. Eight questions had been tabled in the House of Commons and the Home Secretary was now involved.

Tony phoned to say I was going to be arrested. I was more angry than sad. It was a lot of fuss over one small person, which was how I felt: small and insignificant. I didn't believe all the crap about the House of Commons. They just wanted my scalp to set an example.

In the morning, I was formally arrested and taken to Harrow police station instead of Paddington Green – where the main investigation was taking place – so as to be out of sight from the press. I was locked in a cell for an hour, starting to shake and feel nauseous, and then seen by a police doctor who deemed me well enough to be questioned. The questioning went on for two and a half hours. When they were finished, they locked me up again for a couple of hours. When they presented evidence to me that my dealer's boyfriend had implicated me, I fell into their trap and admitted using heroin, even though my lawyer had advised me to admit nothing.

I had never been arrested with any drugs but they decided to charge me with past possession – which does not exist as a criminal charge – as no drugs were ever found on me. Of course, it was a special celebrity charge. A once-in-a-lifetime Boy George opportunity and I agreed to it.

I appeared at Marylebone Magistrates Court on July 29th on what I felt were these trumped-up charges and fined £250 for possession of heroin. I was high on methadone and brazenly carrying a hash joint in my pocket.

Marilyn was arrested but no charges were brought because, evidently, in the real world you can't charge someone on press rumours. I laughed when I saw Marilyn poke his tongue out on the news. My brother, Kevin ended up spending a few hours in the cells, and Michael too. Michael and I stayed together for eleven years after that, but in the end we had such separate lives. We are great friends now though and I love him like a brother.

eigh has played a big part in
y life, it feels like our lives
ad been woven together.

# 6

# CREATING TABOO

**A**nyone who is involved in fashion, especially *avant garde* fashion, will know who Leigh Bowery is. If you don't, google him because he was inspirational. He came from a small suburb of Melbourne called Sunshine and brought that sunshine to London in 1980. You could describe Leigh as a club kid, but he was more than that. A living, breathing, shitting art form. He was a fashion designer who preferred to only make clothes for himself. I was lucky to get some of his designs but he was uncompromising and made them how he wanted to. Like any cool designer, there were hints of Vivienne Westwood. In the nineties, a coat that Leigh made me went missing on a photoshoot. A checkered A-line coat with huge padded wings on the back. If you have it: Give it back!

Leigh has played a big part in my life, it feels like our

lives had been woven together. Leigh was born a few months before me in 1961 and grew up in a very conservative family. His family had connections to the Salvation Army. I've seen some pictures of Leigh as a schoolboy and he looks the spit of Oscar Wilde. He was a talented piano player and attended fashion school before breaking free and doing his own thing. Leigh was looking in magazines in the late seventies and seeing the likes of myself running around the London clubs and was aching to be part of the London scene.

In a bizarre TV interview with shamed rocker Gary Glitter, who had his own chat show called *The Leader Speaks* on ITV's Night Network, Leigh Bowery said, 'London seemed like a melting pot of the most exciting things in the whole world so I had to jump on that Jumbo jet and get myself here.' In the interview, Leigh is wearing a face harness with light bulbs where his ears should be. His body is corseted in red velvet and he appears to have billowing breasts. It is almost impossible to describe his look but watching Leigh flirt shamelessly with Glitter is worth a trip to YouTube. At one point Glitter asks him to explain his look, to which Leigh responds, 'I'd rather leave the explaining to you.'

When Leigh arrived in London in the early eighties, I was enjoying the early days of fame with Culture Club. I remember spotting him at the clubs and I was dismissive at first. During what was labelled the New Romantic period, there wasn't any outrageous look that hadn't been tried –

I used to paint my face blue when it was fashionable. Leigh and his sidekick, Trojan, were going to have to pull out all the props to make an impact on the London club scene. It's hard to imagine that Leigh was ever shy but in the early days he used to dress up Trojan because he was too embarrassed to wear his own creations. Trojan was actually Gary from Croydon and, like many people on the scene, was his very own creation. He was skinny, like a pretty, queer Sid Vicious.

Once Leigh saw how much attention Trojan was getting wearing his creations, he pushed him to the side and took over. I think Leigh was in love with Trojan but Trojan started dating film-maker John Maybury and they drifted apart. Trojan's life took a sad turn as he got heavily into drugs and at one point sliced off half his ear like Van Gogh. On a trip to Paris he shaved the front of his hair off and tried to get a tattoo artist to ink the word 'cunt' on his forehead. He was, thankfully, unlucky. There were stories of him throwing a cat off a balcony and famously scratching the words 'Those below us know nothing' in the lift of the council block where he was living in Camden. The loud music and coming and going in the middle of the night did not endear him to the neighbours. Trojan sadly died of a heroin overdose at twenty-one.

Conversely, from what I hear, Leigh was never a big drug user. A sniff of poppers now and then. Dressing up and getting attention was his drug of choice. His outfits defied both logic and gravity. And at six-foot three and seventeen stone he was hard to miss. He started a club night called Taboo, which quickly became everyone's favourite den of iniquity. It was held weekly at Maximus, a dying seventies disco in Leicester Square. Lots of old clubs were being hired for specialist nights, a model initiated by Steve Strange and Rusty Egan when they opened Billy's in Soho in 1978, followed by the legendary Blitz club in a wine bar in Covent Garden a year later. New clubs like Le Beat Route and Hell were popping up everywhere. The post-punk New Romantic scene needed spaces to dance and preen. Punk had become a bit of a cliché and some of us drifted into a more flamboyant way of dressing. This didn't sit well with the hardcore punks and I remember having beer thrown over me because I was wearing a ruffled shirt and too much eye make-up. My own look changed daily but I was always very fond of dressing like Siouxsie Sioux from The Banshees.

David Bowie came to the Blitz to hand pick freaks for his 'Ashes to Ashes' video. All of a sudden the cool kids turned to jelly. They were screaming and he was mobbed and ushered upstairs to a booth where he sat with Steve who helped him choose the best freaks. I think someone from Bowie's entourage had spotted me even though I was tucked up the back in the cloakroom. But I'd heard my hero might show up and had turned it out visually. Steve whispered in my ear, 'DB wants to see you,' but I couldn't get up the stairs, there was a sea of preened sycophants ruining my bid for stardom. But despite my sadness at that, it made absolute sense for Bowie to come to the Blitz – we were all his children. Rusty Egan, the loudmouthed DJ would play tons of Bowie tunes every week.

I had met my drag mother, Philip Sallon, in the mid-seventies and established myself as one of the freak faces *du jour* on the scene. By the time Leigh arrived from Australia, so much had already been worn and expressed. But the legend of Leigh Bowery was almost overnight. He quickly became the centre of attention everywhere he went.

At Taboo you would spend most of the night in the toilets. Everyone was high and openly taking drugs. There was lots of heroin, and ecstasy had arrived from New York. The drug-taking was so brazen it attracted the attention of the media and Taboo was closed within a year. Before that premature end there were queues round the block and people fought to get in. My friend Mark Vaultier would stand outside with a vanity mirror, holding it up to people asking, 'Would you let yourself in?' Mark and Trojan would ask people if they had drugs and let them jump the queue if they did. Leigh would create a fake guest list every week full of the most unlikely characters you could imagine, like Des O'Connor or Shirley Bassey. British showbiz royalty who would never step into Taboo, but now and then the most unlikely celebrity would show up.

Leigh had his own unique relationship with the truth. He would sit on the phone in his flat and pretend to be talking to famous people. I wasn't super close with Leigh but I admired him. We were disco friends. He lived high up in a tower block in east London with Nicola Bateman, who became his wife in an art ceremony. He proposed to Nicola in the back of a taxi on the way home from a nightclub.

'Shall we get married?' he asked. 'You arrange the whole thing.'

They were married quickly in a registry office with Nicola's sister Christine as bridesmaid and artist Cerith Wyn Evans as best man. I remember some people being horrified that Leigh had got married. It was certainly an unusual thing for a gay man to do. But that was the point really. Leigh did everything for a reaction and he loved Nicola – she is an amazing seamstress and was responsible for beading and sequinning many of Leigh's extravagant outfits. She's also an amazing person. Leigh was often surrounded by formidable females, like Nicola, fashion designer Rachel Auburn, and Sue Tilley, known as Big Sue, who was Leigh's neighbour and best friend and worked as a benefits supervisor.

Despite being married, Leigh was active on the cottaging scene and would often spend an entire day having sex with married businessmen in public toilets. He claimed to have had unprotected gay sex with at least 1,000 men. During the day, Leigh would dress like an eccentric trainspotter, wearing the most dreary clothes with shop-dummy wigs. He convinced himself he blended in, but with his pierced cheeks he was the wrong side of regular. His mannerisms were overly affected and he spoke in a clipped, posh voice. But he was embraced by the London art scene – he was immortalised by painter Lucian Freud in a series of paintings that are considered some of Freud's best and, in 1988, he became a living work of art at the Anthony d'Offay Gallery. For a week he lived in a glass box, changing outfits and posing on a *chaise longue*. I don't think I appreciated it at the time. In fact, I remember rolling my eyes. But looking back, it was pretty genius. Leigh would give performances where he sang, well, shouted, and gave birth on stage to his wife, Nicola. It was a sight to see – Nicola was harnessed upside down against Leigh's body, sometimes for hours before a performance. She would appear from between his legs while he sung 'All You Need Is Love' covered in fake blood with a string of sausages attached to create an umbilical cord. He would vomit Campbell's cream of chicken soup into her mouth. One of his other party tricks was doing enemas on stage. He once shot the contents of his bowels all over the audience at Daisy Chain, a gay club in Brixton.

Leigh was heavily influenced by the drag queen Divine, who'd become famous as a pop singer around the same time Culture Club was exploding. In 1984, Divine appeared on

*Top of the Pops* in full drag and got more complaints than any act in history. Singing 'You Think You're A Man', Divine shook his hips and slapped his butt.

During a live performance at Heaven nightclub he said, 'I'm going to buy myself a Rolls-Royce so I can run it over Boy George,' followed by, 'Oh, he's alright.' When interviewed by Muriel Gray on *The Tube* TV show in 1983 he was defensive because Muriel Gray was unkind to him. He said, 'Boy George wears make-up and no one seems to mind.'

Sadly, Divine had no idea how much I loved him. For me he was a total queer pioneer. I actually have a tattoo of Divine on my left arm and couldn't believe it when I once met him on the King's Road when I was with Marilyn. We ran up to him and he was with the jeweller and artist Andrew Logan. I think we said, 'We love you.' I remember he was so sweet and had kind, beautiful eyes. It's all a bit of a blur because Divine was such a big part of our lives. Marilyn used to call me Dawn Davenport, which is Divine's character in John Waters' cult classic film, *Female Trouble* (changing it to Dawn Pigport if he was annoyed with me!).

In that film, Divine picks up dog poo and appears to eat it; she was a total punk. John's movies truly turned convention on its head. The actress Edith Massey played Divine's estranged mother and threw acid into her face. In that same movie, Divine's mum begs her nephew, Gator, to be gay.

'Why can't you be a nelly. Think of all those hideous anniversaries. I'd be so much happier if you were gay,' she says.

I can't imagine my mother begging one of her sons to be gay.

When I first went to New York I thought everyone would be like John Waters characters. Trust me there were some, but New York in 1982 was still very much in the seventies in terms of fashion. We must have looked like aliens walking around in our Sue Clowes clobber.

We used to go to the Scala cinema in Fitzrovia to watch all the night shows of John Waters' movies. One movie, *Polyester*, even came with 'scratch and sniff' cards with rotten egg and fart smells. You were supposed to use them during the movie but we kept them as souvenirs.

Leigh famously ran up to John Waters in New York and screamed, 'You're a sell-out.' He was disappointed that Waters had made the commercial film *Hairspray* and told him to his face. John was understandably hurt but I told John, 'Leigh must have been drunk or something because he loves you.' When I first met John in LA he wasn't that friendly to me. But I now have dinner with him once a year when he comes to London.

Christine, Mike Nicholls and I went to dinner at John's flat in New York. Mirroring a scene from *Female Trouble*, John said, 'We're having spaghetti.' Both Mike and I replied, 'My husband and I rarely eat any kind of noodle. Do we look

Italian?' I guess it's John's party trick. He said to us, 'Don't you hate people who come to your house and say, "I don't eat wheat"? I always say fuck off then.'

I was heavy into drugs at this time. The night we went for dinner, Christine's foot was bleeding out of her big platform shoes. She'd had a terrible accident in the flat a few days earlier when the shower door exploded and cut her to ribbons. Mike and I were in a nightclub when I received a panic phone call from Christine.

'I need to go to hospital,' she was shouting.

We rushed back to the flat, off our nuts, and helped her pick glass out of her skin. She went to hospital but not all the shards were removed so there she was, bleeding onto John's carpet. I don't think he noticed. Mike – a John Waters obsessive – and John were having the most amazing conversation about John's career. It was like a mental tennis match. Rather like the time I met Pedro Almodovar in Madrid. I think he was surprised how much I knew about him and his movies.

At dinner recently we discussed the trans LGBTQI+ situation in the world right now. He said, 'As far as I'm concerned all these queers arguing with each other is ruining the brand of pervert. We all used to get along united by our differences.'

Leigh Bowery spent a lot of time in New York living with his friend Charlie Atlas, who made a documentary called

*The Life and Times of Leigh Bowery*. Things were really taking off for him when he was sadly diagnosed with HIV. It was before effective antiretroviral therapy was introduced and we lost Leigh on New Year's Eve, 1994. Some of the work he did when he knew he was dying was out of this world. The series of photos shot by Fergus Greer for his book *Leigh Bowery Looks* were surreal and beautiful. Seeing them hung in a gallery was breathtaking. Since his death there have been many tributes and exhibitions of his outfits. His impact on fashion is still evident.

His widow, Nicola, has since remarried and now lives in tranquil Eastbourne, Sussex. She is the guardian of Leigh Bowery's legacy and has all the costumes stored in the loft. I've been up there, it's amazing. I was gifted the legendary merkin that he used to wear and some other choice bits and pieces. But she's not become a 'suburban mum'; she's definitely the mum you'd want if you were a cool kid. As important as any Velvet Underground album. But you can't carry Nicola under your arm. Not with those exploding headdresses.

In terms of freak chronology, Leigh came after me. Gary Glitter asked Leigh if I'd copied him and Leigh said I was an influence. But Leigh also had an influence on me. He made me want to be more outrageous and that's when I created my musical side project, The Twin. It culminated in my album *Yum Yum*, which is a little sexually explicit for me these days. It certainly wouldn't pass the PK seal of approval. But I didn't make the album for commercial purposes. I was going to electro-clash clubs like Nag Nag Nag in London and was influenced by the sound. DJs like Jonny Slut in London and Larry Tee in New York were making punky electronic music that hinted at Kraftwerk and The Normal. The clubs were small but packed and the crowd danced to records that no one outside the club had ever heard, like 'Do I Look Like a Slut?' by Avenue D or 'Modelling Is an Ugly Business' by Larry Tee. I was doing a hybrid look of myself and Leigh, and enjoying being musically *avant garde*. I would have given Sam Smith a run for his money at that point but I never got my tits out (except in *Taboo*).

Before my pop career I was far more outrageous and experimental. The world thought my look in Culture Club was outrageous but it was a toned-down version of my club persona. However outrageous my looks, I was only ever concerned with looking pretty and feminine. Leigh distorted his body, using his flesh as part of the canvas. He would plaster over one eye with prosthetics and give himself a club foot or extend his belly to look pregnant. He would say, 'What's disturbing about distortion? The agenda isn't beauty or ugliness. That's all your ideas.' One time he was filmed outside Buckingham Palace and said, 'Rather like Boy George, I prefer a cup of tea.' Of course, that wasn't true for either of us.

I'd been on a Culture Club hiatus for a few years focussing instead on my deejaying and dance music. But in 2001, I was approached by director Chris Renshaw with the idea of doing a musical based on my book, *Take It Like a Man*. We met on a barge on the River Thames with writer Mark Davis Markham and hatched the idea for *Taboo*. I was clear from the start I didn't want to do a juke-box musical of Culture Club hits. I wanted to pay tribute to all the different characters who had shaped my life; the likes of Leigh Bowery, naturally, but also Philip Sallon, Steve Strange and Marilyn. Glam Rock was the first thing that took hold of me as a teenager, then punk into the New Romantic scene.

My musical *Taboo* was a celebration of seventies and eighties club culture. It was the story of my early clubbing days before fame. I wrote songs about my friends and enemies, telling our story. Philip Sallon was brilliantly portrayed by actor Paul Baker and was our master of ceremonies. He opened the show with the songs 'Ode to Attention Seekers' and 'Give Me a Freak'.

> Give me a freak
> Any day of the week
> I'm comfortable with those you call demented

The music of *Taboo* was critically applauded but the book was panned for being too safe. Our writer, Mark, was under pressure from the producers not to make the show 'too gay'. It was an impossible task and I felt the show became a screechathon, heavy on jokes but low on substance. The main characters, Billy and Kim, were a young straight couple designed to broaden the appeal. Billy, played by Luke Evans, was meant to represent all the straight boys we foolishly fell in love with. Kim was based on my friend Kim Bowen, a fabulous eccentric who would dress like Queen Elizabeth I with her breasts exposed and nipples painted gold. The Kim in *Taboo* was more constrained. The real Kim was amazing when you wanted to go shoplifting. She would walk into the corner shop and distract the staff while we stuffed cheese and ham into our coat sleeves.

Characters like Marilyn and Steve Strange were cruelly hammed up in *Taboo*. When Marilyn initially saw the person playing him, he said drily, 'If I was anything like that I'd slit my wrists.' One of the best portrayals of Marilyn was by John Partridge, and young Boy George was brilliantly played by Scottish actor Euan Morton. In the first production of *Taboo*, Leigh Bowery was played by Matt Lucas. I had seen him play the drums on TV comedy panel show *Shooting Stars* dressed as a baby in his George Dawes persona. It was my idea to cast him and he was perfect. I spotted Luke Evans at an open audition and said right away, 'That's our Billy.' Luke has an amazing talent and has since gone on to become a Hollywood leading man.

The plot of *Taboo* was chaotic but my life as a teenager was quite chaotic. So much happened in a short space of time. *Taboo* starts with me as a teenager leaving home. I meet Philip Sallon who takes me under his wing and shows me around the London clubs. I join the world of weirdos and quickly become a face around town. Billy was an everyman character. A bit Jon Moss, a bit Kirk Brandon. The compromises we were forced to make on the script made the show a bit tame. Even so, we ran for almost a year in London at the tiny Leicester Square Theatre.

After Matt Lucas, I took on the role of Leigh in London. Some of the young cast were taking drugs and I started to indulge again. I had been clean for ages but I was starting to go off the rails. I can't blame Leigh but playing him put me into a very distorted reality. I was on stage with a younger actor who was playing me as a young man. He was getting all the love and I was inhabiting the distortions of Leigh Bowery. He was a brilliant character to play but I feel that we should have made him darker. I would go into the audience dressed as Leigh and pick on people. One night I was taunting the crowd when a woman shouted, 'You've ruined yourself.' I was terrifying everyone while the young Boy George was making mums cry. Every night 'Stranger in This World', sung by Euan Morton, would create an emotional ripple. There was so much great about *Taboo* and so much wrong with it too. (I am actually currently working on a new version with Hope Mill Theatre in Manchester. Our original book writer, Mark Davis Markham, died in 2023 so the new show will be a tribute to him.)

Things only got worse when Rosie O'Donnell – an actress and TV legend in America with her own chat show – took us to Broadway. Rosie was at a matinee in London and came backstage: 'I'm taking this show to Broadway.'

Rosie told us she didn't want to change anything about the show but I never believed her. I sat in a café with Christine Bateman, who designed the make-up, and Mike Nicholls, the costume designer, and said, 'New York will probably be a nightmare but we have to go.' Even though I had strong reservations, who could say no to Broadway?

Broadway was a nightmare from beginning to end. At first Rosie was super brave and put a massive poster of Leigh Bowery at a urinal on Times Square with the slogan 'Your son will come out tomorrow.' She also decided to come out at the same time and made the fatal mistake of putting her own money into the production. This is apparently a no-no on Broadway. The theatre world screams out for new talent and brave productions but they kick you in the teeth for trying.

Even though Rosie's intentions were noble, the critics started to tear her apart. We had so much negative press before we opened. Rosie replaced Mark Davies Markham with New York writer and drag queen Charles Busch and kept telling the press that *Taboo* was like *Pippin*. But it wasn't – *Pippin* was a family show and *Taboo* was more of an *Addams Family* show. In my first scene, I appear from a toilet singing 'I'll Have You All'. The shock on people's faces was delightful. I was slated by the critics for not being a real actor and yet we had many packed nights and amazing shows. It just felt like the critics wanted Rosie to fail.

Yes, Rosie could be brash and aggressive, but she also made us laugh. She was under so much pressure and was forced to shut the show after three months. Our stint at the Plymouth Theatre was exhilarating and frustrating. When I found out the show was closing, I quipped on stage, 'People said we should have been off-Broadway. I'm fucking off Broadway now.' I decided to make jokes about Rosie on stage too. One night Raul Esparza, the actor playing Philip Sallon, had to ad-lib because of an altercation in the balcony. Security had to be called to remove a crazy woman with a ton of bags. It went on for ten minutes and I could hear it over the Tannoy. When I came on stage for 'Ich Bin Kunst (I Am Art)' I said, 'Did you enjoy all the drama earlier on? I love it when Rosie O'Donnell turns up unannounced.'

The crowd roared.

'Don't think of it as the show closing. Think of it as Rosie's purse shutting.'

She lost $10 million on the show but, according to Philip, she had $190 million left.

Things were unravelling for me too. Towards the end of the run, I was going on stage on ecstasy. I have no idea how I managed it. I was clubbing every night and running myself ragged.

I was deejaying around America and flying to Europe. I made a bunch of new friends in New York and started my B-Rude fashion label. I was even selling clothes to Patricia Fields who supplied costumes for *Sex and the City*. For a while I stayed in the flat Rosie had rented for me on Broadway that I shared with Christine and Mike Nicholls. We renamed our flat Cinnamon Hall because we lived above a café and you could smell the spice everywhere. I was hanging out at clubs and having the time of my life. At least I thought so. I was also taking cocaine, ecstasy and drinking whisky sours.

There were moments of wonderful creativity. I was doing art, taking some amazing photographs, and making printed T-shirts and sweatpants to sell. I have creativity in my bones but my spirit was becoming a shadow of itself.

But life got darker after we moved to Broome Street in SoHo in 2005 and the partying took over. Leaving Cinnamon Hall was sad. Christine was always in her room painting her face but she was clearly keeping out of my way. We partied together and went to clubs and even pulled off a fashion show for my label B-Rude after Mike brought designer Tim Perkins to New York. We created a very cool collection; blending my crazy ideas with Mike and Tim, we had our fingers in every part of fashion. Rubber shorts and rubber dresses. Sheer tops with beaded tattoos from the fluid fingers of Christine. Fifties full-circle skirts printed with huge lobsters. I printed and bedazzled hoodies and sweatpants with naked guys and anarchy signs.

I was also exchanging ideas with New York fashion label Heatherette but they were as insane as we were. Ideas were flying out of everywhere but there was zero business sense. Heatherette was run by club kid Richie Rich and his friend Traver Rains, a hot queer cowboy. The Heatherette crew included legendary transexual Amanda Lepore, Paris Hilton, Aimee Philips and Drew Elliott, a former judge on *America's Next Top Model* and now Global Creative Director of Mac Cosmetics. I once upset Drew by calling him 'corporate' but these days he seems to be running the free world. Aimee fell in love with Ian Chaloner, a producer at Radio One, moved to London and has an adorable daughter called Sunday. She kept her maiden name because, in her own words, 'I fought hard for my reputation.'

I met Aimee, Drew and Drew's boyfriend, Macky Dugan, in a nightclub run by Eric Conrad called Beige. On Tuesday nights the restaurant wine bar would turn into a nightclub. It attracted ageing movie stars, elderly beat poets, rock and rollers, lesbians and screamers.

Eric is like Kojak in drag: bald headed with big seventies

glasses fit for a mobster and a very unique sense of purpose. Eric is one of the funniest men I've ever met. Arch, slightly diva-ish, non-compliant, and unnervingly charming. He has run clubs and thrown parties for years and knows everyone. At Beige he would happily move a couple of millionaires to seat Amanda Lapore in a coveted banquette. Aimee, Drew and Macky were also worthy of the banquette and I'm sure that's where we met, thrown together by Eric because we simply had to meet. Aimee, Macky and Drew called themselves the trinity. It was love at first sight.

I know I put Aimee and Drew through hell in New York. They didn't do drugs and hated being around me when I was a mess. (We didn't speak for a little while but now we are close again, thankfully.) I have so many stories from this time, it's hard to know which ones will tickle your pickle. The night Drew revealed that he could do the entire dance routine from Michael Jackson's 'Thriller' video? It happened in the kitchen at Cinnamon Hall. It was a side of Drew I had not seen. It was genius. What about Aimee? She absolutely did not try to kill Christine, whatever Christine claims. Bateman was sunbathing on a window ledge and Aimee tapped her and she jumped out of her skin. For days after, Christine kept saying, 'Aimee tried to kill me.' She got over it when her young Spanish builder boyfriend popped in from the construction site to have a noisy word with her in the bathroom. There were times in Cinnamon Hall when

I thought to myself, 'How many shelves is Christine's new boyfriend going to put up?' One day I came home from a DJ trip and caught them at it on the sofa. I spotted some pert Latino buns running into Christine's bedroom.

'Don't mind me.'

The first B-Rude fashion show was a riot, held in a nightclub during Fashion Week. Debbie Harry was in the audience as hot guys sauntered down the catwalk in glittery underwear. A pair of underpants with a glittery skull on the crotch almost brought the house down. I wanted to revolutionise the male underwear market. I was ahead of the curve but now it's everywhere.

A journalist asked Debbie why she was there and she said, 'I was invited.'

'Do you go everywhere you're invited?' he asked.

'Not always. But I'm definitely here.'

Debbie is fantastically sarcastic and probably over being asked anything. I've known her for years and I love her. Whatever you think about her, stop. She is close with my musician, make-up artist and photographer friend, Miss Guy from the band The Toilet Boys – one of my best friends from my New York days. Once I was in Debbie's dressing room in Australia and Miss Guy texted, 'Debbie Harry hates you.' I showed Debbie and she said, 'Tell him to get a new line!'

One night in Broome Street when I was really off my head, I thought I was being burgled. I thought I saw someone entering the bedroom. I was in the flat with my young Japanese assistant, Kyoko Barbie. I called 911 in a moment of madness and then hung up when I realised what I was doing. I was having a psychotic episode. When Kyoko realised I had called the police she told me to get out of the flat. It wasn't long before the police arrived and caught me running out the door. I was arrested outside in the street, handcuffed and put in the back of a police car and taken to Precinct 5 near Canal Street. Being arrested in America was the thing I never wanted to happen. American cops are terrifying and anything can transpire. I was taken to the police station in bare feet wearing a Misfits T-shirt. I was off my nut and convinced my life was over. At the police station I bent down to tie my shoes laces and I was bellowed at, 'Sir, don't move, don't move.' The police searched the flat and took Kyoko into custody. She wouldn't tell them anything. God bless her. I had been kind to Kyoko and she was an angel for me.

They claimed they found thirteen tiny bags of cocaine, which wasn't true. There was half a gram in a sock in the drawer. The rest had gone up my nose. Everything else in the police report was fiction. They said they walked into my apartment and saw bags of cocaine and a coke-making machine, which was actually my T-shirt press. The way they described the flat in their report was shockingly inaccurate and, luckily, once the New York police have filed a report they can't alter it.

They put me in a cell without realising my phone was still in my pocket so I quickly called Christine in London and shouted, 'I've been arrested, call my sister.' She called my sister who called my then manager, Tony Gordon, and he contacted a lawyer.

Even though I was wasted, I had my wits about me. My foot had been cut during the journey from the flat to the police station so I was taken to hospital in handcuffs, still tripping from the drugs. I remember hearing one of the nurses talk about her new hair colour. I begged the cops to remove the handcuffs because I was totally freaked out but they ignored me. I heard one mumble, 'He's faking it.'

Some hours later, back in the cell, a lawyer turned up and tried to get me to sign a confession. I said no and insisted I get my own lawyer. They kept threatening to send me to Rikers Island, the notorious New York prison. I was kept in the cell for most of the night and the following day before being transported to the courthouse. It was a surreal time in there. Three Mexican guys were put into the cell with me. I couldn't understand anything they were saying but they had a fight and one of them fell on the floor and was having what appeared to be a heart attack. The guards came with a stretcher and were giving him CPR. It felt staged to scare me. I was still coming down and nothing seemed real.

I was put in the back of a police car and handcuffed to the back seat. They made the handcuffs so tight that they were cutting into my wrists. I was wedged in between two cops and then there was one driving and another in the front. They pulled me out of the car at the courthouse as if they were going to beat me up. It was intimidating and designed to terrify, which it did. While I was in the cell at the courthouse I was constantly called names by the guards. Faggot. Queer. I heard one say 'Marvin Gaye was a fag.' I was given milk that was off and I had to sit up on the stone bench because they were throwing buckets of dirty water over the cell floor. At one point I noticed that one of the guards had a small crucifix round his neck. I asked him if he was a Christian.

'I am,' he said.

'Why are you being so hideous then?' I asked him.

He stared at me with bland contempt. When you're arrested in America there are no niceties. You are criminal scum and the idea of innocence until proven guilty really is just an idea. At that point, I felt slightly protected because of my fame. I wonder what they would have done had I not been me? When they first arrested me I was just some crazy punk in a Misfits T-shirt. The atmosphere changed when they realised I was Boy George. People look at you in those situations and think, 'Why are you here? You have it all.' It can also remove some compassion and I think it did. My New York arrest definitely felt heavy-handed.

It was only me and Mum I was really hurting. I'm not

suggesting other people don't love me. I know some of my fans get very affected at these times. The only thing you can say about getting fucked up is that it's utterly selfish. Less selfish when you share the experience. But you always end up on your own at some point.

I can't remember when I was taken in front of the judge. It was early evening and I just nodded while the charges were read out. I think I pleaded Not Guilty and then I was released. My friend Tracey and her husband, Nick looked after me until I could leave New York. Tracey and her mum, Laura were allowed to go to the apartment and collect some of my clothes. I had two passports but the police had taken one. If they hadn't found my spare one, I would have been trapped in America. I was with Tracey and Nick for a few days and then was allowed to fly home. I couldn't wait to leave. After the few months of debauchery I'd enjoyed, New York now felt like Russia. On my way to the airport, I imagined every cop car was following me. I was convinced I would be arrested at the airport. The joy when I took off was beyond. I'm not a fan of flying but that day I was fearless.

At Heathrow Airport all my brothers were there to meet me. Their faces said everything. We drove to Mum's, stopping at McDonald's on Old Kent Road. McDonald's felt like freedom. Comfort food, however bad, always has a vital role in a crisis.

Coming face to face with Mum after such moronic behaviour was always difficult. Mum hugged me and put the kettle on.

'George, son.'

You knew it was serious when Mum said, 'George, son.' The use of the word 'son' was like she was trying to dig deep into me to make it resonate.

I rented my friend Sebastian Scott's flat in Holland Park and tried to stay away from drugs and the papers. I was determined to stay clean and, for a while, I was successful. Being arrested in America felt like the end of my career. I had to return at some point a few months later to face the charges but I didn't want to go. When I told Mum I might not go back she said 'Don't be silly, you love America, you won't feel this way forever.'

It's true, I do love America. It was only the fear of possibly going to prison that worried me. All the time you see people there given these ridiculous possible sentences like ten years for what seems like nothing. My crime was against myself. Addiction is an illness.

I stayed clean for a few weeks but then moved to a rented loft in Shoreditch and it quickly went haywire. It was from that darkly-lit space in July 2006 that I watched the band try to replace me with a new lead singer. I mean it makes sense, but Culture Club without Boy George? They found a singer called Sam Butcher who looked and sounded more like Marilyn. I have no gripe against Sam, he was grabbing a chance, he should feel no guilt. But after one gig, the band dropped the idea. There are quite a few adventures before I got back to working with Culture Club but, as insane as it seems, I still did it. I was a battered wife returning to a bad marriage.

To this day, the rest of the band and I have never discussed Culture Club without me and it remains a kind of dusty elephant in the corner. I doubt they would have forgiven me so easily. Tony Gordon was still in the picture at this point but after a meeting to discuss a Culture Club tour in Australia, I walked and decided to fire him. Roy quickly followed suit. Unfortunately for everyone, a tour without me is a non-starter. I am the face on the Culture Club cornflake box.

I flew back to New York for my hearing and was given a $1,000 fine, which I, or someone, forgot to pay. It's no excuse but, being at the height of my fame, there were many people at that point being paid to do many things for me yet things often never got done. I was reprimanded by the judge and there was a suggestion in the media that I was getting special treatment. Not so.

My subsequent community service in August 2006 ended up being more of a fashion show, though I probably never looked worse, dragging a broom and a bin around the streets of New York in a hi-vis vest and cut-off sweatpants.

Naomi Campbell got sent to a private bathroom with a toothbrush. I clearly had better PR value. I was followed by hundreds of paparazzi, TV crews and reporters over those five days and I have to say it never got boring. I was even commended for my hard work and good attitude by the sanitation department. I was weirdly proud of it. Sometimes you just have to accept where you are. That doesn't mean I didn't shout 'fuck you' at photographers. I remember telling a journalist, 'My mother was a cleaner and I'm a scrubber.'

I went to a nightclub the day my community service was over. It was full of all the coolest New York people, with Lady Bunny deejaying. She must have alerted the door because I walked in to the tune of 'Clean Up Woman' by Betty Wright. Typical Lady Bunny laughing at your expense but I appreciate the twisted humour of a drag queen. There's an honest brutality to drag-queen shade.

*don't know what I was thinking, wasn't in my right mind, but know that's all I did.*

## 7

# AT HER MAJESTY'S (DIS)PLEASURE

**N**othing on this earth can prepare you for the news you are going to prison. Even the handful of Valium that I stole from Alison Hay who was my house guest at that moment. I necked it before going into the glass box in court and had to listen to a rundown of events that I did not remember.

At this point, what does it really matter what happened? His version of events and mine have never matched up. He said in court, on oath, that I attacked him because he wouldn't sleep with me. I have always said that I had paid for his company, but he wasn't my type and I did not find him attractive. I had hired him to model for some pictures and he looked better from behind. He was bitchy about my weight in court.

As I told the police, I pushed him onto the bed and handcuffed him because he wouldn't leave. I don't know what I was thinking, I wasn't in my right mind, but I know that's all I did. It was stupid, aggressive and regrettable but it was less than 30 seconds before he pulled himself free and ran out of the flat and down Ravey Street in his white vest and underwear. What he told police is now in the ether and it was printed in newspapers and is regarded as fact. He hates me, but I beg him to get on with his life. I was wrong and I am sorry but, at some point, I must move on. So, I move on now. I'm not an evil queen just an idiot who did too many drugs and made a massive mistake.

As I told police, I did not beat anyone with a chain and there were no radiators in Ravey Street. Well, only tiny ones close to the floor, and I did not handcuff Toulouse-Lautrec. Once I admitted handcuffing him, I was guilty of assault. The police had no choice but to charge me.

The day I went for sentencing, in January 2009, I went through a surreal moment of surrender. Going from the cell to the van was like being in a seventies movie. I had watched it hundreds of times and now it was happening to me. I was taken to Pentonville. They looked up my arse and sent me to a shared cell. The dreadlocked guy I was holed up with seemed quite pleasant and within about thirty minutes of being there I was offered every drug on the planet. I made the smart decision to turn it down, thinking running out of drugs in here would be worse than hell.

That first morning in Pentonville, I got a letter from my sponsor Beverly. God bless Beverly and God damn Pentonville. On my second day, a prison guard took my photo illegally and sold it to the *Sun*. I was set up by an inmate who asked for my autograph while the officer took a picture. It was disgusting but the upside was being moved to solitary – my friend Amanda had threatened to sue Pentonville and so they moved me from my shared cell. I was happy to be on my own. I like my own company and there was no one to distrust. The prison officers on the whole were nice to me. I think we were all finding our feet. But the food stank like feet. I got to go out in the prison yard once a day. Luckily, you could smoke in your cell but it was still good to get outside. The theme of being in a seventies movie continued. One afternoon the door opened and there was an Italian priest. Father Carmello di Giovanni had previously been the prison chaplain so he had access to the prison.

'Do you know John Themis?' he said.

'Of course,' I said. 'How do you know him? You're Italian, he's Greek.'

John was my writing partner and guitarist for a number of years. Turns out the priest knew a woman who knew John, which is very Greek, like most things in life. Seeing Father

Carmello was massively helpful and I was thankful to John for sending him in. Priests, like churches, have an energy and I am Catholic after all. It encouraged me to write to Mum. In prison you worry the most about your family and I worried what my incarceration was doing to her. But Mum was delighted to hear from me.

> *Brothers, sisters, lovers, united in grief,*
> *They would give you anything,*
> *But they can't set you free.*

After six days in Pentonville that felt like a year, I was taken in a prison van to Edmunds Hill Prison (now called Prison Highpoint North, ironic) in Suffolk. I had to put up with other inmates singing 'Karma Chameleon' incessantly and calling me a batty boy. When I got out of the van and realised some of my detractors were going elsewhere, I put my head back in the van and shouted, 'Goodbye, cunts.' Well, it made the guards laugh.

When I landed, they must have been thinking, 'Here comes trouble.' It felt very different to Pentonville. We were in the middle of the countryside surrounded by green fields. Quite a contrast.

As soon as I could make a phone call I called Mum, but I had to wait to earn privileges before I could make that call. At this point I felt like I was in someone else's life, even though everyone was treating me with kid gloves because 'I'm Boy George'. I got my own cell, which was unusual but they didn't know what they were dealing with. I had my own cell for a while and then was put in with a Muslim prisoner. I didn't know how committed he was to Islam, but he was praying in the cell and he wasn't talking to me. Only the main door to the wing was locked but not individual cells and the first night I was there he took his sleeping bag and slept in the corridor. It was clearly personal. Another prisoner – who listened to the most girlie Turkish pop all day long, clearly a romantic – had said, 'I sleep with my hands on my balls in case Boy George comes in.' In the end I asked to be moved to another block, but before they moved me they said, 'It's a pretty rowdy block, are you sure you want to go there?'

'Yeh,' I said. 'If I have my own cell, I'll just lock the door.'

My dreams of peace were short-lived, though. My cell door was rattling constantly with inmates wondering if I had any drugs, but also wanting to meet Boy George. Across the hall there was a big muscly black guy who was finishing a very long sentence. He was friendly and told me right out, 'Anyone bothers you, come to me.' Next to him there was another Muslim guy, who had a fight with officers after he complained of the smell of bacon coming from the officers' mess. They tried to reason with him but he started punching out and he was wrestled away.

It was the biggest life lessons I've ever had to learn.

When the alarms go off you shudder. You have to be super alert at all times without showing fear. They try to put you with people who are compatible, but who is compatible with me? I made friends quickly with two guys, called Terry and Justin (who was the spit of Philip Sallon). Terry was a run-of-the-mill convict. He was institutionalised. For him, it was easier to be in prison. And, selfishly, I was glad because he made life in prison so much more fun. His energy was hilarious and having been at 'the hotel' many times he knew how it all worked. I was quickly swapping sponge cake for extra milk and Cornflakes. Another towering black guy on the floor below would swap me milk and Rice Krispies for my cake or any pudding. I think people thought he was bullying me but he wasn't. It was fair trade.

I had my first run-in with a guy who was on the phone arguing with his girlfriend. I caught his eye and he shouted, 'What you fucking looking at, batty man?' I pulled open the door of the phone booth and shouted, 'Proud of it.' And then ran quickly to my cell. People heard what he said and everyone came to my defence, especially Terry: 'If that cunt says another word I'll put one on him.'

It was also Terry who made a prison officer blush when he said, 'Boy George fancies you. He's asking for a strip search.' Occasionally cells are turned over by the guards to see if untoward is going on. I had an early-morning raid and, guess what, the cute officer was involved. It was embarrassing when I had to lower my pants but probably more embarrassing for him. Nothing was found and life went on. You weren't supposed to swap food or have extra pillows or blankets but if you keep your mouth shut and behave nothing is said.

Who you are outside will follow you inside. Flawed people are my currency and I know I'm one myself. Before my arrival, I think the prison governor was expecting an absolute nightmare. But for me it was a question of survival. Everyone in prison thinks they're innocent, and the law has no room for nuance. Most things in life are neither. Often, it's the circumstances you find yourself in and not some black stain on your soul. You learn quickly that prisoners are just like relatives. In fact, in the same prison was my brother's brother-in-law, John, who I saw from time to time.

I remember a fierce, black, notorious shoplifting queen from Brixton was sent to Highpoint. I saw her in the yard thinking we might have a connection but she gave shade. She was having none of the Boy George business. She wanted to be the only gay in the village and she wasn't holding back. She eventually got moved because she was sharing a cell with a straight guy and decided to be a naturist 24/7. Bending over while making the bed and showing her meat and veg to this poor bloke. I don't think the guy was homophobic but it was a lot for anyone. Off she went.

Blake Fielder-Civil, Amy Winehouse's husband, was also

at Edmunds Hill. One day I went for coffee in his cell. He was still married to Amy at the time and played me her version of 'Will You Still Love Me Tomorrow'. He said he had Donkey Kong tattooed just above his pubes and I have to assume he was telling the truth. Blake had that Sid Vicious vibe about him and I could see why Amy fell for him. Who doesn't want a punky boyfriend who loves ska? They were like star-crossed lovers, a tragedy waiting to happen. At that point it hadn't happened. Terry came running into my cell a few days later and said, 'They're moving Blake. The love affair's over. You took the dairy off him. He couldn't take the competition.' As usual, Terry was paraphrasing Cockney slang in his unique way but I knew what he meant.

I got myself a job in the kitchen. The most coveted job in prison. If you're not a psycho, your chances of landing a washing-up job are definitely higher. Anyone known for throwing around knives may struggle. I met Justin smoking outside the kitchen block. He gave me a roll up and I said, 'You look the spit of my friend Philip Sallon.'

'Correction, he looks like me,' he said.

He was quick-witted and a bit camp, and I knew we were going to be friends. Justin is Jewish like Philip and had an affair with an orthodox Jewish married woman that went terribly wrong. He sent videos of them having sex to her family and chopped off her hair in the back of his car. He was a hairdresser. It was one of his worst hair-cuts. I used to hang out with Justin in his cell. He got special kosher food and would often give me a pot of lokshen. Like Philip, he was a hoarder. Under the bed it was like Kosher Kingdom.

My first day in the prison kitchen was steamy and tense. I was in the pot room using a big jet cleaner to wash pots and pans. It was good doing physical work and, like I've said, I like being busy. I stayed in the pot room for about a week before I was promoted to vegetarian cook. One of my quiches scored high praise. A guy in the kitchen said, 'Who made this quiche?'

'It was me,' I offered.

'Batty man make a nice quiche, you know.'

It's hard to be offended when someone is being so poetic.

Making good vegetarian curries came easy even with the animal-food vegetables they supplied. Those carrots had an attitude and the knives weren't sharp enough to take them on. I remember hearing Pink's 'So What?' blaring around the kitchen and everyone singing along.

*I want to get in trouble, I want to start a fight.*

Writing about prison is weirdly exciting in hindsight. I don't remember it being particularly exciting at the time, it was more numbing. I remember when the football or boxing was on how all the inmates would scream and bang the doors. It's the stuff of movies.

My first visitor was John Themis and then after that my three brothers visited. I remember thinking, 'I'm glad it's me in here and not one of them.' It's hard not to rail against things in prison but you have to keep your head down. Some inmates drove the guards insane with requests for this, that and the other. The guards are just ordinary men and women with families, and who needs more stress in an already stressful situation? There was no gay sex, whatever people think. No one was particularly homophobic but there was an undercurrent. I've been gay long enough to be able to read the room. I learned to manage, just like I've always done in any situation. When people were aggressive to me, I was aggressive back. You have to send out the message 'leave me alone' while being super friendly. You create your little clans: me, Terry and Justin, thick as thieves, except I'm not a thief any more.

In prison I read so many books. Not things I'd normally read. I had time on my hands and I wanted to push myself. I read all the books I pretended to read before I was locked up: *Catcher in the Rye*, *Catch-22*, *Middlesex* by Jeffrey Eugenides, all the *Harry Potter books*, *Wuthering Heights*, and *A Visit from the Goon Squad* by Jennifer Egan. When I couldn't find books in the prison library my friends sent them. I also received hundreds of insane gifts I wasn't allowed to have and they were stored in the prison basement like some mad treasure trove. I was even sent money and left prison with a ton of money that I didn't really need. I also had sacks of letters but I didn't keep them. When I left, all I wanted to do was forget my time there – I was told, as long as I never come back, I would forget it in days.

But I remember the funny moments, as recorded in this book, just not the hours of mind-numbing boredom and loneliness. I remember the music. The boredom was broken by other people's music and sometimes my own would break theirs. A prison favourite was The Killers' 'Are We Human?'. I can still see Terry singing, 'Are we human or are we gangsters', jumping around my cell like Bez from the Happy Mondays.

I remember that one of the prisoners was shagging a female prison officer. They were at it in the giant fridge and outside where you smoke. Getting away with it must have been thrilling. The guy was cute, but I had no cigarettes. Another prisoner called Pat said to me, 'I really love one of your songs.'

'Only one?' I said. 'Hope it's not "Karma Chameleon".'

When he said 'GI Josephine' I nearly fell over. It was a song I wrote about the American military gay ban: 'Don't ask, don't tell.' I wonder sometimes if people know what the words mean or if they just love the melody? I never did find out which one Pat was.

I was asked to smuggle out contraband but I refused. They used potato to make pocheen, some weird alcohol.

One guy got extra time for smuggling out eggs and bacon in his trousers. A muscle guy, he was going to cook the bacon on the window and eat the eggs raw. We were allowed to work out in prison. I pushed myself to go to the gym, even though it was the most testosterone-heavy part of the prison. I even had to do a test before I was allowed in. It was like being back at school. We had to carry boxes, learn how to do CPR, thankfully with a dummy. Though there were a couple of inmates I would have resuscitated willingly...

I got amazing letters, hundreds in fact. Stephen Fry wrote to me very sweetly. John Themis wrote to me almost every day, and I got a bunch of letters from my DJ friends Princess Julia and Dusty O. It was much better when people wrote to tell me what was going on in a nightclub or some party rather than trying to comfort me. Fat Tony wrote too. He has the biggest handwriting. He just scribbled on pieces of paper and cards. In one he said, 'Right now I wish I was disturbing you while you are watching *The Weakest Link*.' It makes me smile to think of that. There was a time when you couldn't call me during that show. Anne Robinson is my favourite TV wicked witch. She was even bitchy about me once on the American version: one of my friends and long-term fans, Terry Howard, won the show and made a pretty sum. She told Anne her hobby was following Boy George. Anne said something like, 'I'm surprised anyone remembers him.' No worries.

Like Tina Turner, Janet Jackson, Prince and many more, I've forgiven her.

I love so many of Janet Jackson's records and I still play them. But when it comes to me and Janet, let's wait a while. The first time we met was on the American TV show *Solid Gold*. I brought a handful of 12-inch vinyl records to take back to London of her latest single, 'What Have You Done For Me Lately?' I love that record and know every single word (not the dance moves). I walked up to Janet backstage without my face on and said, 'Oh, I love your new song.' She wasn't friendly and didn't try to be. But I just walked off and got myself into my best 'Boy George' and was walking around backstage to make sure I was seen by everyone. One of her crew approached me with a video camera and said, 'Will you record a message for Janet?' So I did.

'Next time you meet someone, be nice,' I said.

They looked shocked but I carried on. I don't remember what I said but, shortly after, I was summoned to her dressing room. She said she didn't recognise me and I said, 'That makes it worse. Are you saying you would have been nice to me if you knew who I was? What if I'm just a fan?' We parted on awkward terms.

I saw her again in London at *Top of the Pops* a few years later and she looked straight through me. I thought, 'She's never going to change.' In December 2019, I was performing at the Royal Albert Hall for the British Fashion Awards and when I looked over to her table she had her back to me and stayed in that position throughout my performance. I was already fuming with Naomi Campbell because she had asked me to sing for her after she accepted a major award. But she did her speech and then walked off without introducing me. I had to walk on like a numpty and sing 'Everything I Own'. Seeing Janet Jackson sitting with her back to me really capped the night off.

When someone is a bit rude you never get over it, which is an important Post-it note to myself. Be nice. When someone is weird and rude it's a different story. There are always artists you're going to forgive because you know they are super talented. But being talented doesn't give anyone the right to behave badly or unconsciously. I'm not always warm to everyone. Actually, past tense these days. But I did have awkward moments, not only with other artists but also fans. It was mostly me apologising for saying something bitchy, whether it was Corinne Drewery of Swing Out Sister or George Michael.

I met Prince in Paris – even that sounds like a lyric. It was Paris Fashion Week and Prince and Madonna had been circling an event in their limos so that they could be the last to arrive. Who's got the time? I think Prince won the toss and he arrived with Mayte Garcia, who was beautiful. All that drama to end up sitting in the corner.

*You went to all that trouble,*
*To be no trouble,*
*So burst your own bubble.*

Everyone was at that party: Prince, Madonna, J.Lo, Puff Daddy, the Propellerheads and maybe Missy Elliott but maybe I imagined that. Missy was at another Versace thing. At that point I found her quite unaware of who she was. 'Who's that?' I thought. 'Amazing.' Not just sort of amazing, completely amazing. The lyrics firstly, because melody is overrated anyway. I next met Missy during the Viva Glam campaign for Mac in New York. I arrived off my nut on ecstasy and poor Christine had to try and paint my face while I taunted her.

'Ooh, why you being so professional? Like you work at the make-up counter at Harrods. Ooh, she's so proper. Look everyone, she's wearing a white coat.'

She was actually wearing a nurse's outfit that I customised, which is far sexier than my recollection. Christine carried on wilfully and then Missy Elliott arrived. She was carried in asleep and placed in a chair. They undressed her in the chair and put her in a robe. Pampered her, preened her, did her nails, started her make-up while Christine was in the full throes of painting me. Christine's make-up was so beyond. She was using an ombre style of fading in and out insane colours and I looked like I'd landed from Mars. Missy woke up for a second, looked at me and said, 'That shit is sick.' And then went back to sleep. How beyond to have shared that moment with Missy, one of my favourite artists, and the fact she probably won't remember it. It's okay, Missy, it's taken me sixty two years to remember anything.

Obviously, I'm being ironic because here I am writing a book. How I remember things is down to me and no one else. Even Marilyn. Whenever Marilyn tells a story, she remembers herself as the hero. I have learned through practising The Three Principles that how you remember things is life's little psychedelic moment. I might remember things in a libellous way so you won't be getting that story. In NA we are taught: speak your truth and make amends, except when it will harm you or others to do so. I know for a fact I'm never going to be best friends with Janet Jackson or Naomi Campbell. She might be furious to hear it but at least she'll call me.

Back at the party in Paris, I was summoned to Prince's corner. I glugged a couple of glasses of champagne for extra courage and off I went with my Slim Barrett, metal earring swinging in the breeze. After exchanging pleasantries – and by the way, I wasn't asked to sit – he said, 'I love your earring.' 'Oh, Slim Barrett would love to give you jewellery,' I replied, saying it like he needed a break. This guy had thirty pairs of shoes made every month by a shoemaker in Hollywood and they had to be vegan.

He certainly didn't scrimp on the wardrobe. There are artists (I won't mention names) that have more money than Onassis and still want a deal. It's their ego that wants a discount. In real life, they don't need it.

I'm not suggesting Prince was one of those people. He was a Gemini with a Pisces moon. I loved him as an artist and as a lyricist. He loved Joni Mitchell and he used to play 'Karma Chameleon' over and over. A moment of madness, surely. Meeting him that time was actually *molto strano* because I was eventually asked to sit down and then he didn't speak for ten minutes. Also at the table was Donatella Versace and some other Italians, but at that point my Italian was super sketchy. I can't hold a full conversation in Italian but I can work my way round a sentence. Trouble with that, if you say anything in Italian to an Italian, they march into the response hands flying believing you can respond. That's where nodding comes in handy.

Prince continued not to speak. Writing about it now fills me with unexplainable hysteria. It was so funny. A plate of carbonara arrived for the wife and Prince started feeding her. I'm thinking, 'What planet are you on, baby?' The arrival of the carbonara gave me the perfect excuse to say goodbye.

'It was lovely to meet you, enjoy your dinner.'

Even he would have appreciated that parting dart. Everone I know that knew him says he had a hilarious side. If he did, he didn't show it to me and I can only work with the script I was given. I've seen him giving shade to people on video so I know he was a number. He turned down the Michael Jackson duet because it started with the line 'Your butt is mine' and he wanted Prince to sing it. Prince could have sung it with such humour and sensual knowing. The track was amazing and would have been doubly amazing with Prince on it.

I never met Michael Jackson, how annoying. Oh, wait a minute. When I was doing *Taboo* in London I was told he was outside the theatre in a blacked-out limousine. He may have been coming to the show but, if he was, Leigh Bowery frightened him off. I ran up to the limousine in a crash helmet and tutu and was screaming in the voice of Leigh, 'Come out, I know you are in there. We love you, Michael Jackson.' He never saw the show.

I loved, loved, loved Michael Jackson. As a performer he was untouchable. I loved his music and some of his antics. He didn't like mine, though. I wish I'd met him. I almost did a duet with his daughter, Paris Jackson. She loved the song 'London Calling Paris' but in the end she said no. It would have been amazing because when I met her at that party in Paris she was so beautiful and warm.

At that same fashion show, Bono crossed the catwalk to give me a kiss. I love Bono. On my 60th birthday he sent me the most beautiful video message. I was in Ireland. I never posted it but it made me cry. The late designer Karl

Lagerfeld wasn't so friendly. He never was friendly to me. He probably thought I was too fat, like he rudely said of Adele. Who knows what he thought? Maybe he didn't think anything, even worse, sitting in his summer castle with a mountain of books indifferent to my existence. However, when I'm standing in front of him with a massive Westwood hat covered in Dior badges, he better know I exist. Again, I loved Karl Lagerfeld regardless of what he thought of me. The fact that he ignored me every time I saw him was a bit John Waters. I still think he was major, with his high-collar haughtiness, like an amazing fashion wizard.

Every time the Propellerheads played something big, or one of Madonna's records, she would get up and dance. The floor might be empty but once Madonna was on it everyone surrounded her like a new cloak she didn't like. They left the dancefloor with her and she didn't say hello to me, which didn't help her cause. My friend met her once and he said, as he extended his arm to shake her hand she said, 'Ugh, I don't know where it's been.' He replied, 'By my side all night.' I told him he should have poked it in her eye.

I actually wrote about that Versace party in my *Sunday Express* column at the time. I caused a lot of pain with that column because I didn't do my research and I was using it for revenge and scandal. What is the world without revenge and scandal? My friend Maria Smith said to me just recently, 'Oh, when I hate people I'm never sad.' If you divorce yourself from the feeling of hatred for another person, you might as well not bother in the first place.

Madonna is everything it says on the tin but she adds new ingredients every day. I know for a fact she's too full of herself to even mention me. She once said, 'Boy George was mean to me in the eighties and he's still mean.' To be fair, I haven't really been given the opportunity. I found Karl Lagerfeld fascinating but Madonna tips the scales. I like loads of her records. Scrap that. I love some of her records. Not knowing anything about her I would assume she'd have issue with the word 'some'. She came to see *Taboo* in New York but didn't come backstage to say hello. We had previously received a cease-and-desist order on our version of 'Vogue'. Let's just say I abbreviated the lyrics to the song. When anyone sends me up gloriously, I appreciate it. I have a sense of humour, I don't think Madonna does, despite some of the clothes she wears (LOL). Every gay man loves Madonna and there's no one gayer than me. Her fans always try to defend her when I make a joke or a jibe. They are mostly missing the point. Madonna's no wallflower. She took on the world in a cone bra. When I went to see her in New York with Marilyn she was writhing on top of a ghetto blaster saying, 'Everyone has a box, only mine makes music. Like Bette and Joan, we should have been friends. There's still time.

It was the same with Pete Burns – he once said to me, 'To think all this time we could have been friends.' In the eighties we all wanted to be the only queer in the village. Instead of supporting each other we bitched and insulted each other's music. After years of bitching, we shook hands at the Daisy Chain in Brixton. I saw him walking towards me and I was ready to knock him out if he started. 'Put it there,' he said in that unforgiving Liverpool accent. I took his hand and he said, 'How do you do it, all that fucking press torture? I have nothing but admiration.' The thing is, I loved Pete Burns the minute I set eyes on him. I paid for his funeral and it was an honour. I almost said 'pleasure' and Pete would have laughed his head off. We had our wars for years. My publicist in New York, Susan Blonde, took Pete to one side and told him, 'Boy George is our biggest star. You don't say bad things about him.' I never knew this happened and I would have been appalled. As friends we would have had scandalous fun. Pete appealed to my dark sense of humour.

My only worry when people are fierce is whether they are happy too. You can be arch and fun. Someone should tell Madonna. I'd love to receive that phone call and I would record it.

⚱ ⚱ ⚱

Soon after prison, with my electronic tag freshly fitted, I was deejaying at a daytime event at the Egg Club in King's Cross.

My frenemy Laurence Malice owned it at the time and Fat Tony was putting on an event. There was drink and there was drugs, but I had been clean for fourteen months by this point and felt comfortable being there. To my surprise, I saw a guy from prison who had always ignored me in the gym. He came up and said hello.

Another time I was recording in Bromley with Kevan Frost, my musical director and friend. I saw someone from prison at the train station. He was on his way back to Edmunds Hill. It was almost like I couldn't escape it.

I saw my mad friend Justin a handful of times and I stayed friendly with Terry for a while, but in the end we lost contact. Terry was just what you need in prison. He was hilarious. Didn't give a shit about anything until it actually happened. But on the outside he was too much of a reminder. A trigger. He went back to prison a number of times and I went back to Pentonville to see him. It was super weird being a visitor. They put you through the security process of locked doors and holding spaces. At one point I thought, 'What if they don't let me out?' They were nice to me, though, and I got a few winks from officers. It was a quick visit.

Going back to prison, if only briefly, reminded me I never wanted to be there again. I often say to myself I would have done it so differently had I known what was possible. I changed a lot inside prison but I didn't know it at the time. When people asked me if it changed me, I got very defensive. I didn't realise the changes until I was free. When you're in prison you're just going through the process. The good news was I knew roughly when I might get out. I did everything I could to get an early release and when they released me after four months into my fifteen-month sentence I was thrilled. The press were there to meet me, of course, and in the photos I looked like Peter Gabriel. I looked like I'd put on loads of weight but I was just well rested. Once we lost the photographers, we drove into a service station and I bought myself a Snickers bar and a Gingsters cheese-and-onion pastie. It tasted like freedom. But it was weird to be free.

The truth is I wasn't entirely free. I was heading home to be put on tag for the rest of my sentence. It led to another surreal moment, though. The women that came to tag me were so sweet and were mad fans.

'We don't want to do this,' they said.

I told them, 'Just don't make it too tight.'

I heard stories about people removing them and gallivanting. But I didn't conceive of doing anything like that. Even when I went to Brighton Pride to deejay I made it home by 7pm. The idea of going back to prison was not an option. I would even smoke in the garden by lying in the French windows with my legs in the house.

I went to the Notting Hill Carnival in 2009 with my

Peckham Rolex and wore cut-offs. It was the one place in the world I knew I wouldn't get shade. If people believed what I was accused of, they certainly didn't show it. I don't want to come across as disrespectful of what happened but equally I don't want to appear moronically compliant. I have opinions about what happened to me and, even in all the ugliness, you can hopefully see that there was humour, there always is. I can't spend the rest of my life defending or being sorry. I did something bad but nowhere near as bad as it was portrayed. I was charged, prosecuted and found guilty. I can't escape that. At this point I do feel less weighed down about it. I knew in prison I was going to have to rebuild my life, brick by brick, and I have.

You wonder at times, 'Am I as bad as the tabloid headlines?' and only you can answer that question. You have to know who you are deep inside. You have to forgive yourself first and take your seat at the table. When I went to the Brit Awards in 2011, they wanted to put me in a side room and I agreed, knowing that when I turned up that wouldn't happen. I ended up getting shout-outs from Arcade Fire and Gnarls Barkley and I was so relieved. When you've broken the law and been convicted you can never fully get past those people who believe you can't change. I've realised now that you don't have to get past them. Richard Gere once said in a movie, 'Good people do bad things.' If I'm bad, it's James Brown bad. And if you can't be forgiven in rock and roll, you might as well be a lawyer.

When the tag eventually came off after several months, I was put on probation and had to meet with my probation officer, Dave, in Islington. He was a nice guy, asking me ridiculous questions, but I had to play along. Most of it was a nonsense and I had to fight my instincts to be sarcastic. I was attending NA meetings close by, which was a good counterweight. I'd love to know what Dave thought about the whole thing. He seemed like a Mod or someone who would like The Small Faces. It was like having probation with Paul Weller. I would often wonder what Dave did when he was having fun. A lot of insane things came into my head during that period. I wondered what the Queen thought of my going to one of her hotels. I wondered what Madonna thought. She definitely said something. If I heard she went to prison, do you think I'd have nothing to say? I'd probably write a song.

8

# CULTURE CLUB – ALIVE AND KICKING

I guess **2010 was the start of another** comeback, or at least I had crawled from the wreckage and shaken myself down. I had left prison in May 2009 but had been on house arrest until September when I heard the BBC were about to make a TV film about my life. *Worried About the Boy* – starring the very sweet and handsome Douglas Booth as me – was being made without my consultation. Because my story was public domain, I had no say and I had no one to really represent me. I wish I had met PK because he would have made sure I was respected and consulted properly. And probably paid.

In the end they did a pretty good job and Mathew Horne who played Jon Moss was uncanny. He spent time with Jon, and he was brilliant. They had great people on costume and make-up which really made the film. Annie Symons, who was part of the actual New Romantic scene did the clothes and I lent her some actual stuff from my wardrobe. My friend Donald McInnes was head of make-up and he hired Christine Bateman as part of his team so that side of things was spot on. My dad was turned into an Irish leprechaun, my mum was dreary, and I had no brothers, or a sister. 'Who's that supposed to be?', my mum asked.

Steve Strange was Shakespearean and Malcolm McLaren was like Toad of Toad Hall. That said, I quite liked it and it was good to see something positive on TV after a couple of years of horror headlines. I actually visited the set in Manchester and was amazed that Douglas looked a bit like me. Such is the power of make-up and of course great acting. It all got me thinking about my time in the band and the people we'd sang and played with. It actually served as a great reminder of what I loved about singing and performing, and how many incredible opportunities I've had over the years.

It's very rare that I ever sing a song that I haven't written unless it's an already classic song like 'Everything I Own' or a hidden gem like 'The Crying Game'. I recently sang on a song, 'Let Me Down' by The Lottery Winners who I met on Twitter. I love the internet because as ghastly as some people can be you can meet interesting people. They sent me the song and

I liked it. It was catchy, tropical and could have been about Jon Moss with its sarcastic lyrics and joyful melody. There was no talking to my people or their people, we just did it.

Over the years I have always wanted to bring in different people to perform with us. I have a vision of Culture Club being like George Clinton and parliament with a circus of performers running around the stage. One of my greatest finds was Helen Terry who sang on our early hits and brought a raw soul to our sound. I met her outside Heaven Nightclub one night and my friend Christine Binnie said, 'You should hear her sing'. So I said, 'Sing for me' and she snapped, 'I'm not a performing seal'.

I brought her in to the studio with Steve Levine and she was amazing. The boys obviously liked what she did, but weren't sure they wanted her in the band. I didn't see it like that – I just saw it as a great person making us greater. I am happy for people to shine on the stage because it's not a competition. Do you think I would care if Roy did a backflip or surprised us with a moonwalk?

I'm not insecure about a singer hitting higher notes because I can do what I can do and I'm good at it. I care more about the song and anything that elevates the music. There is a generosity and warmth to letting people share your limelight.

I have shared the stage with singers who did not respect the moment but it's always on them. God bless Luther

Vandross who had a voice like silk. I sang with both Stevie Wonder and Luther at a Motown tribute at the famous Apollo Theatre in Harlem. I had stupidly taken a line of coke and I was shaky and nervous. I sang 'Part Time Lover' with Stevie after managing to get out of singing 'Signed, Sealed, Delivered' because I was in full fear. I was taken to Stevie's dressing room and we went through both songs but I felt I sounded better on 'Part Time Lover'. I pretended I didn't have the words to the song but Stevie said, 'You have the lyrics in your hand'. I have no idea how he knew.

The performance with Stevie went well but Luther barely looked at me. A young kid asked for an autograph as we waited backstage. 'Not a good time, honey,' he snapped. We performed the Jimmy Ruffin classic, 'What Becomes of the Broken Hearted'. Both George Michael and Rod Stewart sang that night, and they were amazing. Rod's version of 'Dock of the Bay' was sensational.

I've already told you about the time I sang with Jocelyn Brown. Working with Jocelyn was amazing and what a powerhouse voice. I met her when she released 'Somebody Else's Guy', which Fat Tony always played at The Wag Club. Jocelyn sang with us for a few years and came to Monserrat when I recorded my first solo album, *Sold*, produced by Stewart Levine. We wrote the song 'Keep Me in Mind' together and I also wrote a few songs with the Motown legend Lamont Dozier.

I flew out to Monserrat after getting clean from my heroin addiction. Stewart Levine helped me put a new band together and that's when I met one of my favourite drummers, Ritchie Stevens. I recorded a cover of 'Everything I Own', a Bread song that Ken Booth took to Number 1 in the seventies. Most songs can be given the reggae treatment and even though Stewart only knew the hippy version, we cut it and it went to Number 1 again.

Richie Stevens has played with some of my favourite Reggae artists like Linton Kwesi Johnson and Horace Andy. He can play anything, but reggae and dub are his passion. He is the son of Avant guard jazz drummer John Stevens. I worked with Richie for many years, and he produced my album *This Is What I do*, an album I am very proud of.

My favourite duet is with Anohni, formerly Antony from Antony and The Johnsons. We recorded his song 'You Are My Sister' in New York and performed it on *The Jonathan Ross show* in London. I remember I took some black-market Valium to calm my nerves and I collapsed backstage. I managed to pull off a pretty good performance and the scandal was hushed up. I felt terrible and vowed to make amends. It wasn't my first car crash performance for Jonathan. I sang 'Time Machine' with Amanda Ghost, and I can't bear to watch it. No wonder he never asks me to sing.

I got to sing 'You Are My Sister' live with Antony in Australia and he cried. I was there on a DJ tour and saw a poster for the show and offered my services. It was a perfect redemption. I am writing about Anonhi in past and present context. I guess everyone who reconfigures their identity is living in future and past context. Or do they find a middle?

I have been lucky to sing with amazing legends like Diana Ross, Dione Warwick, Smokey Robinson and others. I wish I could do those performances now because I know I'm better and more confident. You learn from mistakes and back then I was distracted by drugs and the unhelpful aspects of fame. I have a new respect for making music.

After I came out of prison, I was asked by Mark Ronson to sing on a song called 'Somebody To Love Me' with singer and musician Andrew Wyatt. My voice wasn't at its peak, and it took a while to nail the vocal. The song sounded like I could have written it, but I wasn't involved in the writing. I did a bunch of live shows with Mark and his band, and the song was well loved all over the world. I appreciated Mark reaching out to me when I was in a difficult spot. They did a video for the song with actress Diane Kruger playing a young me. I heard she was upset because they dragged her to some working men's club in the middle of nowhere with no luxuries and she was kicking off just like I would have. For one day she really was Boy George.

It's not always easy to work with other artists. With Kim Wilde we just swapped songs. She wrote one for me to sing and I did the same. I love her and I love her voice.

We made a strange video for the song, but PK hated it. We were floating around in astronaut costumes and looked a bit comedy. When PK spoke to Kim's manager he said, 'It's just two old eighties stars floating around the moon'. That was it.

Some of the dance people are the worst and they say the weirdest shit. Hot Since 82 asked me to write over a track and I sent him my idea. 'I don't want you to sing', he said. I was annoyed briefly but then thought outside my own limitations. I ended talking about the year 1982 and our song 'Body Control' is quite emotive. I worked with Groove Armada before they were famous and one of them made a bitchy comment about me in the press. If I turn up in the studio in sweatpants and a baggy tee without my eyebrows people get very confused. All you have to do is remember what your girlfriend looks like first thing in the morning. Even the most beautiful people in the world can look like shit but I do, as they say, 'scrub up quite well'. Boy George is a creation, five parts hat, twenty parts outfit and thirty five percent make up. Lots of people dress up like me but they never really look like me. I have created an almost cartoon image of myself. Anyone who wears a hat gets called Boy George. Some people feel insulted.

My friend and official impersonator Keith George does a brilliant job. I love that he makes a living being me and that he is so respectful. He was once asked to throw puppies into the Thames for a comedy skit and said no, 'Boy George would never do that' although I probably would for the right price. I have seen other artists complaining about being impersonated but it just doesn't bother me. I asked Keith if he stopped working when I was in prison and he said, 'I have never not worked'. People love those classic songs and I feel proud that I have created a legacy for someone like Keith to make a living from. There are other people who do me, but Keith is the most successful and I give him my clothes and hats. If the look is right that's half the job done. You need to be able to sing and Keith can hold a tune. People think it's weird that I'm friends with Keith but he's very sweet and smart and not the least bit creepy. Like me he has a quick tongue and striking eyes. His other act is a drag queen called Mandy Gap who I'm told is a vile creature. If you've not seen it, go check it out.

have no rules, but I try to
remember to do helpful things
to get myself loose.

# 9

# ROCK AND ROLL
# PARANOIA

**I** **love it when someone famous say's 'It's**
really exciting,' but no sign of excitement can be seen.

I love open people and I don't care if they are left or right.
Lots of people take a political stance because of who they
fear to be emotionally. Ha, who doesn't love a generalisation.

I have no rules, but I try to remember to do helpful things
to get myself loose.

*On stage*
*Don't forget to concentrate*
*Get over yourself or fully commit to the you*
*that you have created.*
*Did you create yourself or are you created?*

*Everyone wants to be Little Richard*
*To sing Like Aretha*
*And express like Nina Simone*
*Tell another story like Bowie*
*Steal from everyone and make it all yours*

Pretending you've never met the make-up artist after they've spent three hours making you look human does not make you Dame Joan Collins.

Stars radiate and they mess up and they are forgiven because, if you want to live in a fabulous democracy, you have to play by the rules.

I think I've evolved but I think a lot of things.

It's hard to be a star if you are too self-conscious.

I hear all the references and I think all good music sounds like everything you love but served differently. Revenge is a dish best served soul.

Soul is subjective but so is everything. Bitter people can make a pretty sound. Anger with a melody is a kind of peace. This is my bible, not yours. I use the term 'bible' because emotionally it resonates. Jesus loves you, loves me, loves us all because God is only love and love is God explained.

The word 'seminal' is used a lot in music but seminal is selective. You like what you like because it follows a musical grid that sits nicely in your ears but adds new shoes and panties.

Everyone in music thinks they are doing something new when they are just doing something differently. Musically, my hero, David Bowie, threw it all together with both respect and distortion.

This is not an absolute musical map, but every guitar twang is the cousin of another guitar twang. How you tell your story is up to you and can define you and then become a musical nightmare.

Success is amazing and suffocating. Fame is gorgeous and confusing because you have ideas about what it is as a concept. You can't know it until you do. Like your first kiss. First orgasm. Falling in love. Getting your heart destroyed by someone who turns out to be a massive projection.

There's only so much you can do with your arms on stage. Little Richard would be a good starting point, then Elvis, Mick Jagger and, of course, Bowie. You can't do Ian Curtis.

## 10

# ENTER PK

The headlines over the years have always used the cliché, 'The calmer chameleon.' But it's only now that it's true. I've always had the ability to laugh at myself and be self-deprecating but my ability to pull myself out of a mood is shocking. When I first started working with PK, he couldn't believe how explosive I was when I came off stage, cunting everyone off and throwing my hat across the room.

'The gig was complete shit. I was awful.'

I cannot tell you how much I've changed in that respect. When I walk on stage now, I have a respect for the experience that I never knew was possible. The days of taking my bad moods on stage in the name of artist integrity are long gone. PK, like Roy Hay, is a Leo, who wants to tell you what to do and be your best friend. It took me a long time to realise how sensitive PK is because he can be so insensitive. I suppose, like Philip, he can give it but he can't necessarily take it.

I met PK through Amos Pizzey, alias Captain Crucial, who called me from LA saying there's some bloke called PK who manages Pele and wants to do some branding deals with you. It was very vague but, though I had no interest in football, even I knew who Pele was and I was impressed.

PK and I had the most awkward conversation on the phone and then he sent me a text apologising for the phone call and suggested we meet in person. It was August 2014 and I was going out to New York to promote an upcoming Culture Club tour and appeared on *Late Night with Seth Meyers* with Taylor Swift. I did a quick photo with Taylor because my niece was a fan. Let's just say it was a very swift meeting. I don't think she had any idea who I was, which was a shame for her (LOL). Having said that, I think she's fabulous and talented. I admired the fact that she took a political stance against homophobia and prejudice when some of those around her were telling her it was bad for business. Having an opinion is always bad for business.

PK and Dorit rolled up late to the Seth Meyers show and then disappeared to a restaurant round the corner like Bonnie and Clyde. I still hadn't met him. I thought, 'Who is this guy? He's so rude.' But when we finally met, I loved him. He reminded me of one of my brothers.

Straight talking, loud and charming. I took my Italian friend, Maria Smith, with me to meet them at the ABC Kitchen. It turned out Dorit is fluent in Italian, so while they chatted I started to get the measure of PK. He confessed that he used to ring my doorbell and run away as a teenager and that he was the world's biggest George Michael fan. We often joke, 'Sorry you got to manage the wrong George.' It also turned out that he loved Haircut 100 and once waited outside Nick Heyward's flat to get an autograph.

To say PK is a character is an understatement and our early conversations were hilarious. The next day I went to meet him at his office in Times Square, which he was packing up to move to LA. I was mostly deejaying at the time and I wanted to keep my DJ career separate from my music career, to which he replied, 'I can't manage the donkey if I can't get hold of the tail. It's all or nothing,' he said. 'I want to manage Boy George, not half of him.'

I remember him saying, 'Do you know who the hell you are?' Because at the time I was very British and dismissive of my legacy. He kept saying, 'You're Boy George and that means something.'

PK's background was in real estate and before the 'Credit Crunch' he'd had a portfolio worth a billion. He was briefly vice chairman of Tottenham Hotspur Football Club and was on *The Apprentice* with Lord Sugar. I wouldn't describe PK as shy and, since Dorit became a reality star on *The Real Housewives of Beverly Hills*, he has achieved greater notoriety. In fact, now he's a social liability: he gets recognised everywhere and, unlike me, he loves being recognised, although I am much less stressed about it myself these days. My policy now is to be nice to everyone I meet, and not in a false way. I used to get really uptight when people recognised me and ask for photos when I wasn't dressed up but now I couldn't give a flying plate.

I actually love being Boy George and I have discovered the more you try to hide, the more you tend to be seen. Wearing sunglasses and a baseball cap is a sure way to stand out but being open and friendly removes so much of the tension. If you tut and roll your eyes when somebody asks you for a photograph, no one walks away happy. When you are warm and friendly, the world is a much better place. I don't ever want anyone to walk away and say I wasn't friendly, and if they are happy to have a photograph of me in my sweatpants, it's all good. I'm not going to pretend I was always nice. Some of my best friends I told to fuck off when I first met them.

So what about PK? He came into my life like a hurricane and changed everything. I still don't have anyone to bring me an espresso in bed like he does, but I'm working on it. He is strangely undemanding, but he encourages it in others. He's like a little boy who likes setting off fireworks in the house. He's a Leo on the cusp of Virgo and I tell him that at times he is like Jon Moss and Roy Hay: Jon being a Virgo and Roy being a double Leo. He will be less flattered by the Moss comparison but it's more about mannerism than the soul.

Very early on I looked at PK and said, 'You have sadness in your eyes,' and it's true. Lions are more sensitive than you realise. I joke that he swipes me with his big clumsy paws when he opens his mouth, but he is equally complimentary. I have learnt to communicate with him with more sensitivity and grace, but both of us can still be clumsy.

It was him who told me, 'You need to fix your teeth.' Ha, I was furious, but it turns out it was an act of genius. Getting my teeth done has changed my face and my life. I used to pout to hide my teeth which were rodent-like. Thank you, Dr Sam Saleh, for giving me back my smile. Not for free, of course. I paid. I call my gnashers 'Keith the Teeth' and say they used to be the backing singer, but now they are right up front stealing the applause.

PK comes with lots of baggage but none of it is Louis Vuitton. That's all in Dorit's closet. He brings a circus of assistants and people who do this and that, and you don't need them until you need them. He redesigns your life until it looks like his. He likes to watch other people shine, which is why he is a good manager and a good friend. Of course, he loves to be complimented and told how good he is and that's tough for me because I expect everyone to read my mind.

A bit like Dad when Mum said, 'You never say you love me,' and he replied, 'I'm here, ain't I?'.

When I met PK he said, 'I know nothing about music management.' 'Good,' I said. 'I don't need that kind of help.' I only have one arm in the music business these days and I am excited about what I can do next. At sixty-two, they advise you do a covers album, or work with someone young, do a duet with Post Malone or call up Calvin Harris. With all due respect to everyone, please fuck off. If I do a jazz album, I will write it and not do the classics. We need more songs to be written. Just like we need more flowers for the bees.

I have become a successful artist and now have my own studio where I create art, make videos and do photoshoots with my team; Ben Fletcher, Dean Stockings, Leigh Carter, Nicola Bowery, Sally Nunn-Hammond and now Vangelis poly-Glamorous. I love creating and write songs most days. Sometimes more than one. This book has inspired a ton of lyrics and brought back incredible and sad memories. The hope for the future comes with Jagger and Phoenix who are PK and Dorit's adorable children. Phoenix is strong and sassy and Jagger sharp and super sensitive. I can't wait to see who they become.

I have an honest relationship with PK and I trust him. His bones are more commercial than mine, but creativity is key to everything I do. He will tell me not to post stuff or say this or that and most of the time he is right. 'Who are you entertaining?' he will ask.

It was because of PK that I had the opportunity to work on *The Voice UK* and then in Australia. It was great to be on TV again, even if dramas still ensued. You probably read of a few bustups with Seal and Delta Goodrem on *The Voice Australia* but, all in all, I really enjoyed it. In 2017, I joined the cast of *The New Celebrity Apprentice* in the USA. I thought it was a good way to reintroduce myself to America but Donald Trump had other ideas. When I say reintroduce myself, I mean create greater awareness of my fabulousness. I had toured America a lot with Culture Club but it's a big place. You can do an extensive tour of the West Coast and easily miss the rest of the country. One of the reasons why MTV was so powerful in the eighties before the internet was because it put your pop videos everywhere and I wanted to reembrace that power. Radio may no longer be quite so effective but TV still packs a punch, so many people are glued to reality shows nowadays.

Trump left *The Apprentice* in 2015 to pursue politics. As a politician I think Trump has the least in common with his followers than any other politician, but a huge part of his popularity was purely down to his presence on TV for so many years. I find him fascinating and, while I'm supposed to be vigorously anti-Trump, I really don't have the time. I was in Los Angeles the day Trump won the presidential election. PK was throwing an election party at his house in Beverly Hills. My friend Sadie and I went out to get more alcohol and headed to West Hollywood. I saw an obviously gay man sitting outside Starbucks sipping a Frappuccino wearing a 'Gays for Trump' badge. I thought to myself, 'I bet he wins.' In a liquor store on Sunset Boulevard, Sadie had a run-in with the guy at the till, who had made some acidic comment about my tattoos then proceeded to smack a box that a young black kid was carrying from the storeroom and shouted at him for no apparent reason. Sadie flew into action: 'Don't you talk to another human being like that. You're rude.'

There was tension in the air – everywhere. I thought it was going to kick off so I went outside to be helpful. But I could tell Sadie was angry. In her mind, it was whether the old ideas were going to dissolve or be voted in. Well, we know what happened.

Wrongly or rightly, I find myself outside of politics now. Taking sides never seems to solve much. What I do care about is social justice. It's boring to say I came from nothing but it's true. I know I came from great personality and strong character, which is definitely something in the bank. But, though I believe in compassion, I also like cash and cowboy hats. The suggestion that being compassionate is a sign of weakness doesn't sit with me. I have a lot of time for activists like Beverley Palesa Ditsie, a South African lesbian who has tirelessly campaigned for LGBTQI+ rights throughout Africa. And God bless Peter Tatchell. Peter is gung-ho for gay rights. He once tried to arrest Robert Mugabe and had a face-off with Mike Tyson. Why is it strange when people care as much as Peter does? Even those of us who consider ourselves bold remain tight-lipped in the face of politics.

I wasn't close to Jimmy Somerville in the eighties but I was impressed by both his voice and his political courage. I would have been too self-concerned to give such compliments back then. Between myself, Jimmy, Pete Burns, Holly Johnson, Marc Almond and Marilyn there was a battle for who was the most important queer. The good news was that we provided some of the vast spectrum of queer culture. But what I sang about was wholly innocent compared to what Frankie Goes To Hollywood were suggesting. I wanted a nice, straight boyfriend. Holly wanted water sports. Jimmy Somerville's 'Smalltown Boy' was the haunting reality. That song still sounds brilliant. As soon as you hear that opening refrain, you know how gay you are.

Looking back, I should have been best friends with Holly and Paul Rutherford. I actually got close to Paul during the acid-house explosion. I should have been friends with a lot of people.

One night, I had a run-in with the straight boys from Frankie. I was working at Sarm Studios in Notting Hill with the legendary P.P. Arnold and Frankie were recording upstairs with Trevor Horn who owned the place. After that, I wrote an insane letter to Frankie's Holly, which he still has. My letter was pretty rambling; I should have signed it 'From Karen'. I'm not sure I can blame that all on drugs but at least I can feel sorry for that.

✢ ✢ ✢

The host for my series of *The Apprentice* was Arnold Schwarzenegger, another right-wing person I'm supposed to not like. What can I tell you? I did like him and he absolutely got me. I tried – like I always do – to be myself. When it comes to creative ideas, I'm not shy in giving mine. We were put into two competing groups. They give you tasks where someone has to be team captain and, if it goes wrong, the captain gets the blame. My first task involved make-up and I had to do a sales pitch to supermodel and TV mogul Tyra Banks. We won the task but my presentation was weak and Tyra told me so. As wounded as I was, I realised I could have talked about make-up until the cows came home in high heels. This is my world. I am the one-liner on the eyeliner.

My team kept winning. The funniest task was for a motorbike company and I hired a drag queen called Alaska Thunderfuck. We photographed Alaska in full drag in various poses on the back of a motorbike. They said they wanted a male, early thirties, as their target audience. When I was questioned by Arnie about using a drag queen, I pointed out that Alaska was actually a thirty-three-year-old male, which was the perfect target audience. The television personality Brooke Burke had used her then-husband, David Charvet from *Baywatch*, to model on the bike with her. He didn't ride pillion and so Brooke lost the chance to make a powerful female statement. She should have been in the driving seat but apparently he wouldn't allow it. She's married to someone else now.

Throughout *The Apprentice* all the other celebrities kept telling me I was unorthodox and weird. 'You have your own way,' was their polite way of saying it. I noticed early on there was a lot of keyboard-tapping on computers. They liked to look busy even if they weren't. Whereas I was happy to get my hands dirty and I was lucky to get lots of songwriting tasks. I won all of those. I wrote a song for the Los Angeles Clippers basketball team and another one for a drinks company using the unpoetic word 'polyphenols'. I had a brief skirmish with Vince Neil from Mötley Crüe. We were doing a task together and I accused him of being drunk. Looking back, it was none of my business and he had every right to scream at me in the boardroom. 'Keep your sobriety to yourself.' I upset him but he won the next task and took hundreds of thousands of dollars off me for his charity. Sometimes you're set up to not like someone and you fall in line like an idiot. I actually like Vince, even though he never calls.

*Queer Eye* presenter Carson Kressley was my team partner and 'the other gay'. We got on brilliantly. He knew where to get everything. There was an electricity whenever he was around. My next run-in was with Porsha Williams, a fierce, beautiful black woman from *The Real Housewives of Atlanta*. Apparently, you never put a lady's handbag on the floor, especially if it's Gucci. I also got to know Kyle Richards, who is Paris Hilton's aunt. These days Kyle is on *The Real Housewives of Beverly Hills* along with my manager's wife, Dorit Kemsley but I didn't know her at the time.

I had an hilarious encounter with a young kid in a hardware store who pointed to my hat and said, 'Are you a Pharrell fan?'

'Yes, I am, but that's not why I'm wearing a hat,' I replied.

He wanted an explanation but I didn't give him one. I wasn't prepared to google myself. Often, when I'm in a taxi, the driver will start talking to me asking what I do. If they don't already know who I am, I tell them right out, 'I'm Boy George,' which normally cuts out the small talk. Once, while deejaying, a pretty girl said, 'Are you Boy George?'

'Yes,' I said.

'Are you really, though?' she said. 'You're not really Boy George, are ya?'

I told her to piss off.

The most difficult thing on *The Apprentice* was asking strangers for money. I was blown away by how much people were willing to give. A couple of people gave me $100,000. I even called Rosie O'Donnell and she gave me $10,000. I enjoyed working with the public, and lots of gorgeous fans did wonderful things to help our charities. I offered to perform gigs for people to raise money and I kept my promise. Our last task was the most fun. It was for a cruise-ship company and we had to perform a song. I managed to get Natasha Bedingfield and Mel B to pitch up. We also had to create certain products and sell them, which was a lot of fun. We created our own candy recipe, which was delicious. One of our team was sent in a private jet to charm Warren Buffett, but we lost that task. He preferred the other team's candy.

Both myself and comedian Matt Iseman (who hosts *American Ninja* Warrior) avoided the boardroom right until the end. I felt like I just sat there watching people get sacked. In the end I came second to Matt but he was such a nice guy I was happy for him to win. Annoyingly, the ratings were a disaster because of Donald Trump. He had an online spat with Arnie – you'll probably have read about it at the time – and middle America switched off.

Alaska Thunderfuck issued a statement in the wake of Donald Trump's presidency distancing herself from the show. She didn't do it for Donald, darling, she did it for Boy George.

But irrespective of all of that, I enjoyed *The Apprentice* for the experience. Doing things you don't normally do is good for the soul. I'm not sure if it was helpful in terms of profile but those who saw it seemed to love it. Lots of people even told me I should have won it. (That's like someone at Kiss Radio saying they should have played 'Generations of Love', a single I released in 1990, which, despite universal critical praise, didn't get enough airplay in the UK to make it the hit it 'deserved to be'.) There were lots of early mornings and endless outfits to create. I tried to look presentable at all times but there were moments when I had to pretend I was regular – that's a lot easier said than done. Even when I ended up on a basketball court during a live game, I managed to customise the outfit to look edgy and cartoon. As I've got older, I've relaxed more physically. I've never hated my body, but I don't often stand naked in front of a full-length mirror. Getting dressed is what it's all about. I have rules about what I wear. I like shirt sleeves and a smart, well-cut jacket, even if it is covered in spikes. Take a bit of rabbi, add a bit of Rasta, throw in some dandy and you've got my look. I like a chunky shoe because I've got short legs and a long body. But if you're looking in my eyes, you won't notice.

swear the first thing he said
was, 'How's that miserable
it, Marilyn?'

## 11

# SOUND AND VISION – BEING AN ARTIST

**M**y idea of beauty has always been quite wide. Often, I'll hear someone described as ugly and I won't agree. For me, ugliness is in the character of a person. There is no point being a pretty arsehole. No one stays beautiful but a person's true soul will shine through wrinkles. The jazz singer and cultural commentator George Melly once ribbed Mick Jagger, 'That's a lot of wrinkles.'

'Not wrinkles, laughter lines,' insisted Jagger.

'Mick,' came back Melly, 'nothing's that funny.'

I am the biggest Mick Jagger fan on the planet. I've only met him once, at Mandy Smith's wedding to Bill Wyman in 1989. Fat Tony was DJ and I tagged along to keep him company. Mick Jagger walked up, shook my hand and said, 'I like your shoes.' Apparently, he's a keen shoe freak because I've heard similar stories.

The first time I met any of the Stones I was in Paris with Marilyn on my way to a party. I saw Keith Richards and Ronnie Wood and said to Marilyn, 'We are having a drink. I need to meet them.' Marilyn rolled his eyes.

'Hurry up then.'

Eventually, I got speaking to Keith, Ronnie and drummer Charlie Watts. Later, Marilyn and I spent a day with Keith and a lot of cocaine in Jamaica. I didn't see Charlie for years after that until I bumped into him at WHSmith at Heathrow. I swear the first thing he said was, 'How's that miserable git, Marilyn?'

I laughed: 'Still a miserable git but he'll love that you remembered him.'

Being a star is a responsibility. There is no handbook except for what you see on TV or read about in the press. I think film stars and pop stars are quite different, but I used the likes of Marlene Dietrich, Liz Taylor, Carmen Miranda as well as David Bowie, Marc Bolan and Steve Harley to create myself. No one ever gave me a script but growing up in a heteronormative world you do go through a kind of conversion therapy. Because the world wilfully ignores who you are so as not to encourage you, you are forced to create a false self. I'm not suggesting straight kids don't create a false self, but they have more reference points. Democracy is about majority rule and what's best for everyone.

Seeing David Bowie in the seventies was the beginning of my re-education. I don't think anybody can say for sure whether Bowie was straight, gay or bisexual. It might even be a nonsense to say it about yourself. Such labels limit an idea of who you are. Even if, for a young gay kid, it seems absolutely fabulous to swirl around in a beaded kimono, someone is always looking at you thinking, 'Absolute poofter.'

Once you realise you're 'one of them', you have to explain yourself through every situation you find yourself in. If you're naturally camp, the work is done for you, but we are all more than our gesticulations. I think if I was straight I'd still wear mad hats and make-up. My friend Kenneth from Denmark is married with kids but he's a fellow dandy who wears big hats, cravats and Vivienne Westwood tracksuits. Bowie's ambiguous stance was powerful because he might have been straight. Who would choose to flounce around in the gay world if it was going to affect record sales? As big as Bowie seemed in the seventies, he sold fewer records than Elton John but his impact was colossal. Great artists pick up on the mood of the times, sometimes long before the moment has arrived. With Bowie, you have to factor in people like mime artist and dancer Lindsay Kemp, who pulled Bowie into a queerer world. Bowie wasn't just turning up in a frilly blouse like some bands. He added mime and kabuki to the mix, and it was dark and sexually suggestive. Dick Emery's comedy camp on seventies TV was one thing. David Bowie was another.

In her book, *Man Enough to Be a Woman*, trans punk Jayne County suggests that Bowie stole a lot from her. No question Bowie was enthralled by the likes of Jayne and the Warhol crowd, but Bowie was always going to be Bowie whoever he saw. Jobriath was an out gay American performer who was meant to be bigger than Bowie, but he never had the songs. Even if you hate the clothes Bowie wore, his songs are amazing. Bowie was a fan of Anthony Newley, Scott Walker, Kurt Weill and Jacques Brel. All consummate wordsmiths and melodicists. He sang about Bob Dylan and the mystic poet Khalil Gibran.

Culture Club's struggles to get a record deal were partly about finding the right song but mostly about getting over people's first impressions of me. I wasn't turning up in a frilly blouse. The reality of me in person was powerful to witness, even for me. There was nothing apologetic about me in 1982. When people made comments about me in the street, I cussed them like a fishwife. No one who met me thought, 'Now there's a nice straight lad dressed up for rag week.' I wasn't in your face, I was in your mouth. I had to learn not to be so aggressive. A bit of success can help in that area.

There is still a currency now in being a bit queer, especially if you are mostly straight. Matt Healy from The 1975 often kisses guys on stage. I'm not sure if they use tongues, but recently I saw a clip of him kissing a male security guard. I think it was the Arctic Monkeys who started this trend and I think Matt definitely wants to be a queer Arctic Monkey. I wouldn't mind myself. I enjoy a bit of ambiguous sexual behaviour in rock and roll, and I've always said it's easier for a straight artist to be a bit queer. Rod Stewart was brilliantly convincing when he went through his camp phase. Singing 'The Killing of Georgie' on *Top of the Pops*, he was like the hot boy at school telling you it's okay to be gay. Mum bought me that record and put it in my pants drawer in a brown paper bag. Up until that point I'd just been highly strung and theatrical. Now it was clearly out of the brown paper bag.

There is so much mythologising about music and songwriting, but it turns out it's not that difficult. 'Steal like an artist' is a great template since every guitar twang is the cousin of another guitar twang. In fact, writing a song is not as difficult as getting it played. In popular music, they write you off at a certain age, even in a world that is screaming about diversity and inclusion. You don't run out of ideas, you run out of options. The way we dismiss older artists is so wrong. The last couple of Alison Moyet albums have been some of her best work.

I think you make great music when you stay connected.

I like being out in the world, whether it's on the bus or the tube, because even if I had a wine cellar, it wouldn't stimulate much. I look at posters on the walls and find lyrics, my iPhone always handy to record melody ideas or write down lyrics. I write things like 'Hanging out with flowers is one of my secret powers.' Once you add a bit of delay and a reggae bass line, you can sound unexpectedly profound. These days the sonics are equally important. Words or sentences don't have to make sense if they are sitting inside an interesting chord structure. I used to sneer at musical theatre until I realised how much of it Bowie used in his work. The chorus of Pink Floyd's 'Another Brick in the Wall' is absolutely musical theatre.

In fact, since I've learnt to get out of my way creatively, I have been so much more prolific. I'm not hoodwinked like some people when I hear a song.

'Isn't it amazing?' people say.

'Maybe for you,' I think.

Sometimes I hear pop songs and think, what possessed them to use those bland chords? The music industry wants you to believe that only a handful of people can do what you do successfully: Adele, Ed Sheeran, Harry Styles, Lewis Capaldi, with Dua Lipa holding up the Kylie pop/disco side. In America they have Beyonce, Pink, Lizzo, Katy Perry, Lil Nas X. In some ways America seems more diverse because the black music industry is so strong and

**Above left:** I'm not a drug addict, I'm a drag addict. Fucking up in public. © Andre Rela

**Above right:** Blondes have more fun! © Andre Rela

**Below:** Konnichi wa. © Andre Rela

With the other queer George from London. © Shutterstock

On stage with Elton Joan at the Prince's Trust concert at Wembley, 1987.

© Shutterstock

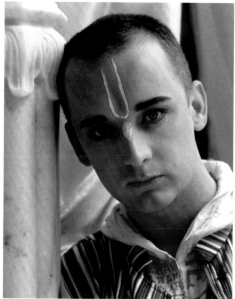

*Above left:* Golden. © *Dean Stockings*

*Above right:* Bow down mista. © *Shutterstock*

*Below:* Me and Leigh Bowery, at the Limelight club in London. © *Shutterstock*

By Royal Appointment.
© Getty Images

Put your hands up.
© Dean Stockings

On the set of the 'Funtime'. My favourite video. © Shutterstock

With Rosie 'move that building' O'Donnell.

© Shutterstock

On Broadway, as Leigh Bowery, in Taboo.

© Getty Images

In London with some of the cast, including a young Luke Evans and Matt Lucas, who played Leigh in London.

© Shutterstock

***Above and below left***: I had the best time on *I'm a Celebrity* — well, I didn't enjoy the cuisine so much but it was a worthwhile experience! © *Shutterstock*

***Below right***: With fellow judges on BBC hit show *The Voice*. © *Shutterstock*

Evolution: my life has seen me wear many outfits and play many roles, but at the end I'll only ever be George Alan O'Dowd from Eltham. And I'm happy with that. © *Anton Corbijn / Getty Images*

vibrant. Everyone is still making the same record, though, and pretty much saying the same thing.

As a writer, I've been developing lots of new ways to create lyrics and melodies. I use the Bowie model of cutting up words – which goes back to the surrealists – and very often I'll have the words long before the melody. I never understand artists who start with a melody because I only care what someone has to say. When I'm advising people about songwriting, subject matter is everything. It doesn't have to be about anything and you can change the subject matter any time you like. If you know what you want to say, you'll find a way to say it.

So many of my favourite songs make no sense. I've always thought 'Itsy Bitsy Teenie Weenie Yellow Polka-Dot Bikini' was a stroke of genius. Because of that title I wrote songs like 'Is Your Mind Still Prepared To Be Blown?' I grew up with songs like T. Rex's 'Salamanda Palaganda' and 'She Was Born To Be My Unicorn'. The more insane the song title, the less chance Gary Barlow is going to write it.

Some of the most brilliant and loved songs start with the simplest lines: 'Tonight you're mine completely. You give your love so sweetly.' Being understated can be part of the magic in a great song. Look at Burt Bacharach. He knew how to keep it simple. Hooks are everything but learning not to follow the structure can result in magic. 'The Crying Game', my 1992 hit produced by the Pet Shop Boys, is not a structured song but it sticks in your head.

Often with Bowie, particularly later, he placed bridges or choruses slightly off centre. On the album *Low* he had incredibly long introductions, instrumental tracks and random chants. People say to me, 'You turn everything into a song,' but that's what songwriting is, taking words that already exist and lining them up for dramatic purpose. I have my go-to references, like Bowie obviously, Bolan, Dylan, Joni Mitchell, Morrissey, Scott Walker, but also bands like Glasvegas, Nirvana, Cowboy Junkies, Rod Stewart and the Faces for sure, Paul Weller and Nina Simone.

There is an incredible musical pantry where you can choose ingredients and flavours. There are so many things in there you sometimes can't find what you're looking for. That's when you stumble across a new band or even someone older you've never heard of before, like Little Jimmy Scott. I like finding out about foreign bands as well, especially French, Italian and German artists. I never understood a word Edith Piaf was singing but every word struck a chord.

In the last two years I've released about 47 tracks. I started the pandemic by writing a song called 'Isolation'. I was talking to writer and director Sacha Gervasi, who had been hired to write a movie about my life, and he introduced me to his friend who owns satellites. That was impressive in itself, but the line 'I met a man who owns satellites' felt very Bowie-esque.

The punk singer Yungblud was doing camera tests to play me. At first, I was horrified. My friend's kids asked if I like Yungblud and I said that he's a punk wannabe. Then I discovered we had the same publicist, Shoshanna. She has a rule: we don't slag off Britney or anyone else that she works for. Why would I slag off Britney? During her recent dramas I wrote a song called 'Free Britney'. I haven't heard a better song about her. Unfortunately, Shoshanna wouldn't tell her about my tribute. She'll hear it one day and I hope one day she'll truly be free.

Anyway, I decided to meet Yungblud and I loved him. I had to call my friend's son and say, 'Actually, I was wrong about Yungblud, he's really sweet.' I went to see him at Alexandra Palace and he ripped the roof off. I left thinking, 'I want that audience.'

Unfortunately, Sacha Gervasi left the project but I wasn't convinced about his script anyway. He'd wanted to pretend that Jon Moss had visited me in prison when he didn't even write to me. They wanted a cast of inmates singing 'Karma Chameleon' as Jon and I skipped out of the prison. Trading the facts for theatrical fun. I hope any movie about me is truthful but I have my fears.

Leading an abbreviated existence is the stuff of fame. Those introductions on TV shows where they play snippets of five songs and mention your highlights are as aggravating as they are uninformative. Why are we all so frightened of being interesting and complex? Why does television fight so hard to under-explain you? With PK, the thing I argue most about is music. With my many years of experience I feel I am more than equipped to know what's what. I write in a very classic way, heavy on surrealism, heavy on melody.

I started the project '60 for 60' to celebrate my 60th birthday. I haven't reached the number 60 yet but I have hundreds of songs. So many I can't remember. Powerstudio, where I work with my main co-writer Benny D, is like a pyramid full of hidden musical treasures. I feel the more you write, the better you get. There is no formula, although listening to Ed Sheeran and Adele, I sometimes feel otherwise. I could get away with writing the same song over and over, but I've got no interest. If I can't think of anything to write about, I'll write a song about that. Such a dilemma created my song 'Ride':

> *What do I care about today/*
> *What really matters to me/*
> *Write down what comes into my head/*
> *Hold your kids and say I love you/*
> *Tell me what you're feeling/*
> *It ain't rocket science/*
> *What about if happiness was your greatest*
> *act of defiance.*

Lyrics can come from anywhere and they do actually come from anywhere. I try to explain this to young artists but it doesn't make sense until you get it. It's impossible for me to be in a writing situation and not end up with a song. I once wrote with Mark Ronson and left the studio with nothing. I think Mark is so hell bent on being cool nothing is good enough. I just write the song and regret it later.

There are songs I used to roll my eyes at that I now love, like 'Ça Plane Pour Moi' by Plastic Bertrand. When Kylie recently released 'Padam Padam' (which she didn't write), I thought, 'She's nailed it.' There's no logical reason why you would prefer one cheesy song over another. Sometimes it's just the weather or the fact that you're cruising along a beautiful coastline. I try not to hate things the way I used to but there are some artists who just never change the record. They find a formula and suck it dry. As a writer I can always tell when they've run out of ideas.

The music industry is full of self-appointed experts who have never written a song and never will write a song, but they are so ready to tell you how to do it. I can't tell you how many times I've been told, 'You should do a song with X or Y because they're younger.' I don't want to be down with the kids. I prefer them to look up at me.

o, disclaimer. Upfront. This
s my story about Marilyn and
t him write his own.

12

# I'LL GET YOU, BLANCHE – THE STORY OF MARILYN

**M**arilyn was a live wire even at sixteen.
I don't remember him coming out. He was just out from the moment we met. He entered our lives through the Robert Gordon window. Probably his car window, since Robert drove, and when you're a sixteen-year-old boy dressed as Marilyn Monroe you need someone with wheels. I tweeted a section of this story on X (formerly Twitter) rcently. Marilyn was very quick to bitch. So, disclaimer. Upfront. This is my story about Marilyn and let him write his own. I will absolutely get facts wrong, but I also might make him more interesting. Marilyn is interesting. Thoughtful and smart until self-destruction takes over.

My friend Robert Gordon met Marilyn at the Bandwagon disco in Kingsbury Circle, a local disco in outer suburbia north-west London. Both Robert and Marilyn considered themselves straight at the time, which, looking back, is hard to imagine. Robert was with his straight mates and Marilyn with a bunch of girlfriends. Robert's mates wondered why he was chatting to this girly boy but they clearly recognised each other on a cellular level.

Robert's dad had a shop in the local high street and Marilyn had been in there. Being Marilyn, he did a bit of detective work and subsequently found out where Robert lived. Marilyn arrived at Robert's family home in full drag and Robert's mum warned him not to 'fall in love with that boy.' That night Marilyn opened a white-chocolate Easter egg when Robert left his bedroom to put the kettle on. Robert had been given it by a friend and was saving it, but Marilyn broke it into pieces and, after devouring a chunk, said, 'Ugh, it's disgusting.' Nothing gets in Marilyn's way when she wants something.

Marylin invited Robert to a party at his mum's house in sleepy Borehamwood but, when Robert arrived, he discovered he was the only guest. Marilyn pulled him into his bedroom, which he had decorated with black bin liners, and a life-long friendship was established. Marilyn and Robert had a thing for a while but in the end became best friends.

We all flitted between the queer and straight worlds. Happily leaving a punk gig to go to a gay club like the Sombrero in High Street Kensington or Global Village under the arches at Charing Cross station (which became Heaven in December 1979), which was more mixed but still an open-minded disco. So-called proper gay clubs were tiny and frequented by a much older crowd. Vile old queens would look down their noses at us in our punk garb. We were spoiling their bid for assimilation. They looked far less straight than they imagined.

I met Robert through Philip, and Robert had met Philip at the Sombrero. Robert had a car so he naturally became Philip's new best friend. That's not to suggest that Robert was less than his car. He had the best wedge haircut, with a fringe that covered one eye, and seemed laid back until Philip pushed him too far. Philip treated Robert as his personal chauffeur and often instructed him to drop people off on his way home. One night Philip met two cute boys and tried to get Robert to drop them somewhere he wasn't going. They refused to get out of his car. 'Drop us home,' they demanded, so Robert drove to the nearest police station and they agreed to get out.

Robert was more of a soul boy than a New Romantic, but he upped his flowery game quite quickly. If you arrived at Philip's to go out and he considered your outfit dreary, he would style you instantly whether you liked it or not.

One person Philip never needed to style was Pinkietessa Braithwaite, who once had a regular name that you can no longer use. I won't dare say it because the last time I did she bit off my head. Pinkie dresses like a 1940s movie star but she would probably eyeroll at such a description. I have never seen Pinkie looking less than splendiferous, and if she owns anything casual, I have never seen it. The first time Robert met her was at a house party and she was wearing a cowboy outfit like Jane Russell in *The Outlaw*. Most people who dress up are doing it for attention but not Pinkie. She is the queen of self-promotion in some ways but always says no to pictures. I used to say no if I wasn't dressed up but now I always say yes unless I'm in a toilet. I find it's actually more time consuming and stressful to say no.

When Pinkie lived in Los Angeles I took her as my date to the 1986 Grammys and the press wrote that she was Marilyn. It was the night Prince won everything and John Travolta blew me a kiss. Marilyn was furious and rang a few news channels to put them right. I let Pinkie steal all the glamour that night and I dressed down in a suit with light make-up and Clark Kent glasses – my Clark Bent look.

Pinkie changed her own name, but most people were given disco monikers by Philip or me. Philip always called Robert 'Gay Robert' but we no longer use that title because it annoys Robert (even though he is the gayest person I know). He's a couple of years older than me but still looks amazing. He still goes to gay clubs where you can only wear your boots. He even makes music with Marilyn. Robert does it more as a hobby and, when I suggested he should work with other singers, he said, 'God, no, I don't want a job.' He has worked hard for years, though, and has now retired and just wants to have as much fun and sex as possible.

In the early days of our friendship, Marilyn considered Robert his soul property, but then so did Philip. Poor Robert, having to pick sides between two of London's spikiest specimens. He's mine, he's mine. No, he's mine. These days I am very close to Robert, and we often share Marilyn stories. I think we both love Marilyn, but we bear scars.

It's difficult to know where to start with the Marilyn story. Her version of events is heavily weighted towards her own complexities. She remembers, loosely, every act of cruelty I have ever inflicted but there are holes in her holiness.

So let's go back to the beginning... I first met Marilyn, or Peter Robinson, at Punk Jayne's council flat in Swiss Cottage in 1977. Jeremy Healy was going out with Punk Jayne and I would hang out in the living room while they had sex upstairs. It was during the time of my first feud with Philip and he came over with Peter to rub my nose in it. 'Doesn't he look like Marilyn Monroe?' he kept saying. 'Go on do the face,' and Marilyn pouted but he was wearing a hacking jacket and jeans. Hardly Hollywood. That night some local skinheads threw bricks through the window and everyone was screaming. We were always running from skinheads or Teddy Boys.

The first time I saw Marilyn in full Marilyn Monroe drag was at the Sombrero. Philip accidently said hello to me because I was working an entirely new look: a bowler hat and channelling Sally Bowles. He tapped me on the shoulder, I turned, and he ran away screaming. Marilyn approached me and said, 'Do you actually like Philip?'

'She hates me, love, so it would be rude not to hate her back,' I laughed.

I thought Philip had tried to turn this young starlet against me but his plans ran foul. Marilyn wanted to be on the winning team. I was fast breaking free of Philip's hold over me and getting myself into clubs. That night it was my friend Ashley who got me into the Sombrero, but I was working on it.

I befriended Philip again and we moved as a threesome through the night. Philip, Marilyn and George. A gleesome threesome, always on the edge of falling out. We hung precariously off Philip's one-liners, for he was the queen of the barb.

'Hey, Philip, meet my new girlfriend.'

'Hello, what's your name, love, and what's he going to do when you get the sight back in one eye?'

'Hello, my name is Ben, what's your last name? Dover?'

Philip was a relentless hoot with the off-the-cuff quips

and he was always the loudest presence in any space. I can still hear Marilyn torturing Philip. 'She's old news. Beauty eclipses wisdom. Nothing she has to say is of any interest to me. She's a fool. An old fool.' Marilyn loved calling Philip 'old'. Philip would say, 'Marilyn is funny, she's like Benny Hill, but don't trust her.'

Marilyn's party trick was to steal the boy you fancied from under your nose and then push him away when he showed interest. Straight boys fell for Marilyn because she was in heels and a dress. Her body was very masculine, but she swished through the room looking believable. She had a sense of humour about it, kicking off her heels in a taxicab and sighing, 'I can't wait to get home and take off these ridiculous clothes'; pulling an electric shaver from her handbag and shaving at the bus stop. It's insane that we got on buses and trains, but this was life before Uber. Marilyn wasn't shy and always made an entrance, even on the bus. She would fix her hair with hairspray, wiggle and say, 'Enter my aching body.' She used that line when she jumped on David Bowie's lap at the Embassy club one night when we merely believed we were famous.

I once did an online chat with Bowie in the nineties when the internet was wind-up. It was a fascinating, hilarious conversation, which I only recently saw as a transcript. At one point he asked, 'How's that dreadful creature, Marilyn?' Which is funny because Marilyn insists she slept with Bowie.

Marilyn was very cat-like with her friends. She had some 'glitzy' older friends that she kept away from me. People like photographer Johnny Rozsa and Stevie Hughes, who was a brilliant make-up artist and aspiring photographer. They were older gay men and very advanced in the queer universe. Marilyn ran off with them even when he lived in the basement of my squat in Carburton Street. It's hilarious to say 'my squat' but I was there first so I suppose that's what it was.

Marilyn talks about my perfectly crafted public image but is insanely protective of his own. Let's discount the YouTube rants because Marilyn thinks these rants are his divine truth. If he really believes I sabotaged his career, then he is certifiable.

You'll remember the story of Marilyn walking away from the cabaret. Soon after that he moved to America with John, Robert and Pinkie. They went to live in LA and I got on with my life. I resented him leaving because we had been inseparable until then. Partners in slime. But we always seemed to find a way back to each other. We travelled the world together. We did alot of drugs together. For a time, when you saw me, you saw Marilyn.

A few years back, after she went through rehab and was looking surprisingly amazing, I was helping her financially. I don't think she was grateful – she implied I could give |her more, but I had my limits. Don't die but don't take the piss. It wasn't a one-off. I have helped her loads and, no, I haven't kept count. Before we investigate what I've given Marilyn over the years we should look at how the universe keeps giving her chances. Her mother won the bloody lottery. I was told by Marilyn that she won it but I thought to myself, she'd be straight into a bikini and heels to hold that cheque high in the local paper. I still don't know if it was Marilyn or her mum that won, but whatever, Zeus parted the clouds again and said, 'Hey, Marilyn, here's another opportunity.'

As soon as Marilyn got some of that money, I barely heard from her.

I have no idea how much her mum gave her but it was enough to buy a house in Margate and a new car. (Both the house and the car are now gone.) I kept seeing posts of shopping bags. She booked into The Ritz hotel in St James's with her new man, a naked yoga teacher who had previously been straight and had kids. Marilyn sent a text to my sister, Siobhan, who had been sending him money on my behalf. It said, 'Hi Shoe, I no longer need George's money.' Siobhan had already sent him money and asked for him to return it. Which he did. Shiv didn't much like being called Shoe and I thought the least Marilyn could have done was send her a bunch of flowers. If the gender pronouns are fluid, it is intentional.

At this point, in 2016, I had been helping him financially and paying for recordings, musicians and a video for our track 'Love or Money'. I even hired my friend, Hamilton, to do Marilyn's make-up and hair. She wore a pair of my vintage Vivienne Westwood bondage trousers and a sequin jacket I bought her in Las Vegas. The only thing I didn't do was hold her up with a gun. I insisted I got those trousers back at the end of the shoot.

This was all going on as I was taking Marilyn on a bunch of TV shows to promote his record and create a buzz about him. He clamped up on TV and came across as cold and moody. I guess he felt controlled, but how is that my problem? PK never wanted me to do the TV shows with Marilyn and, when he saw how miserable he was, he said, 'Well, you tried, now leave it.'

I was soon going to be heading out to Australia for |*The Voice* and had my head in a book called *The Path*. I was probably reading two books, jumping from one to the other. I read something about psychic vampires and I thought, *It's her!* Bloody Mongerleeeesh. I have a string of names for Schmazda (Marilyn). She calls me Dawn, after Dawn Davenport, or Dawn Pigport, and I call her Abnormal Jean or Mongerleeeeeesh! Jon Moss used to call Marilyn Melon Head.

Back in London, Marilyn took me to a studio in Earls Court and introduced me to Benny D, who was trying to make music with Marilyn. We tried to work on some ideas but nothing really came of it. I knew Benny from NA meetings and we later become great friends and writing partners. At first I thought Benny was a weirdo but that's how most great friendships start.

Writing with Marilyn was very stop-start and everything was a problem. I never struggle to come up with an idea but Marilyn hated everything. The truth is she wants to be Mary J. Blige but she hasn't got the range. I wanted to create music that suited her vocal abilities and, with 'Love or Money' I think I nailed it. We recorded 'Love or Money', with John Themis, who was my musical director for years and my writing partner. I would argue that I wrote the words and melody, even though Marilyn was in the room pulling faces. She did contribute but you had to stab her in the neck to get her to say she liked anything. She was still smoking heavily, just cigarettes, and I kept telling her to stop if she really wanted to sound any good. There was talk at the time of Marilyn doing the Rewind Festival, which is a huge eighties live shindig. Marilyn was showing interest but that's what she always does and then fear kicks in.

I can't fill in the gaps in Marilyn's logic or how she remembers things. The YouTube videos she posts seem to be done when wasted or in some sort of emotional state. I guess when anything goes wrong in Marilyn's life, she thinks of me and believes I haven't done enough for her. I can say all sorts of things about Marilyn and still feel a degree of love. When Marilyn decides to focus her rage against me it seems to be all consuming. The first YouTube video she did was from outside my house during the pandemic. The intercom went and all I saw was Marilyn's mane filling the screen. She was buzzing like a brat. I didn't answer and when I saw how crazy her eyes looked it was an easy decision. Plus. No mask. This was in the thick of the world crisis. I saw the video once it was posted, and the comments were flying. Most of them hoping for some peace mission between us but this drama, this war, is only in Marilyn's head. Well, most of it. You only hear about how Marilyn is treated but never how she treats everyone else. Who knows what will happen with us now?

## 13

# FALLOUTS

Fallouts are not much of a working theme, and I usually make up with everyone because war is stupid. My worst fallout was with Caron Geary, aka McKinky, known these days as Feral. Talk about a perfect new name.

We were as close as you can be for several years after meeting at Fred's bar in Soho in the late eighties. She was tiny with ringlets, a sparkly halter neck, cut-off jean shorts and platform shoes. She played me a 7-inch record she had made called 'Reggae-Gone-A-Kinky' and I loved it. The words were filthy and provocative, and we exchanged numbers using an eyeliner pencil.

I got her in the studio to add her white-girl Jamaican rapping to my track 'Kipsy', which was about a model agent who got arrested for selling ecstasy. I had written the song purely on hearsay about cops raiding her flat and finding drugs hidden in the washing machine. Kinky was able to write the entire story in quasi-Jamaican patois, which was less of a scandal back then. Kinky, like Amos Captain Crucial, was dedicated to reggae. A white-girl reggae obsessive with a penchant for saying something slack. The lyrics to 'Reggae-Gone-A-Kinky' are so good, but if I print them I predict more legal action.

Kinky is litigious and holds a grudge longer than anyone I have ever known. A few years back she put out a new song and added 'Kipsy' to the package. I got calls from the regular shit stirrers but I felt a reaction was what she was after. She didn't get one and, anyway, these days who makes money from music?

While signed to my dance label, More Protein, in the nineties, Kinky made some great records like the acid-house classic 'Everything Starts with An 'E'', released under the name E-Zee Possee, which celebrated the use of Ecstasy.

Jeremy Healy, Simon Rogers and I created the track in Jeremy's home studio in Camden but Caron added the spice with her controversial rap about taking ecstasy and 'rubbing up with a stranger'.

More Protein was distributed through Virgin Records but I don't think they were seeing its full potential when the acid-house revolution started. They suggested removing Kinky's rap but I got the record to the now legendary DJ Paul

Oakenfold, who dropped it at Spectrum. Then DJ Graeme Park dropped it at midnight at the Haçienda in Manchester. It spread like a bush fire through the acid-house club scene. But even with huge club support the tune was never supported by Virgin. Meanwhile everyone was jumping on the vibe: The Shamen came up with 'Ebeneezer Goode' with its chant 'E's are good, E's are good', then Scritti Politi arrived with a dance mix of 'Take Me In Your Arms' and the ragga-house fusion felt hijacked.

I loved my dance period – my song 'Generations of Love' was a huge underground hit, despite Virgin never getting behind it. Some fans say my dance period is their favourite. My dance project, Jesus Loves You, which I set up in 1987 after I first left Culture Club, was an exciting way to find another audience.

I loved experimenting during this time and made a bunch of tunes with Kinky. She came on tour and we had a very intense friendship. Like a love affair minus the love and without sex or real affection. Is that called a marriage? I took her all over the world and she made a decent living from me. She was my plus one for everything and, despite her spiteful mouth, I adored her. But we fought like crazy and everyone found it painful to be around.

We had alot of arguments and one night we got into a squabble with a rocker who wrote for Guns N' Roses. I had been on the American actor and comedian Arsenio Hall's show and said I liked Guns N' Roses. Arsenio's response was to call Axl Rose an 'ignorant racist' and I jokingly spat.

I didn't actually care if they are homophobic or not. Homophobia is a self-fulfilling nightmare for those who suffer from it. You kind of expect a band like them to be a bit queer-ful.

Anyway, this rocker guy on the show who apparently worked with Guns N' Roses took offence at my TV spit and we had a few words. Kinky got involved and it turned into intense screaming and drinks flying. Kinky was thrown out and I left with her.

And that's how life continued for a while until Kinky was invited to rap on Erasure's *Abba-esque* EP. I agreed to let her do it, even though she was signed to More Protein and, by then, owed the label a decent sum of money. The song went to Number 1 in the UK and Caron made a few bob, which I asked to split because my understanding was that all third-party royalties were supposed to be shared with the label. It was Virgin's money, but I asked to share the royalties 50-50. No chance. She wanted it all, it got a bit ugly and she cussed me: 'Berry Gordy and Babylon thief.' In the end, Virgin gave up on More Protein and handed the entire label to me when I was dropped by them in 1994.

It was then that Caron decided to leave More Protein, kicking and screaming, and tried to sue me until her lawyer checked the contract.

After I fell out with her, so many people fell in her artistic wake.

Caron and I never made up and then she accused me of assault, resulting in my arrest. It happened on the top floor of Harvey Nichols when I foolishly tried to say hello. Kinky screamed, 'You're a fat cunt,' and I left. Calling me 'fat' was as deep as she could go. Fortunately, her friend Danielle got her to see sense and the charges were dropped.

Now, every time anything good or bad happens in my life, she takes to Facebook to have her say. When I went to prison she was clearly delighted, but not so happy when I got my job on *The Voice*.

I often chant for her, and I find thinking positive things about Kinky Caron very helpful. She did say something nice about me in a dance magazine, but she must have had a karma relapse.

It feels funny to say but I wouldn't know how to feel if she was friendly. I wouldn't trust it. I think she is a great talent, and I could have done so much more with and for her. I often work on tracks and say, 'Imagine Kinky Caron on this.' Our work together on More Protein and with Jesus Loves You remains some of my favourite work. Completely of a time when Kinky Caron knew how to smile and had a sense of humour. Someone should tell her that hatred is like drinking poison.

The second Libra down was John Themis, who was my

friend and writing partner from 'Bow Down Mister' (the fourth single released by Jesus Loves You in 1991) onwards for almost thirty years. John played acoustic guitar on 'Bow Down Mister' and a spiritual moment was born. He worked with me when I wrote songs for my musical *Taboo*, which was considered by some as my crowning musical opus. That's what a wonderful review said. Reviews about my music are rarely complimentary. I cried. Good tears.

John had hair when we met, only at the back, and he was wearing cowboy boots, tight jeans and a George Michael BSA leather jacket. His playing was tight and skilful, and we jammed a few old classics. I was impressed. He joined my band, quickly became my musical director, and we started writing. I have no idea how many songs we created but we just didn't stop. He had a tiny studio in his house and for a while a larger studio at the bottom of his garden where we recorded 'I Specialise In Loneliness', which is a total jam.

I even brought John into Culture Club when we decided to do some live shows later in the ninteies. It was good to have him as a musical referee between me and the boys and they grew to adore him. We toured for years, and I watched John's kids grow up and even helped with Candy Rock, the band he created for his daughters, Emily and Katerina.

I loved John like family and I still don't fully understand why or how he left. Actually, I get 'why' because I am told he was tired of touring, but he did it without leaving a door open for friendship or the occasional guitar solo.

I know that he now works for his friend, Lenny, whose family owns the Brunswick Centre in Bloomsbury. Among his various duties in the company, John runs the Brunswick Art Gallery and puts on live shows, which look like fun.

My friend Maria Smith, who has a Libra son, always jokes of Librans, 'They walk over your dead body.' I have yet to meet a Libran who doesn't piss in their own handbag. I do have one surviving Libra mate, producer Kinky Roland, but so many have fallen by the wayside. Kinky Roland is the Libran that stayed. We do most of our work over the phone and the internet, so that possibly helps.

I met Kinky Roland when I was deejaying in the nineties, when he made records for the label Heidi of Switzerland. I went through a hard phase where I was playing banging techno and Kinky fitted in. I'd got in touch with the label and asked him to do a remix. The guy running it said, 'That bloke from the eighties wants a remix.'

A long relationship with that bloke from the eighties came from that phone call. Now Kinky is my dance guy and he knows that world, but we do pop and funky stuff too. I push him to be less linear and he pushes me for detail. He is super talented and completely unreasonable but then so am I. I love him and it's proof that when a Libra meets a Gemini it can be a match made in four to the floor.

I love Librans and they appear in my life like moths around a flame. But they love the good life and will elbow you out of the way to get a seat on a private jet. They put their comfort before everyone, but it does depend on their moon. Let's get it clear. I love Librans and they sometimes love me.

ϟ ϟ ϟ

It's my fallout with Philip Sallon that has been nuclear. I went to his 70th birthday party in 2022 after much back and forth. I did the right thing and was not rewarded.

We fell out over a boy who still doesn't understand why or how. Philip might say I stole his band but it was really all about the keyboard player. There is a chance (however vague) that, after years of nibbling away, the tree might have fallen but it's unlikely. I mean, can we accept that some boys are straight? Being straight doesn't mean you have to act or look straight. Just as being a drag queen doesn't mean you have to be a boy.

The band in question were called The Electric Flowers, which I said was a disaster of a name, and they became We Are Brando. It was 2014 and Philip was managing them, among his many other skills, and asked me to give them musical advice. My first advice was to run as fast as you can from Philip, who had apparently told them he was like Simon Cowell. Who knows where he got that idea? But Philip asked me to help these three kids and that's what I did. I pride myself on being honest and, when it comes to music, I'm brutally honest.

We Are Brando are one of my favourite bands that no one really knows about. They will now and not just because Philip was madly in love with one of them. We have made some incredible music together and my dream is to take those boys on the road.

They had previously been managed by former MP Lembit Opik and, while the name is a song title, the concept of him managing even The Cheeky Girls is out there. Brando's management life got no sweeter under Philip, who, they told me, constantly made them change songs. Rather than just saying 'rubbish', he thought moving the bridge and changing one word would do the trick. He played me stuff and I said, 'Rubbish songs. Great ideas but trying too hard to be radio.' But that was exactly where Philip wanted them. Bleeding over a well-crafted pop song so that Philip could say 'Look, I'm like Simon Cowell if he wore Westwood.' I asked the boys who they wanted to sound like, and Morrissey was way ahead of Rihanna. My advice was to invest in a sound that told people who they are and I agreed to write with them. Philip hated my advice and kept screaming 'Rihanna, Rihanna, Rihanna.'

I told them to leave Philip and, as far as I know, they

needed zero encourage-ment. The lead singer, Luke, had already relocated to Cornwall and was having a Philip-induced meltdown. Once they said goodbye to Philip and his misinformed musical ideas, he sent me a scathing email dripping in contempt and accusation. It was along the lines that I had ruined his entire life and stolen every bit of sunshine from his sky, and he would NEVER forgive me. Hence the continued crow's feet.

I guess music killed our friendship and it often does kill friendships. Look at me and Joan. I love Philip and always will, but hell will need to freeze over before she gets a grip. I could indulge him and pretend I take this feud seriously, but I just don't.

In Philip's mind, I stole his band and his potential boyfriend. And then he accused me of stealing Laura Fireman, who I met through Philip and hated on sight. We were going to Bagley's, a mid-nineties rave club in an old warehouse in King's Cross before it became slick and cool. Philip called me and said, 'I'm sending this mouthy Jewish girl called Laura to pick you up. You'll love her. She's very you, she's very us.' Laura, who was a music PR, arrived at my house in Hampstead in her sleek Mini Cooper with Philip and two other friends in the cramped back. As I tried to climb into the tiny car, Laura quipped, 'Can't you fit in, skinny?' I got out of the car, slammed the door, told her to fuck off and went back in the house.

She kept ringing my doorbell and in the end I started laughing and came out, got in the car and said, 'Don't say another word.' Needless to say, we became good friends, but it wasn't until I did my first season on *The Voice* in Australia in 2017 that I got to know Laura really well. She moved out to Sydney with her husband, Lex, and her twins, Flo and Cassius, after living briefly in Brazil. Philip was furious that I was hanging out with Laura on the other side of the world and accused me of stealing her. I immortalised this moment in a song called 'Clouds' where I say:

*The day I stole Laura was the day I grew*
*to adore her.*

Philip won't allow me to be mentioned in his presence and shakes like Little Richard every time he hears my name; although he allowed me to go to his 70th birthday in 2022 because, after all, I am Boy George. I went to his party dressed up to the nines because I knew that's what he wanted, even though he didn't really speak to me. I have to love him from afar now and I do love him. He's been such a huge part of my life. Even writing this makes me quite tearful. I've had many a cold war with Philip but never one that's lasted this long. I don't write this about Philip to be bitchy, although he trained me in the art, and there's a lot more I could say and maybe I will. I guess my real point is that you can love someone even though they don't love you.

I often see Philip out and he avoids me like the plague. At my friend Robert Gordon's birthday recently, he sat as far away from me as he could but jumped into every photo as if we were best Facebook friends. Maybe we are but he just hasn't realised? It is deeply frustrating for me because I know I'm a much better person now and potentially could be a better friend to Philip. I think of all the fun and laughter we're missing out on.

All this is to say that I know I've evolved because in the past I would have been a mindless adversary, but my love for Philip is as all-consuming as his hatred for me. Philip might go round telling everyone who will listen that I'm a terrible person but he doesn't really know who I am now.

*Philip Sallon*
*Holding court*
*Philip Sallon*
*Down at Heaven*
*Philip Sallon*
*Walks through Soho*
*Philip Sallon*
*She a legend*

## 14

# JUNGLE IS MASSIVE

*I still can't believe I went into the jungle.*
I watched *I'm a Celebrity... Get Me Out of Here!* –
the South Africa version with its 'All Star' cast of former
contestants – and thought it's a show you watch, not a
show you do. Yet I did do it, the original, in Australia in
November 2022. I thought it would be super challenging
and, in the spirit of Andy Warhol, I felt I like I was jumping
headfirst into pop culture. I love how Andy Warhol started
modelling in his later years. No better time than now to
be yourself. I also got paid well to do it and I can't pretend
that wasn't another good reason. With Jon Moss and his
money-sucking lawsuit breathing down my neck, I felt
like it was a gig I couldn't turn down. I kept my fears to
myself, except for heights; I wasn't teetering on anything

or jumping out of a helicopter. I made a promise to myself that there would be no nelly screaming. Paul Burrell she won't be! Maybe just a hint of Gillian McKeith. The odd well-rehearsed stage faint in front of a spitting snake. *Remembering the whole time, your brothers are watching. South-east London is watching.*

I heard that on *Big Brother* there are hairdressers and make-up artists in the next room. Not the case on *I'm a Celebrity...* but you go in thinking there will coffee breaks. When we first landed in the helicopter and started the long trek towards camp, reality-TV star-turned-presenter Olivia Atwood was complaining, 'There must be an easier way into the camp. How do they get all the lights and camera equipment in, they can't drag it all the way through here?' I thought to myself, *Jesus stop moaning*, but she was right. There were easier ways to get into the camp. They want you to feel absolutely stranded. They made each one of us get into separate Jeeps with blacked-out windows. It was the start of the rituals to wind you up and get you rattled.

The day I did my first trial on the beach in a suffocating water tank I saw security give Olivia Atwood some food. I thought it was a choc ice at first and was a bit jealous before I discovered Oliva was feeling unwell and needed a sugar pick-up. It was a protein bar. We were only on day two and Olivia was being monitored carefully. The first task was a baptism of fire. I wasn't bothered about what I had to do but I was bothered about being on TV in a wet T-shirt. I knew I had more to get over but I threw a dry towel over my shoulders and refused to take it off on camera.

'Can we lose the towel?'

'No!'

I nailed that water task and I felt completely fearless. Moments before I was cursing everyone; I hated PK, I hated Ant and Dec and the universe. I tapped it out using EFT, chanting 'I am fearless, I am confident, I am happy, I am strong.' I do these mantras every day, especially since doing it in the jungle because I realised how much it was helping me. My spiritual practices in the camp were amplified in the edits for comedy effect, though. I didn't keep anyone awake. I wasn't noisy, but they taped what I was doing and played it back endlessly to make it look like that was all I did. I did my morning rituals in the treehouse, which was away from the camp. I did hear a loud bird squawking in the morning and maybe my campmates thought the noise was coming from me.

After being in isolation for several days prior to entering the jungle, I was taken on a speedboat for some pre-show filming. We were shooting the *I'm a Celebrity* opening sequence and doing the master interview. I had to try on my jungle uniform and I was terrified. I had cut up one of the hats and created a crown with the help of Ben Fletcher who runs my art studio. It had a bit of a Basquiat vibe, like a punk crown. We customised one of the shirts with big red polka-dots. I wanted to customise everything but that would have meant the show giving away too much control. You quickly realise that, when they say, 'Let's talk about it,' they mean 'NO.'

I get that the show is designed to make you crazy, but they should know that you are already crazy when you step off the flight to Australia. I stepped off mine from Mexico wearing a lion's head I bought on the internet. I was told that my code name for the jungle was 'Lion' so I was being super subtle. An American fellow passenger was the only one to comment on my lion drag. He asked for a picture and, of course, I agreed – I knew I looked good as Simba. I could just about see through the eyes of the mask and had to hold on to the strapping security guard so I didn't lose my Balenciaga. From Brisbane airport we were driven to a posh suburb to stay in a safe house and go into isolation.

I only found out that my DJ friend Chris Moyles was also heading into the jungle days before I flew out of London to join Culture Club for some American dates. My manager, Tiffany, has been living with Chris in London for several years and had managed to keep the jungle news quiet. And, yes, I can confirm they are more than friends. They have two blue cats, and they are constantly refurbishing the house. It's what you get for dating a Cancerian. Chris is a Pisces who has zero interest in Star signs. Tiffany dropped the bombshell about Chris going in because it was about to accidently-on-purpose appear in the press. I was excited. I'd never slept out in the elements with Chris, but he has fixed my TV and brought my weekly shopping over. He is part of my life these days and even if we had a bust-up in the jungle, I know we could never officially fall out. Tiff would never allow it!

I was the only celebrity to have company during isolation. Who knows what the other campmates asked for. Chris got a running machine and was called a diva for it online. But Chris runs all the time. A running machine for Chris is like coffee to me. It turns out that I should stop drinking coffee because my blood type, O, is very acidic. But I have already given up so much. I love my espresso doppio with double cream and a top-up of hot water. I like it sweet with a little sugar. I could live on sweet coffee. Now that sounds like an opening line to a Prince song.

Sadie Turner, who helps run my art business, stayed in the house with me. We are both spiritual seekers and nut jobs and kundalini yoga freaks. I call her, the spiritual gangster'. Sadie is smart and sweet but with an edge. She calls it her 'swivel head'. It's where Brighton meets *The Exorcist*. A more helpful person you could not meet but push her at your peril. She gives amazing advice and seeks wisdom. She's an 'everything' type of person, like all my friends. The recovery sister of a hypocrite. I do drink now. We both do. I think it's under control, but I keep an eye on it.

The producers took our phones, but we managed to get the internet working almost immediately on my laptop. This was how I found out politician Matt Hancock was entering the jungle. The password was at the back of the router, which wasn't even hidden, so I immediately did a search to see who was coming. I watched videos of everyone on YouTube and researched their astrological information. I knew their moons, their dunes and their pantaloons. I was shocked to find out Matt Hancock was a Libran. We had two Librans: Matt and Mike Tindall. 'Oh no', I thought. 'I'm probably going to get on quite well with Matt Hancock.' I knew that I would like Mike.

While we were in the safe house we were taken for daily walks by girls from the production team who actually spoke to us, and even the burly security guys were civilised. Sometimes, halfway through our walk, we would get detoured because of another celeb heading our way. Chris was in a house close by and one day he came to visit, and we chatted through the fence. Another night we broke out for a long evening walk in the rain and went down to the beach at the back of the house. Huge frogs were everywhere. I love frogs.

Sadie and I tried to live on rice for a few days before I finally left isolation after eleven days. But I think we made it too tasty. We added salt, and salt makes everything more delicious. We were getting groceries delivered daily and

Sadie kept adding naughty things like crisps and Tim Tams. She was trying to follow a low FODMAP diet but, even when things were not on her eating list, she kept saying, 'Tim Tams are FODMAP. So are chocolate rice cakes.' I gave up trying to prepare myself because I had no idea what I was preparing for.

I put a little bit of light make-up on before leaving the house for the final time. I'd been awake the entire night, shaving everything. I was freaked out. Off into the unknown. Sadie wanted to follow me and hide in a tree.

The guy who drove me on the day my official journey into camp started wouldn't speak to me. I was getting one-word answers or grunts to everything. I was alone at this point and had no idea where he was taking me. I thought, 'They are taking this whole thing far too seriously.' I was driven to a harbour but had to sit in the car for about two hours. Right from the start I found the silent treatment annoying.

I was eventually taken to a jetty with a red carpet, bowls of fruit, exotic drinks and a 1970s-looking yacht. That is when I first met Sue Cleaver from *Coronation Street*, TV presenter Scarlette Douglas and *Hollyoaks* actor Owen Warner, who asked me my name. I was in full Boy George drag and I had been all over the press, so I must assume he was nervous or lives under a rock? Maybe it's a generational thing. I had to choose one person to join me after meeting them for ten minutes. Owen was out but only because choosing the hot guy was just too gay. I knew that my VIP experience was obviously a trick, so I thought better of inviting Sue.

I chose Scarlette; young, fit, great earrings, glamorous but determined. She looked like she could handle anything. As the boat cast off, we started chatting. 'Save it for the camera,' came the order. Nothing is more entertaining than the truth of the moment. Everything else feels a bit fake.

I nibbled some cheese from the buffet and let Scarlette enjoy all the prawns. After about four hours, some of which we spent alone resting in cabins, we arrived at the location. I had to practice zen because doing things is how I relax.

The yacht stopped offshore and we had to climb into a little dinghy and row to shore. They handed me a tiny lifejacket and I said, 'I am not wearing that.' Scarlette looked like a supermodel in hers. They found me a bigger lifejacket and we climbed into the dinghy. I was excited that my new lifejacket had bright-orange trim. Laughing and screaming, we sang, 'Row, row, row your boat, gently down the stream...' That laughter soon stopped when we found out where we were sleeping.

Walking on to that hot beach in full Boy George drag was hideous. I was hungry and it was late. The nightmare had begun. Marooned on an ugly island, sleeping outside. My mattress was wet. I folded it over like a martyr.

We had just met Olivia and Chris on the beach after climbing clumsily out of the dinghy. Olivia had had to choose someone to jump out of a helicopter with her and she chose Chris. I couldn't believe he had done it. I felt like I already knew Olivia. Her banter had banter and she was having a non-stop bitch-off with Chris. You would think they knew each other but certain people just click; no smalltalk.

The mood changed when the first delicious meal of rice and beans arrived. I'd hardly touched the buffet on the boat so I was up for eating anything. It was bland and Oliva's portion was frozen in the middle. We sat around a man-made fire in our new uniforms and slowly tried to eat the gruel. We all gave Olivia a bit of our food, but she wasn't eating anything. I got the impression she prefers a bit of fine dining. While I was in the camp, I'd tried to prepare myself so was taking the new wonder drug Ozempic, which dampens your appetite, but that night I really felt the hunger. I was awake all night. It got so cold I screamed at the crew to relight the fire. I had a mosquito net around the bed, which added shadows and drama. I could feel them filming me and spotted a tiny red light in the pitch black. So I meditated under the moon on my bunk. It was an amazing meditation and a good time to remember what I was about to experience. I tried to have a spiritual word with myself. Sometimes you need to take your own best advice.

I convinced some of my camp mates to use EFT and all of them said, 'I think that tapping works.' Even comedian Babatunde Aléshé who is an evangelical. Baba was cool with the tapping but resisted my attempts to send him positive vibes. Before our first trial together I was chanting and jokingly tried to throw him a little blessing. 'No, no,' he said, 'keep it.' LOL. I'm not suggesting that his rejection of my goodwill was the reason we only got three stars, but it didn't help. Conceptually, rejecting positivity is an act of self-sabotage. During an early conversation in the camp Baba said, 'You're into black magic, though, right?' He was looking at my tattooed arms making all the wrong assumptions.

The task I did with Baba and Chris Moyles was probably the most intimidating. We were inside a tiny replica of the Angel of the North called Angel of Agony, with Chris right at the top and Baba above me. I took the lowest position and had to put my hand into holes with creatures in without looking, unscrewing stars to try and avoid upsetting snakes or rats. Once I had the stars, I had to push them through a tiny slit up to Baba and then he passed it to Chris. They obviously made it impossible by dropping a ton of cockroaches and ants on us. Baba was screaming and kept dropping the stars. We got three stars, which was cringe.

I decided to chant and sing as I pushed my hand through a membrane and into the first hole towards a snake. I was chanting *Om* and *Hare Krishna* and to my surprise the snake stayed out of my way. In fact, none of the creatures moved. I think the chanting and singing took me out of my state of utter panic. Obviously, I knew the creatures wouldn't kill me, but your head goes completely. I also thought it would be fun to bring a bit of chanting to the masses. One of the animal handlers gave me the thumbs-up when we finished the task. I knew then that I would chant my way through everything.

And it was bloody well I did because the camp was hideous. An utter khazi. The floor is a manmade carpet of wood chippings, leaves and dirt. The beds are open to the elements, the army-style sleeping bags are coarse and damp. The beds are nabbed first-and if you're not fast or female-you get one of the uncomfortable hammocks. I was lucky to get a bed but I kept thinking about snakes and spiders. I did a little prayer every night to the creepy crawlies. 'Dear creatures, can we share this space and leave each other alone?' I think it worked. Politician Matt Hancock should have prayed because on day one a scorpion bit his finger. He let out a scream and turned into a little boy, but he was braver than I would have been. I couldn't help wondering if ITV had planted the scorpion. It was just too perfect.

We named the scorpion Keir Starmer after the Labour leader. I bet if Keir was watching, he was screaming his head off. You would be amazed who watches the show. Later that same day Seann Walsh let out a comic scream as a scorpion crawled up his thigh. Seann screamed much louder than Matt. Mike Tindall came to the rescue with a piece of cardboard and lifted the creature off. When creatures appear in the camp, they send in guys wearing full camouflage with covered faces and industrial visors. It's like an actor from *Dad's Army* crossed with Darth Vader.

My friend Kevin Bishop said Seann Walsh was 'good people'. I met Kevin through Sadie, but I knew who he was because he turned me into a witch in *Star Stories*, which was a satire on George Michael and Wham! Watch it on YouTube. Hilarious. Seann was as lovely as Kevin promised. He laughed at everything I said. If you can make a comedian laugh, that's love absolute. Seann was smart, eccentric, baffled, bludgeoned, satirical, sweet and out of his comfort zone. I started on him immediately, 'Alright, love rat.' He took it very well, but he knew I was on his side. 'It's a bloody tabloid headline, not a fact,' I assured him.

In his mind, he was in the jungle to repair some damage he'd done to his career. He instantly showed people who he was and he stayed in longer than I did, partly because he kept his mouth shut and didn't say any of the things out loud that he was whispering in my ear! He's instantly likeable though, a good Irishman. Technically, he was born in the UK like me. His dad is a glorious Paddy who was a functioning heroin addict for years. He said to Seann, 'Tell Boy George about the drugs. He'll feckin' love it.'

Not everyone was quite as easy, though. Like everyone, I was miffed by Matt Hancock's arrival in the jungle, but I wanted to keep an open mind. It was hard to do that, though.

I remember being interviewed about him and I just burst into tears. I remembered Mum being rushed to hospital during lockdown and how I couldn't be by her side. Seeing him in person just brought it all to the surface and I was emotional and angry. After the interview, I wanted to be alone and took myself away from the rest of the camp. Seann Walsh came to check on me – he's such a peace maker – and I was letting off steam about Matt.

Matt kept saying he did nothing wrong and that it was a technicality. I found this annoying. He should have just said sorry because it wasn't a technicality for the rest of us. We obeyed the rules and he, like many politicians, flaunted them. Matt appeared behind me at that point, and I had to be honest. I told him I'd been slagging him off. He actually took it very calmly. Meanwhile, I had no idea Seann was pulling faces behind our backs as we thrashed it out. Seann had arrived with Matt, which was clearly pointed – the two scandalous celebs entering together – but Seann's scandal was personal. It was between himself and the two ladies involved, not the entire nation. But whatever the producers tried to twist, asking me if I hated Matt, of course I didn't.

Everyone was pretty tight-lipped around Matt until I had my outburst, but even then it was mostly off camera, which I thought was disingenuous of them. I believe telling people straight to their face is best if it is not going to harm them. Matt took it like a politician, like he didn't give a shit. I understand how tough it was for Matt Hancock to enter the camp. He was a marked man because of his Covid antics as (un) Health Secretary. But once I had made my point to Matt I decided to live and let live.

I was accused of bullying Matt, which was never the case. I tried to discuss controversial stuff with Matt, but he was very guarded. We talked about transgender rights and safe spaces for women. I was told he was 'anti-trans', which is quite common right now, but he insisted he wasn't. In the camp, men, women, gays and straights were sharing a sleeping space and a very smelly toilet and yet there was relative harmony. Of course, there were times when the women felt uncomfortable or that feminine needs were not catered for. Sometimes I would catch myself moaning and realise it didn't read well. With the lack of food and comfort, you must be a saint not to moan occasionally but, once you remember you are meant to be having a hideous time, you get over it or get sent home.

Matt had gone in as the villain and was getting it from everywhere. At first he was chosen by the public for every task, and just got on with it. He had no choice because he had to appear fearless. He told us about taking part in *Celebrity SAS: Who Dares Wins*. He surely was looking for love.

ITV put a red chair into the camp right by the fire and Matt was crowned leader of the camp after a leadership contest. He fell back on the chair while trying to adjust it. I did chuckle. Luckily for us, Matt was a well-behaved leader, and I could see his confidence growing. I had my back up instantly and was planning to disobey any of his orders. It felt like a wind-up having him as a leader after everything but all he did was dish out camp chores. He also got to sleep in the retro RV motorhome in the corner of the camp.

The RV was sold to us as a luxury experience. It had comfy beds but it was full of spiders. No one really wanted to go in there but Matt chose journalist Charlene White as his deputy. She refused to sleep in there with him and told us she needed to be 'neutral', which made no sense. But I understood why a married woman would be uncomfortable sharing a bedroom with a stranger. A male stranger.

Charlene was already established as camp matriarch. Such a bossy Cancerian in the kitchen but with a contradictory sweet side that wanted to make sure you ate. I found her strong character challenging but I also took note of how thoughtful she was. I was amazed that she left first. You are not voted out of camp; you just don't get voted for.

Charlene helped stabilise the camp. She was mum with Sue as her trusty sidekick. Two perfect bookends of an opinionated bookshelf. They seemed to personify two books that inspired me: Mary Beard's *Woman & Power* versus *Rage Becomes Her* by Soraya Chemaly. They are both smart, but Sue holds the sarcasm card. Meryl Streep playing Margaret

Thatcher also came to mind. 'If you want something spoken about, ask a man. If you want something done, ask a woman.'

I can be very laid back and I enjoy being taken care of. I'm happy to do anything if I'm asked in the right way. When I arrived with Chris, Olivia and Scarlette, the camp was already almost full. Some things had been predetermined by the force of personality and people were setting up their barriers. There were accusations about camp mates not pulling their weight, but you can't all be in control. It's a fact that some people were very aware of the cameras and being helpful in a way they never were previously.

The younger camp mates have grown up in a pop culture where everyone is self-aware, or at least camera-conscious. I had to get comfortable with being around a bunch of strangers and never being alone. I love my own company. Being on camera without my hat or make-up was a trial. I don't become an entirely different person when I'm dressed up, but the energy shifts and people treat me very differently. I know I have battled for years with my public persona, and I am getting much better at being both Boy George and George O'Dowd. They are both me, of course, but I like how Boy George dresses. Being in the jungle was the most exposing thing on the surface. Because of the editing there was a very false idea of me portrayed but this was true for all of us. The stories in the press just wanted to make me look difficult. It doesn't appear to have worked with everyone. Since coming out of *I'm a Celebrity...* people have been super nice to me. 'We loved you in the jungle, you were absolutely real.'

It matters less if you know you're being guarded and behaving nothing like yourself just to stay in. I cannot for the life of me be anyone but whoever I am in the moment. I have a revolving personality and my perspective can change as quickly as it becomes rigid. I have started to accept that I know less than I realise. Getting high on your own supply of nothingness is a rare gift. Being away from my phone and the computer was life-affirming. I was told my ability to 'self-regulate' was unmatched. I have always been able to fly off the handle then fly right back. A quality I got from Dad. Smash the house up. Break all your records in half. Breathe. Someone put the kettle on. The fact I only lost it a few times in the jungle is massive.

The water situation was hideous. They make you collect water from a pump, which you must then carry up the hill in a bucket and boil on the wood fire. You were supposed to let it cool, but it was put into the dispensers while it was warm. It was Mike Tindall who was carrying everything. He quickly became the in-house lumberjack and water bearer. I could see Mike liked to keep busy. A good way to avoid awkward conversations. At first, he was quite closed and didn't reveal much, which was annoying because we all wanted Royal gossip. He opened up enough to rap and sing and tell us how much he loved musical theatre. He had some Royal stories but none about Harry and Meghan. Shame.

The smoke from the fire is impossible to get away from. If you move one way, it follows you. It's like ITV are controlling the wind. Not everyone's wind was controllable. One day we were sheltering from a vicious storm in the Telegraph Hut and Sue Cleaver let out a 'whatever you ate before you came in' fart. Owen ran out of the door and the rest of us swallowed it. It was tastier than some of the food. It's okay, Sue, my mum used to say, 'Better out than in.' Sue's jungle fart was iconic. Of all the people in the camp Sue was the hardest to read and yet I felt I had known her forever. Everyone in a soap seems like your best friend. Well, maybe not Owen but I've never really watched *Hollyoaks*. I was in it once as myself. I played Boy George the DJ.

Sue is a Virgo, like Jon Moss. I tried not to think about it but they do have some similar characteristics. Right now, I prefer Sue. She was consistent and I don't think she was that bothered about winning. She won me over with her northern sarcasm and biting wit. An eye roll from Sue was as iconic as her farts. She also knows a million poofs and we talked about The Three Principles, which I have been trying to live by. Sue is one of those people I will never have to explain myself to.

I might have pissed her off when I came to Matt's defence

when he was given the cooking task. Sue was backseat-cooking, telling everyone what to do while not lifting a finger. There was a lot of that, including from me. I kept telling them they were over-cooking stuff or not cooking it correctly. I offered advice about cooking certain vegetables but the dash-it-in-the-pan process took over. When the food arrived the mood in the camp became very aggressive. Every night it seemed to arrive later and later. Who had energy for finesse?

Whoever won the stars would read out the menu. There was never any mention of the vegetarian option, but it was mostly some sort of mushroom. Cooking anything is a nightmare. Heston Blumenthal would battle with the fire, the pots and the blunt knives. There is nowhere to prepare anything, and it's just set up to be an absolute nightmare.

One night we had potatoes, mmm, and Matt was talking out loud as if he was at the House of Commons: 'I think I should parboil the potatoes first.' Which is, of course, exactly what you should do. Sue piped up, 'No, no, it will take too long, just shove them in the pan.' And Matt was about to surrender. I went up to Matt and whispered, 'Everyone knows you parboil potatoes, ask fucking Jamie Oliver, not Eileen Grimshaw. Grow some balls.'

Sue's face was a picture for the rest of the evening and I thought, 'She hates me.' It's very possible that Sue didn't even notice me talking to Matt but, later that evening down where the washing up was done in a rusty, leaf-filled bath, I heard there was plenty of bitching about Matt.

'Who does he think he is?'

'He's getting pretty full of himself.'

Not much of this was ever said to Matt's face but we all bitched about each other at times. Scarlette even upset Seann and he blew a fuse off camera. But we had some great times too. Watching Scarlette teaching Matt the electric snake dance was priceless and then there was the attempt to get Matt to sing his favourite Abba song. Sue would serenade Matt in the voice of Margaret Thatcher. 'I Will Survive' in the voice of Maggie was TV gold but, like so many hilarious moments, it was never broadcast.

I asked Matt, 'If you were on *Mastermind*, what would your specialist subject be? Maggie's handbags?'

He looked at me with sulky contempt. I told him about when I met Margaret Thatcher and had my photograph taken with her. He probably thought I was trying to smoulder up. Gagging for the Tory Whip!

After my initial outburst at Matt, it was inevitable that we would get a task together. During our food trial together, he suggested I was flirting with him. I might have been if it was on camera. He did look a bit like Fran Healey from Travis. I thought I was being smart choosing the vegetarian food option for our challenge, but it turns out stinky tofu is even more disgusting than a bull's penis. I thought shoving it in my mouth quickly was the best, but I was soon retching. If Matt was cast as The Villain, I was The Diva and we both felt pressure to get every single star. And we nailed it. I wasn't just doing it for the gays, but I was doing it for the gays.

There was another task in a pub. We all thought it was a nice night out, but the beer tasted like fizzy vomit. We did tasks to win pizza, crisps, French fries, chocolate and alcohol. You had to choose a partner. I chose Seann on another trial and Chris was furious. At the pub, Chris Radio X'd me out and chose Mike. He was calling Seann my new boyfriend. God, I love jealous straight guys!

Luckily for me, I didn't fancy anyone in the jungle. When I came out, all my gay friends were saying, 'What about Owen? He's hot.' He is easy on the eye and, yes, I did have to avoid staring at him at times, but Mike is more my type. Like Owen, footballer Jill Scott was instantly likeable. An Aquarian like Mum and Dad and, like Dad, could talk the hind legs off a donkey. Jill was 'so what?' about being gay, which I understand. She didn't hide it or talk about it all the time.

I wasn't the person who talked most in the jungle, but I was the most outspoken. I did feel that any vaguely controversial subjects were cut short. I felt Scarlette came in for Matt over me a few times but maybe she has political aspirations.

Scarlette was another camp mate whose early exit

surprised me. It made you wonder what the public are being shown. It rarely made sense. At first I thought Scarlette could be a winner because she got stuck into everything. Though she upset me when she asked about my court case and prison. The question was casually and thoughtlessly posed out of the blue, interrupting a terse conversation between me and Matt. At the time, it felt like she had been told to ask the question. She had no idea of the facts and it upset me. ITV will insist they do not instruct conversations, but they plant questions in people's minds. I was even asked to talk to Jill about being gay.

I had just done a task where I was covered in gunk, and I saw Sue and Mike climbing into a Jeep while the rest of us were told to walk. It wasn't any old hill, it was steep and I told them, 'I'm older than Sue and I'm asthmatic, I'm not walking up the hill unless you're filming me.' They insisted there were no Jeeps available, but I dug my heels in. 'Okay,' I said, 'How do I get out of here?'

I found a wheelbarrow and I plonked myself in it with a bottle of water and said, 'I've got the patience of a saint. Fuck off!' I forgot to tell them I was a south-east London saint. I meditated for what must have been thirty minutes. I could feel the camera boring into my soul. I asked the guy to stop filming me. He said, 'I'm not allowed,' so I ran down the hill and found the crew camp, grabbed an apple, took a massive slug of orange squash, went into another tent and zipped it shut. It was exciting and dangerous, I don't even know why I did it. I found aspects of the camp very compliant. But at that point I felt like one of The Slits on the cover of *Cut*, a mud-covered savage in a reality TV nightmare.

A stocky security guard in camouflage pulled open the zip on my hiding place and said, 'You're acting like a brat.'

'What are you going to do, beat me up?' I shouted and zipped myself back in.

It took a while but eventually a Jeep arrived and took me back to the camp and the guy who called me a brat got into trouble. I asked explicitly for nothing to be done to him. But what is this, Hunger Games? Suddenly they can speak to me.

It was a long way back to camp, or did they take me the long way? Outside of the main camp when you went for trials they would give you bottles of water or they would let you drink from coolers. Later they tried to stop it and I said, 'Give me the water or I'm just not going to go on set.' When you arrive for a trial, they cover your head in a towel and walk you towards the set like you're being kidnapped. Obviously, I kept lifting the towel. There was an aggressive woman with a clipboard who kept saying, 'No talking.' So I talked more and much louder.

I tried to incite a mutiny one afternoon because we failed a bushtucker trail and missed out on some chocolate treats. We kept getting the questions wrong because everyone relied on Matt to provide the answers. 'Oh, he's a politician. He must know everything.' Turns out he didn't. My chocolate revolution got the cold shoulder and Matt warned, 'Recently on *Celebrity Coach Trip* the cast tried a mutiny, and they were all fired.' I laughed. *Coach Trip* is budget TV, they flew us in here in helicopters.

There was a trial where four of us were in a massive swirling teacup, which got faster and faster as offal and animal parts flew in our faces. We had to throw hoops onto a target as the teacup spun around. As giblets were hitting me in the face, I started throwing the hoops wildly and chanting, *Hare Krishna, Hare Krishna* and laughing hysterically, which surprised all my camp mates because, when I climbed into the teacup, I looked like I wanted to kill. I always saved it for the camera. When we finally got out of the teacup, I discovered that all my rings had hit the target. I did think to myself, 'Chanting Hare Krishna absolutely works. It must be the universe because I wasn't trying.'

So if the jungle did anything for me it was understanding that my spiritual practices were powerful and worked. I got into a routine of getting up before everyone else and going to the treehouse with my plastic mattress to do my yoga and chanting. It kept me sane, and I made a vow to myself that when I came out I would continue, and I have. You could say *I'm a Celebrity...* improved my kundalini. They portrayed me like a chanting menace. My friend Maxi Jazz from Faithless was watching from a hospice and I'm told he was entertained by me chanting *Nam Myoho Renge Kyo* because he was also a practising Nichiren Buddhist. I had no idea that he was dying but it made me cry to think I made him laugh at a time like that. He was an amazing man, oozing cool and calm, ripping off your tights with his teeth. NMRK Maxi.

⁂

When Ant and Dec appeared in the morning, everyone was tense and desperate not to get sent home. No one wanted to be first, but once it came to it you, it felt like you were beginning the next part of the adventure. Sue was completely delighted when she left, and I was ready to go. My sister, Siobhan and my nephew, Zech, were in Australia waiting for me and I was desperate to see them. The younger ones, like Jill, Owen and Scarlette, were the hungriest to go all the way. I think everyone was surprised by Matt staying in so long and there were people saying the British have short memories, but people are bloody-minded and like to stir things up too. I thought ITV would have secretly loved a Matt win. Some camp mates (and their families at the hotel, I later found out) were speculating that Matt must have a team of professional bots working around the clock voting for him. I laughed at this because it really didn't matter.

Once you walk across the bridge and out of camp you realise just how easy leaving would have been. The press kept insisting I was constantly threatening to leave but I was not. I am annoyingly professional. I *have* walked out of things, like band meetings or rehearsals, but never from anything work-and pay-related.

I was the fourth out of the eleven to be unvoted out. Was I disappointed not to have got further? No. It was a blessed relief. I had (been well) paid (for) my dues. My sister met me on the bridge. It felt amazing just to see her.

As the doctor gave me a check-up, I watched the camp on TV monitors. Despite just leaving, I felt like I had never been there. My sister said she could see me struggling to find my place in the jungle from the first week.

Over the years watching the show, I have always found the letters from home segment cringey. When you tour for as long as I do, a few days away in an exotic location is hardly emotional. Weirdly, though, my sister's letter, with its family titbits, made me very emotional. It didn't contain anything profound, but it felt like a love letter piercing my heart.

# 15

# KENTUCKY FRIED CHICKEN AND PRIMARK – LOSING MUM

They say writing a book is cathartic but some memories are not helpful. This last year, 2023, has been a big one. The Jon Moss lawsuit has been gnawing away at my finances and my sense of security, but losing my beautiful mum on March 12th tops everything. Of course, I knew Mum would die at some point. We all will. Being with mum when she passed was a beautiful and painful gift. Death is the biggest and smallest moment of anyone's life. My calmness was unnerving. If I had been told that I was going to have to be a grown-up at that moment, I would never have believed it. I wanted to fall apart and scream down the hospital walls but I knew Mum deserved more than me making it about me.

I was planning to be at Mum's for Sunday dinner and woke up to a hysterical phone call from my sister, Siobhan. Mum had collapsed and had been rushed to hospital. They had put her into an induced coma and things were not looking good.

'Get here as quickly as you can.'

I could tell from Siobhan's tone that it was that day. The day you always dread. The day you hope will never happen. The night before at around 1am I was shivering and thought I was coming down with a cold or perhaps had eaten something iffy. Was it Mum sending a message?

I had to think quick: order a cab or jump on the Elizabeth line? I knew I would feel awful sat in a taxi so I walked over to Liverpool Street to get the tube. I arrived at the platform to discover the Elizabeth line was closed. I heard a familiar voice: 'George, is that you?'

It was my niece, Millie, who was heading to Mum's for Sunday lunch too. She had no idea I was living in Spitalfields but here we were in the same place at the same time. I told Millie that Mum was in hospital and we headed there together. We talked and talked all the way to Woolwich where we met my other niece, Molly, at the station and she drove us to Queen Elizabeth Hospital. The first thing I did was hold Mum's feet. Maybe I thought I could stop her flying away? My nephew, Zech, was kissing Mum's head and everyone seemed to be in the room. Our family priest, Father Richard Plunkett, was holding a Bible and there were tears. Lots of tears.

Mum did not want to go; she wasn't ready, and watching her struggle to breathe broke my heart. Mum loved life and never asked for much from it: Kentucky Fried Chicken and Primark were her guilty pleasures. She loved her family and her grandchildren, and they loved her.

Mum lived in Shooters Hill, Woolwich, right next to the water tower with my sister, Siobhan, her husband, Craig, and their kids, Molly and Zech, and two yapping dogs, Rupert and Matilda. I bought the house for Mum after my dad left her for another woman. Siobhan and her family moved in to take care of Mum and jazzed the place up. At first Mum hated the changes and would complain, 'My home is being taken over.' But once the kitchen was done, she was delighted. 'Look at my beautiful kitchen.' she'd say. Siobhan and Craig's modern approach often left no room for her knick-knacks. But at Christmas Mum filled the house with decorations and it was biblical – she always went over the top and we all loved it. I have always been completely thankful that Siobhan and her family were living with Mum. Mum wasn't easy but she was an incredible and loving force of nature.

I 100-per cent saw that undeniable force leave her body.

I was cupping the crown of her head with one hand and squeezing her hand with the other. I told her she was safe and that I loved her, then I felt her squeeze my hand, but I have no idea if she could actually hear me.

I was softly singing Hindu prayers and I thought to myself that if she woke up her first words would be 'Shut up!' I can't count the times Mum said to me over the years, 'I thought that chanting was supposed to make you happy.' I always explained to her that, prayer or not, you remain a human being.

'You're a Catholic, son,' she would insist.

'I'm Catholic in my complications and Buddhist in my aspirations,' I would say.

Mum went to church most Sundays and Father Richard has been a close family friend for years and years. I jokingly refer to Richard as 'Father Ted'. His church is very close to Mum's house and across the road from where Stephen Lawrence was senselessly murdered. The church is called St John Fisher & St Thomas More and is where anything spiritual happens in our family.

When my father died in 2004, Mum did a blessing for him in that church and tried to tell us it was just for us kids. Dad had already been buried by his new wife and family, and though we were there, it was like they were describing someone else. After the blessing, she had a little plaque placed in the church garden. A touching tribute to a man she loved foolishly and loyally till the bitter end. I thought Mum was so dignified for doing that. She even asked to share his ashes with the new family but the request fell on deaf ears.

It was a New York drag queen, Tobell von Cartier, who told me to go home from New York for Dad's funeral. I was at a club with Erich, Aimee and Drew, and was telling them there was no point going home for the funeral. It would have nothing to do with my family and be an insult to Mum. On my way to the bar for another whiskey sour I was pulled aside by Tobell. 'Child, you know you have to go to your daddy's funeral. You will never forgive yourself. I don't know you that well but I do know you can't miss your own father's funeral.'

I was glad I went, even though it was awkward and some of my relatives on my dad's side ignored me. One of my cousin's had stopped talking to me, I think because of things I'd said in my first book, *Take It Like a Man*, which is both sad and weird because I was super close to her. I worshipped the way she built up her eyelashes with more and more mascara, her platform shoes and her layered halter-neck dresses. I babysat for her and her husband's kids and listened to their Pink Floyd and Eric Clapton 8-tracks on big, fat seventies headphones. They would bring back Kentucky Fried Chicken and friends from their nights out up the Old Kent Road, boozing at the Thomas A Beckett pub and racing like James Hunt through south-east London to get home. You could sometimes hear the roar of the engine from the balcony of the flat. The same block of flats where ill-gotten goods were stored in the basement. A nod, a wink and a stroke of the caretaker's palm. But Dad wouldn't allow any stolen goods in our house. One time Mum wanted a smoked-glass coffee table but it wasn't something you could add to the room quietly. Dad's tea would go down on that and all hell would break loose.

Sitting next to Mum, clutching her hand, I thought about all those memories with my family, with Dad and how different it could have been. I can't emphasise enough that Dad had many great qualities: he was compassionate, generous, oddly open-minded. He was a handsome fucker. People loved him. I loved him. Mum loved him too.

I thought about everything Mum had been through. What I'd put her through. What we went through together. At some of the most difficult moments Mum was always stoic. Words weren't necessary. Mum could look at you and make you feel disappointing. Mum used to give me the silent treatment because I was probably the most gobby. I hated her ignoring me, preferring Dad's punch-in-the-gob method. Boof! 'Make me a cup of tea, son.' The weight of the punch depended on what was happening. Dad broke a chair over my brother Gerald's back once. But I got away with a lot of verbal with him. You just had to be careful not to go too far. Dad was small but quick. He would punch up at a six-foot man and floor him. At a family wedding a guy was being playful with Mum, and Dad knocked him out. Dad carried a car jack under the front seat and it was wielded from time to time. Road rage was regular behaviour at that time in south-east London. I was told the reason I don't like being in the ocean is because my dad was like a shark. He would attack out of nowhere with the least provocation. It was never important stuff.

Oh, Mum, what you've been through. You kept your sense of humour, even if you did get very cheeky because of the mild vascular dementia. One day, Mum was out with her baby great-grandson, Albert, and a woman approached the table.

'Oh, he's beautiful, innee beautiful.'

When she walked away Mum said, 'Nosey cow. Thought she'd never go away.' Siobhan shushed her as she always did.

Mum would make comments about how people dress.

'Ain't she got a mirror in her house?'

When I was a kid it was me being told off by Mum for being bitchy. I suppose the apple never falls far from the tree.

They gave Mum morphine and eventually her breathing calmed. We all just sat there listening to her breathe. Saying beautiful things. Trying not to sound fearful or too sad.

At one point I felt her stop breathing. I thought she was gone, but then another breath. I was staring at her face, watching her slow down. Her hand went cold and she stopped breathing, this time completely. I wondered where she had gone. I know we never leave this place. We dissolve and become part of the atmosphere because there are no gaps in the universe.

⚑ ⚑ ⚑

At Mum's funeral I told the story about Philip Sallon coming to my family home. We had a picture of Mohammed Ali next to one of Pope John Paul in the hallway.

'Is this a joke?' Philip said.

'No,' my mother replied, getting the measure of him.

Cups of tea made.

'How old are you?' Philip asked my mother.

'Forty-one. Why?'

'You do look like you've lived,' Philip said.

As quick as you can, Mum said in her thick Dublin accent, 'Don't swing round too fast with that nose, you'll take someone's eye out.'

Philip was silent and said to me later, 'Oh, your mother.'

Mum had a long love-hate relationship with Philip.

'Who does he think he is?' she would say. 'Wearing a nappy to a posh restaurant. Look, you can see his arse. Sorry, he's disgusting.'

I was amazed that Philip wasn't at Mum's funeral. I consider myself an honorary Jew and, as a fellow Jew, I found it unforgivable. Up until Philip cancelled me, I attended every seder night feast, Succos. I've even fasted a few times on Yom Kippur. I miss Philip's sister Ruth's kosher feasts with her husband, Zaki, knocking up fresh horseradish sauce, and the sarcasm and wit of their two children.

I didn't write anything down at Mum's funeral; I spoke from my heart. It made me smile when I saw two flowered Kentucky Fried Chicken buckets at the side of the coffin. It looked like Banksy had set it. Beautiful flowers shot up from Mum's casket like fireworks. It was as if her spirit was jumping out. We had spent some time with the casket the night before the funeral. It was mostly close family and I was glad I got to see it, but it made me gasp to imagine Mum inside that box. It was beautiful, though. Lovely wood with brass fixtures. The guys who carried her were dressed for the part and they knelt down. I said to Kevin, 'She's not a footballer.' David had initially insisted on helping to carry the coffin but on the day we all agreed to leave it to the professionals. Mum was very proper. She liked things done in a certain way. Not fussy necessarily, but precise. She was an Aquarius. Some things have to be the same. I have so many Aquarian women in my life: Christine Bateman who does my make-up. Laura Fireman who I stole from Philip. Eve Gallagher, my soul-singing sister from Sunderland who now lives in Switzerland. The nurse who took care of Mum was an Aquarian.

As soon as I saw her I said, 'What star sign are you? And where are you from?'

'I'm an Aquarian from Dublin,' she said.

'Perfect. I know you'll take care of her.'

PK flew over from Los Angeles and asked me if he could bring his friend and Irish footballer, Robbie Keane, to Mum's wake. My mum would have loved Robbie Keane being there.

'Did you see who was at my funeral?'

My friend Christine looked like Joan Collins and my other friend, Hamilton, had an awkward moment with an alien religion. He wasn't sure of the protocol when approaching the casket. The important thing was that most of the people I love were there. It was an absolute celebration of Mum's life.

Though I'd love a permanent cloud in the sky, I talk to her picture in the hallway every day. I can say what I like and she never answers back. Nothing rude. I just sit on the stairs and gabble away about what's going on. I say 'I love you' when I come in and when I go out. I feel Mum's presence strongly. I hear her telling me to get on with my life and have a fantastic time. I definitely had a beautiful relationship with Mum but it was respectful and honest. There was a hint of 'Spare me the details' when it came to Mum. I've always been private with everyone, actually. There's a lot of noise on the surface and some of that noise is pleasant, but in the background insecurity lurks. I'm less insecure right now than I've ever been. I have a lot of the same problems but I approach them in a different way.

The last twenty years of Mum's life, she travelled and did things with her family; she went on cruises, she went to Ibiza many times with me. After we lost Dad there was a coming together, I feel. When I got sober, I got closer to my family too. The idea of being in the world without Mum was incomprehensible. I accept it now but I pull on Mum's energy. I talk about her. I sing about her. I write about her. I think about what she taught me. I hope I made her happier.

As Mum's go, I couldn't have asked for a better one.

feel very strongly that
should write a balanced
ccount of meeting Jon but

## 16

# THE JOAN MOIST
# FUND

I gave Jon Moss the nickname Joan Moist some years ago, long before we fell out. How badly we've fallen out this time is anyone's guess. There have been numerous long silences. I call them 'The Cold Wars'. What did we ever have in common? Who is this bloke I once obsessed over, who has controlled aspects of my life for as long as I can remember? It may sound odd, but I can't say that I know Jon very well, which is actually not surprising because our relationship was very surface. He described it as platonic, ha. I think sexually ravenous is better. Our fights were colossal and the make-ups were always passionate then dark. I think lots of men are awful.

Jon was definitely one of those. He switched off. That's what I mean by 'dark'. Lights out. No more fun.

The saying 'Women fall in love with what they hear, men with what they see,' that's very Jon Moss. I joked in my first book that Jon would flirt with traffic if he could. He was very sexual and confident, at least on the surface. He liked it when I beat my eyes fierce.

I feel very strongly that I should write a balanced account of meeting Jon but most of what I say about his character will be off. I do think Jon is very entitled. Philip always said, 'Jon is bitter because he's adopted,' which is true – the part about him being adopted – but it sounds like a line from a John Waters movie. I never got to know Jon's family, even when we were at the height of our success. Jon was a bit of a rebel, a posh one, but a rebel in his world. His dad owned property all over London. He was involved in men's clothing. I met his mum a few times but his parents never supported or acknowledged our relationship. Jon acted accordingly and kept me away from his family. In modern terms we were fuck buddies. Platonic, my arse!

The songs I wrote at the time I met Jon were the real-life diary of what was going on in my head and my heart. Some of it was fantasy, maybe all of it. I wrote about the love I wanted or felt I didn't deserve. I was my very own Gladys Knight & The Pips. I grew up watching Dad talk badly to Mum so my idea of love was confused and yet I wanted to be in love more than anything. When Jon came to my place he would find an excuse to leave as soon as we had sex. I fulfilled a need in Jon that he did not want to fully accept. Big, stinking closet.

I grew up around control so it's no wonder I lost it so many times. As a kid, my father ruled over every aspect of our lives. He controlled what Mum wore, how much she painted her face. Mum was instinctively creative so it was a mean blow.

I once took my mum on a private jet to Scotland to do *The Mrs Brown Show*. She was her brilliantly raw, honest self when she said, 'Georgie once bought me a real fur coat and I said, "Where am I supposed wear that, Tesco's?" Brendan O'Carroll, the man behind the Irish grandma Mrs Brown, promised not to broadcast it but I found it funny. I remember later that night in the hotel I was feeling bloated, having eaten stuff I shouldn't have. Jet sandwiches. Typical me. I snapped at Mum but she wasn't having it.

'Don't you be cheeky.'

She went down to the car while I caught my breath. When I stepped into the seat next to her, my first words were, 'Sorry, Mum.'

'I know you are.'

Mum learnt to let things go. I'm learning to do the same...

I can't say enough times that I don't hate Jon. Perhaps it's a case of, 'Say it enough times and convince yourself.'

I know what it's like to be riddled with angst and filled with the need for revenge. Letting go is a mindset, just like holding on.

The final meltdown in the Jon vs. me fiasco came on the 2018 Culture Club 'Life' tour, which was originally planned to be 80 dates in that year but we ended up playing 109 gigs. I was waiting to go on stage, I can't remember where. But I remember feeling relaxed, chatting to PK while Christine was finishing my face and my stylist, Mykee Ortiz, steamed my jacket. I was excited. We had a full house and I wanted it to be amazing. These days I always want it to be amazing. Those old pre-show tensions were nowhere to be seen, but I still had stuff on my mind. Fashion mostly, but getting Roy, Mikey and Joan to look presentable was less of an obsession than it used to be. In the old days I was more in control of what everyone wore on stage, but it's harder to dictate when people are married and their wives are their stylists.

In the early eighties when everyone was skinny and drop-dead gorgeous, we had a connected 'Culture Club' look with all the printed Sue Clowes clothes. But success brought greater excess and, once we started making money and getting famous, our look became more fragmented. Mikey always looked cool in everything but he stopped wearing hats because Roy and Mikey would take the piss. Roy loved the *Miami Vice* look because he secretly wished he was in

Duran Duran – a silky sky-blue Armani jacket with the sleeves rolled up and big hair. I loved our early look because it made us look like part of the same tribe.

Jon was always the problem child because he thought being behind the drums meant he could go unnoticed, but I had William Baker knock up some punky casual threads with zips and clips so he looked like he gave a shit.

I remember saying to PK, 'I bet Jon won't wear the clothes we made for him. I bet he hasn't even tried them on and he'll probably walk in any minute wearing the same ill-fitting rags he wore on the last tour.'

'No chance,' said PK with great authority.

On cue, Jon walked in wearing printed track pants and an ill-fitting T-shirt with sparkles on. Ed Hardy for rich housewives heading to the gym.

I went crazy and called him a tramp and he said, 'The zippers scratched my skin. I have to be comfortable on stage.' But it was more about control.

'Do you think I'm comfortable in what I'm wearing?' I asked him.

Being overdressed, hot and uncomfortable is my life's work. Before every tour I try to get myself in shape to wear my fabulous outfits, but I invariably switch what I'm wearing last minute because my clothes are a bit too snug. It drives Mykee crazy but I always have options and my look these days has a twisted synchronicity. The hat is always the focal point and I try to create looks that are individual to me so I look exactly like myself. Or my invented self.

> *I was there when you created yourself from cardboard*
> *& glitter!*

Over the years I have often seen photos of myself and thought, 'Wow, don't I look great,' but at the time I probably thought I was too fat and ugly. You rarely look as bad as you think you do.

Being on stage is about fantasy and entertainment and I think the problem, as evidenced on our 'Life' tour, is that, now that we're all older, Jon is no longer able to just sit there and be God's gift. There was a time when he looked amazing in everything. I never had that luxury. I have always had to over-gild the lily.

There was a bit more screaming with Jon until I decided to hug it out with him. I didn't want to take that energy on stage, but I was far from happy. My attempt to make us look like we were in the same band had failed. There were some complaints from Roy about the tartan Teddy Boy drape jacket he had been given but he wore it and looked great. And Mikey? I don't always like what he wears but he at least makes an effort.

For the rest of the tour I thought that Jon looked utterly miserable and kept complaining about everything.

He hated the food, the gigs, the travel, the hotels, the fans. When we did our 'meet-and-greets' before the show he would say weird stuff about anyone and everyone. Sometimes it was funny, but mostly I just found it distasteful. I wanted to do the meet-and-greets on my own because I know I'm good with people and I know how to make them feel appreciated.

One night on stage around halfway through the tour in America, I was introducing a new song of ours called 'Life' and I thought that Jon had deliberately rattled the drums as I was talking. I turned around and said, 'Are you fucking serious?' I went very Woolwich and it felt like the crowd stepped back in fear. It was mortifying. Jon's drum rattling had thrown me off my stage game and I wondered how much more of him I could take.

I know I can't blame Jon for my reaction, but he was constantly unsettling me and I just thought, 'He doesn't want to be here.' My chatting and laughing with the crowd even seemed to annoy him. Even Roy – who is a typical Leo and always trying to be everyone's friend – started to pick up Jon's constant complaining and started to ask, 'Hey, Jon, is anything right?'

At a press conference in Chile I remember him telling the crowd of reporters, 'I'm writing the memoirs of Adolf Hitler,' and he kept telling journalists in America, 'You know my birth-day is 9/11,' which was a real conversation stopper.

I never understood why he was so childishly provocative, but he was.

Don't get me wrong, there's always been a sense of those 'three straight boys against the crazy queen'. They are the three legs on a sensible table. I remember Philip Sallon once saying to me, 'You take your moods on stage,' when I was just thinking that it made me a true artist. I'm all for playfulness and banter off stage, but this was starting to affect my focus.

We were flying the next day in a gorgeous private jet and Jon and I were exchanging one-liners. Jon can be hilarious. It was a good vibe after the bickering and bad feeling. At one point Jon shouted, 'Oi, one insult at a time.' He thought I was picking on him, and if I was, it was unintentional, just old habits.

So I asked him how he was feeling and he replied, 'I hate these long tours, I want to be with my kids.'

'How is that going to work?' I said. 'Touring is how we make a living and I want to tour more. You can only get better by touring more.'

For many reasons, we'd never toured at the height of our earning potential and we had so much ground to make up. Duran Duran, our contemporaries, were smashing it live and earning far more than us – they'd never stopped. When we were one of the biggest bands in the world in the eighties, we did more TV shows than live gigs. The cult of Boy George's personality had taken over at that time. I take no blame in that, though. Even if I was doing my job madly or badly, I wasn't running the schedule. There was no long-term plan because no one really believed we could maintain our popularity. Radio play for new music had trailed off and we were doomed to be a nostalgic juke box. I remember thinking that, if it was all going to be over soon, we might as well grab all we could. I can't say if this was conscious or unconscious or even how it actually was, but things seemed to be driven by money rather than pleasure or strategy. I'm not suggesting we don't want to get paid doing what we do now, but I definitely put more importance on joy than I ever have. The days of taking my bad moods on stage are long gone. Despite our differences, I've worked hard not to look at Mikey and Roy with negativity.

Jon would have been happy doing a few festivals and corporate gigs – Jon told me very clearly that he hated long tours and thought they were a waste of time – but we had to rebuild our live reputation. I love touring, personally. What can I say, it must be my Cancer moon. Not the travelling aspect, but I love being in new places and I always want to improve my stage presence. If you are smart on tour, you can get into a routine and enjoy the experience.

Jon didn't want to be away from his kids. That's what he said. In the studio it was, 'I have to pick up my son,' or, 'I can't come in till *blah blah* because of one of my kids.' Jon had always called the shots where the band was concerned.

He decided how long tours would be. He was the decision maker and that's how he wanted to keep things. I think it was the concept of doing things differently that troubled him the most. According to Jon Moss, PK was wrong about everything.

So I said to Jon, 'Leave the band then. Or what about your son, can he drum?'

'He's not as good as me,' he replied.

I thought, *is that possible anyone can be that bad?* (LOL.)

I'm joking, of course, but it looked to me that he didn't want to be there so I suggested he leave the tour and go home and get 'match fit'. I was taking singing lessons and working with an acting coach to improve my onstage confidence so I wasn't preaching what I wasn't practising myself. And so, Jon went home mid-tour and I thought that he seemed happy to leave. I had no idea of the fallout that would happen because of that.

We hired a new drummer, Garrison Brown, an American who brought such amazing energy to the show. I remember thinking, 'I love American musicians because they love the gig.' It felt like Jon was over it, but maybe he was never under it? On that same tour, Jon had flown back to London during a two-day break, which I thought was insane. He didn't think about how it might affect his performance either. So when he eventually did leave, I didn't miss him.

The tour went ahead without him and every night got

better because I didn't have to feel that negative energy behind me. We were still fooling ourselves that he might come back, but it was becoming more and more unlikely.

While back in the UK, Jon sent a half-hearted clip of himself drumming, to perhaps suggest he was making an effort, but it felt mocking. Jon's attitude was always, 'This is my band, I started it,' but actually it never was. PK flew to London, where they had an ostensibly amicable lunch and PK said that they agreed that he should take a break. He said he had a bad back and intended to come back for some major shows at the end of the tour, particularly Wembley Arena. In the end, Roy, Mikey and I decided we didn't want Jon back. Two legs on the table were now missing.

PK delivered the news to him over the phone. Jon wasn't happy and wanted to be paid for gigs he hadn't done, being part of the band, so the agent in America refused to pay us and held the money. PK did eventually got them to release the money as they were holding it on behalf of the group and not one individual.

Jon started going head-to-head with PK and it was getting ugly. I think Jon was surprised and hurt that I chose PK over him and, once Mikey and Roy also signed with PK, the battle commenced. If Jon had tried to speak to me or seemed upset, I'm sure I would have taken him back in a heartbeat, but he seemed so unemotional and rigid. Why, at almost sixty years old did I need to spend time with someone who didn't seem to care about something so important to me? In fact, I was realising that without Jon I was getting better on stage and enjoying it in a way I never had or thought possible.

PK set about changing all the financial infrastructure Jon had put in place, including parting ways with our American agents. He secured a massive deal with Live-Nation selling our touring rights for a huge amount of money which Jon was excluded from because he was no longer a member of the band. But Jon claimed he was owed an outstanding balance for the 2018 Life tour and, when he heard about the LiveNation deal, demanded his share of that too.

His lawyers argued that he was still in a legal partnership with Culture Club. Whereas we argued that we'd not been in business with Jon for years as we all had individual managers and had not run the band as a partnership. There were no partnership accounts. But despite this, and the fact that our lawyers thought we had a good chance of winning, we decided to accept that the band was a partnership to avoid a case in the High Court.

We tried to do legal mediation to reach a settlement with Jon in October 2021. It took place in a building in the City, which was like a family court. I remember arriving early and being put into a room with Jon. But it felt cold and the mediator looked like Noel Edmonds. I tried to lighten the mood by writing a message on the board and

|drawing a picture. It was quickly apparent that meeting Jon was a mistake.

'Come back to the band,' I said.

'Why would you want me back?' Jon replied.

I couldn't think of any reason. The truth is I just wanted to find a quick way out of the legal battle. At this point, Jon had the law on his side regarding whether we were a legal partnership. On paper there's less room for nuance, but the reality was very different as far as I was concerned.

Turns out that, even though I'd been working solo from 1986, my money was still going through a company that Jon had set up in 1982 called Sharpgrade. Jon still had control of my money. Who knows for how long? There's nothing I can do about it now but it was frustrating to sit and listen to. When I asked Jon why he made himself the boss of our finances, he said he'd done it to protect me from sharks and that he'd done me a favour. He said I should thank him.

I was livid and said that I'd never asked him to protect me.

But at Sharpgrade, Jon was the boss. I had no idea that I was just playing a dummy role in it. Sign everything and dribble out of both sides of your mouth. I feel like an idiot admitting this, but I was only interested in the creative side. I like working. I know now that I should have asked questions. I realise now that it would have made sense to have my own lawyer instead of using the same one as Jon and our manager, Tony Gordon. At the time, when I was signing away my life, not one of the grown-ups asked, 'Do you understand what this means?'

We went back to our legal teams in separate rooms and waited while Noel Edmonds went back and forth between us. Jon said no to every deal and towards the end of the session he barged into our room with his legal team. I called him every cunt I could and the room fell silent. It was a PR disaster. We were facing the prospect of a court date with Jon, which PK wanted to avoid. I thought I could turn up in a veil and have my say but even I knew it wasn't going to be helpful. Irrespective, stories soon appeared in the press that I had 'conspired to defraud' Jon.

It wasn't until March 2023 that Jon sued me by serving me court papers on my doorstep. To add insult to injury, it was just a few days after Mum died. His timing felt cruel. I know he's not in control of when the papers are served but it was a huge time for me and I felt gutted. I almost sent a text back saying, 'My mum never liked you.' But I stopped myself, knowing Mum would have gone mad.

'How dare you tell anyone I said such a thing?'

She probably wouldn't like to see it in this book, but the truth is Mum never knew Jon.

Mikey Craig was served on the same day as me. Roy, being in America, was harder to get to. Even with the hurt I felt and the internet at my fingertips, I was proud that I managed to not react to the tabloid stories. Instead, I posted a new song, 'Dirty Little Limited Company', on TikTok – it really says everything I need to say. Well, there are other songs – 'Watching the Lotus Bleed', 'Bitchy but Soulful' – but I'm sure Jon would say they are more about me.

There was also an argument over the value of the Culture Club name. PK argued it was worth £750,000, Jon said it was worth £35 million. Again, to avoid it going to court and all the costs and risk that involved, in March 2023 we settled on the Culture Club name being worth £1.75 million. In return, Jon agreed to 'relinquish' all rights to the Culture Club name.

We assumed that Jon and his lawyers would allow us to pay him over a period of time but instead he issued a statutory demand for payment in twenty-eight days, which if we'd not paid meant that Jon could have petitioned for bankruptcy. That could have meant me losing my house.

I just didn't have that kind of money to pay Jon immediately. I'd put most of my money into my home in Hampstead, and who knew there would be a pandemic? Post-pandemic we were killing it, rebuilding our live legacy and stepping up into glory but it was slow going.

PK – who had faced bankruptcy himself – found a solution for us and we're paying that all off now.

✦ ✦ ✦

It's too soon or too late to fix my communication with Joan. The last time I physically saw Jon was in an alley off Hampstead High Street. He was sitting with Sacha Baron Cohen. Yes. Borat. Not so weird. As I said, people know each other and Jon is considered the mayor of Hampstead. The few times I've been in the high street with Jon we have been well attended by strangers and shopkeepers alike. My dad was just the same, loved by strangers.

I wouldn't want to come across like I hate either my father or Jon. But there are similarities; I felt both were cold and unavailable emotionally toward me. Dad, I forgave him years ago and I also thanked him: some of my better qualities come from him. He was my dad – I had no choice in the matter – but because of him I can see that indifference was an aphrodisiac. Don't you want me baby?

I have less to thank Jon for but lots more to forgive. Smitten by love, I just let Jon run the band. He set up a company to 'protect us' but made himself sole director and sole shareholder. It was PK who fulfilled my dream of being financially free from Jon Moss, who lost his bid to bankrupt me in the High Court only recently, which is a huge relief.

I think the reality is that Jon was shocked when we fired him and then secured a huge touring deal with LiveNation. I remember going into LiveNation with PK and saying, 'I want to take Culture Club up to the penthouse.' It sounds cheesy now, but I wanted to put fire under myself and the band. I must have convinced LiveNation too. And the latest tour has been incredible.

We used a couple of new drummers on the American tours and then settled for British drummer Jermaine Whyte. Having a drummer who is confident and wants to be there really changes the vibe. No musician or singer delivers a perfect performance every night but having the right attitude, wanting to improve, knowing it's possible: it makes a massive difference. And I hope it continues for another thirty years!

n an ideal world I would look
ow people think Boy George
hould look and at least have
ew eyebrows drawn an

## 17

# FANNING THE FLAMES
# OF FANDOM

**F**ans. *Can't live with them, can't live*
without them. I love fans because I am a fan. I am mostly
friendly with everyone I meet but if I'm not friendly I'm
always real. I try not be ratty but sometimes my insecurity
takes over. Mostly it's about not being dressed for a photo
and thinking do I want a picture of me looking like this on
someone's fridge. Feeling fat, looking ugly. In an ideal world
I would look how people think Boy George should look and
at least have my eyebrows drawn on. More like Dolly Parton
and less like one of the O'Dowd boys. I realise after years of
pointless tension that no one actually cares what you look
like. If they do, so what? If I can I like to take the photo
myself because I know how to angle an iPhone.

I have struggled with my weight most of my life and being under public and media scrutiny doesn't help. We are all guilty of saying, 'Hasn't so and so got big,' even when we are carrying extra pounds ourselves. I love food and I can't control my appetite, but I think I have finally got it under control. Well, I'm on Mounjaro. Isn't everyone? Trust me anyone who was fat last year and is now skinny is on the wonder drug.

I was having dinner on New Year's Eve 2016 in Bangkok with my friend Amanda Ghost, her husband Gregor and some of Gregor's family. We were with Princess Narisa Chakrabongse and her son Hugo, who is a Prince and a Thai rock star. Amanda took us to a very hip Indian restaurant called Gaggan Anand, named after the chef who owned it. The staff were bowing to Hugo and his mum and we got an amazing table. The food was delicious and it was all going so well until Gaggan came to introduce himself. He looked at me and said, 'Oh, you look like a plump Boy George.' My friends went crazy but I hushed them and said, 'I am Boy George and the food is amazing'. It was probably more embarrassing for him than me, and Amanda said I was magnanimous.

I met Amanda in the nineties when she was doing Philip's door at the Mud Club with her friend Lisa Hanlon. The Mud was dying on its feet because Philip wouldn't pay to hire cool DJs. Jeremy Healy had cancelled at the last minute and all

DJs were 'a bunch of cunts', apparently. But Philip's themed club nights were legendary. You couldn't fault him on the atmosphere, even if he broke everyone's back to get it done. He screamed at people like he was Faye Dunaway in *Mommie Dearest* when they were working for virtually nothing. Or in Philip's words, 'The privilege of being screamed at.' Philip accused Amanda of siding with his partner, Debbie Lee, but all she really did was give a dying club an extra shove. When people came to the door and the club was empty she'd say, 'Oh, it's rubbish in there. Go somewhere else.' If you have any disco dignity, you don't charge someone to come into an empty club just because Philip Sallon might scream at you. He was paying Amanda peanuts, and peanuts weren't going to keep her in Vivienne Westwood.

Amanda was the first 'official' friend that I was accused of stealing from Philip. Before I met Amanda, Philip told me we were going to get on, and we did. Every weekend after a successful night, Amanda's friend, Lisa would pack the boot of her car with bin bags full of cash. What Philip did with it was his business. A year later Lisa found a bundle of cash under a spare wheel. When she told Philip, he screamed, 'I knew you'd stolen it. I knew it was missing.' Of course, it must have fallen out, and I asked Lisa why the hell she gave it back, especially as he didn't say thanks. People who love Philip collect these stories. One day someone should make a film about him where people are telling stories but he never appears. Hilary Arse! With all this taken into account, it was amazing Amanda had the grace to invite him to her wedding in 2008. Philip had spent years telling anyone who would listen how she ruined his club. People from the Saatchi Synagogue in St John's Wood would tell me what he'd said. Luckily, Jewish people like to gossip, especially after they've been to shul. Philip has never had social grace or awareness when it comes to gossip. If he hates you, everybody has to.

Before Amanda was married, we were as thick as thieves. So many crazy, brazen, drunken nights. I used to joke that one day she would have her own skyscraper. After trying her hand at being a pop star, she has a songwriter credit on James Blunt's 'You're Beautiful' and co-wrote for Beyonce, then went on to be the President of Epic Records. I loved her album *Ghost Stories* and especially the single 'Filthy Mind' with its trippy video. How she became President of Epic I don't know but Cancerian's can walk through steel walls. I was sadly barred from travelling to America during her Epic reign, so I never got to visit that skyscraper. Now Amanda runs her own film company with her husband, Gregor – they made the hugely successful movie *Tetris* and work for Len Blavatnik who owns the Warner Music Group. A long way from the days when Amanda walked into my kitchen head to toe in Westwood wearing dark glasses. She never ate vegetables and only drank Cherry Cola. These days she's a supermum, juggling world domination and making sourdough.

✝ ✝ ✝

It's never a good idea to comment on anyone's appearance, even if you know them. I would never judge anyone on their size but to be human is to be a hypocrite. I know I don't enjoy being overweight and it's something I really want to deal with. By the time this book is out I will be Kate Moss. I keep telling myself: 'self control is sexy'.

Geminis love a fad. I have done every diet and bought every useless piece of plastic on the market to try and get in shape. The less I eat the better I feel. Fasting is something I have embraced, and I try to eat my first meal around 2pm. I have recently given up dairy and wheat but for about the millionth time. I'm not a fire starter, I'm a twisted sourdough starter.

I love bread and yes, I will eat it again. I walk most mornings and stretch daily. I talk to myself and I try to be positive. I feel like I'm watching my life through my own eyes. I have a new awareness of my behaviour as I enter every situation, meeting strangers, walking on to the stage. I am constantly talking myself through it like I am my own life coach. Fans have commented that I look happier and seem at ease. I have found a new way to talk to myself. A new way to change my own mind. If I fuck up sometimes it doesn't make me a bad person. If I fuck up all the time, maybe it does.

You should talk good about yourself and think you're

sexy. But you also have to do some work on yourself. If you love someone, you have to water them like a flower even though sometimes you'd rather stamp on them. Most of the things I got vexed about in old relationships were pointless, unhelpful, and never going to make a thing right. I'm more careful what I care about now. It really is the fleeting moments that make everything beautiful. I prefer simplicity to special effects, except when it comes to my eyebrows and my hats.

Though I will admit that getting my teeth done has changed my life. See, I'm a walking contradiction. And even though some people say they preferred my old teeth, my response is, 'Give me your address and I'll send them to you.' It's time to confess I had three hair transplants around 2015–2018 – two in Ireland and a final one in LA – and the weird thing is no one remembers I was bald as a shaved badger. I had a tummy tuck not long after, which was the most painful thing I've ever done because I went on tour straight after with Cyndi Lauper with the blood bag attached. I'd previously lost seven stone doing the metabolic balance diet and I needed to get rid of the excess skin. When anyone asks about my scar I say I had twins by Caesarean. I've never had botox, though, and I might be the only person in showbusiness with my own face. I'm not frightened of getting old and I think I've grown into myself. It might seem weird to say I feel sexier but I actually do. I used to joke over the years, 'Sexy at sixty.' That was my ambition.

I think nudity is the enemy of fashion and, while I don't hate my body, I prefer to be naked in private. Being in *I'm A Celebrity...* was a continuation of me getting over myself, and of course I enjoyed the money. I certainly didn't do it for the cuisine.

However, don't just plonk yourself into an outfit because I'm the kind of queen to tell you to your face I expected more from the look. The drag world has come on leaps and bounds since me and Marilyn were running around Soho in ripped tights. Some of the drag queens on *Ru Paul's Drag Race* wear and do incredible stuff. The make-up is exquisite, the costumes verging on couture. Ru Paul has harnessed drag for herself, hundreds of drag queens paying commission to Ru Paul's empire at DragconUK and other locations to be named. I think people like Sam Smith are being provocative, but that's OK too. Just understand that you are going to get a reaction and not necessarily one you like. Ricky Gervais says, 'How arrogant are you to think you could live your life with no one ever saying anything horrible about you.'

I tap myself and say, 'Be nice, it's good for your health' and it turns out there is scientific evidence that being nice *is* good for your health. Geminis hate surprises so don't jump out on me at the airport and please don't follow me. I know it's hard for fans because they want to show respect, but they feel like they have to seize the moment. I was watching Anthony and the Johnsons at Joe's Pub in New York and sitting across from me was Lou Reed and Laurie Anderson. We didn't speak but as he left Lou gave me a little wink. A fan with a camera asked Lou if he could take a picture. The kid wasn't prepared and was fumbling and Lou snapped, 'Anytime this week.' I would be happy if Lou spat in my eye.

I once got spat on by Ari Up from The Slits who are my favourite girl group of all time. I was standing in a doorway next to them outside the Roxy club and I said hello to Ari and she spat on me. It only made me love her more. Years later, I tried to sign Ari to my dance label More Protein. She came to see me with two of her sons and they were all wearing matching purple track suits. She had long dreads pulled up into a pineapple, exploding from her head. A cheeky white punk Rasta. Ari had made a reggae track called 'Rent A Dread' which I wanted to license. I always thought Ari was beautiful and stylish and in my early Culture Club days I was putting myself together in a similar style and fashion, and moved from channelling Siouxsie Sioux to Ari Up.

Visually I have been influenced by many people, but I put myself together in my own way. As a teenager I was very experimental and would completely change my entire look every day. When I discovered make up and what it could do to my face, I went for it, shaving off my eyebrows like Ziggy Stardust and drawing them high and wide and every which way possible. I have pretty eyes. Can I say that? It's my best feature but my face is quite plain and wide, like a peeled Irish potato. I can rub soot into my face and throw on a handful of glitter and I look quite good. Some people have a great face for radio, and I have a great face for make-up. You would think I would have my own make-up line by now.

When it comes to meeting people, I prefer a direct approach. None of that, 'Are you who I think you are?' You know who I am so let's cut out the small talk. Sometimes it's awkward when people approach you and they are nervous, but you can always turn it around. Just remember everyone is human. You are only famous because other people know who you are. Fame is a kind of myth. A liar and a fire you need to keep stoking.

In 1982 there were no smartphones and the selfie was an alien concept, but there were always paparazzi and they loved getting a picture of Joan Collins fetching her milk from the doorstep. We lived in constant paranoia of being snapped out of drag. Everyone wanted to see just how awful I looked without make-up. Why did I care so much? It has taken forever to develop a sense of humour about it.

My sense of humour has always been my best weapon. Laugh at yourself or be like Dolly Parton and make the joke before they get the chance. 'It takes a lot of money to look this cheap.' Genius. I love Dolly Parton.

I'm not a fan of fans outside my house, airports or hotels but I know what I was like with Bowie. After seeing him arrive back from Berlin at Victoria Station in 1976 I ran to the tube to get to Capitol Radio to catch another glimpse. I screamed and tried to touch him, and he stuck to the script, dashing from the car into a side door. Every inch the unreachable star. I wasn't offended because part of the thrill was wanting to see Bowie as an extra-terrestrial entity. He didn't talk to people. He was too busy being extra. I loved Bowie and I always will, but I'm just more fish and chips.

The chase was part of the excitement but it's not 1976 anymore. Maybe for Harry Styles or Taylor Swift fans. The music industry has been smashed open and everyone has seen the wizard behind the curtain. So much of the mystery that was created around stars in the past seems trite right now. You can't be nebulous when you are doing the floss in your kitchen on TikTok. I don't have to pretend to be down to earth because I already am. If I have ever been rude to you, I'm sorry.

When I went to see Adele in Vegas, she sent me a beautifully signed tour programme saying, 'I can't believe you are here,' but she did not meet me. I thought it very odd. If I'm edgy before a show I say hello to people after. Tom Ford was there too with his kid, and she came up to where he was sitting and hugged him. I was seated behind with my niece Molly who asked, 'Do you think she did that deliberately?' I don't – after all, she might have known him – but it's what I would expect from Madonna. How other artists treat you at their concerts is super important. Your people may only represent you but it's always on your head.

Morrissey treated me and my friend Mike Nicholls like royalty and we were looked after by Sam Smith. Let's put aside the fact we lived next door to each other for a few years but never really spoke. Sam had parties in his garden that I was never invited to, but we are at different ends of the life and fame experience. I could smell the weed wafting over the garden fence. I love the smell of weed especially with a bit of Clint Eastwood & General Saint. I have watched Sam have his existential crisis with fame and I recognise it. I have been that woman.

One day Anohni, formerly Antony Hegerty came to visit me in Hampstead and freaked out when I said Sam lived next door. He dragged me round and we rang on his bell, but no one was home. It's sweet but naive to assume that being gay and being in the same business is a reason to be friends. I can count my famous friends on two fingers. I can only imagine what it would be like living next to Marilyn or Pete Burns.

'Did you want sugar or cyanide?'

I have been guilty of being standoffish with other artists, but I have a pretty good radar on what to expect long before I meet someone. Most artists are uptight and worried about how they look but it's the people around them that are often the worst. The stuff around fame is like the stuff around God. Lots of people get God and fame confused. It's easy to think you're a genius when you're just lucky.

Most people's reputations dance ahead of them. At this point I know fame inside out and I know all bullshit around it. Writing a song is not clever or difficult especially if you are just saying the same things as everyone else. Getting a song played on the radio is difficult but the only difference between a hit and a non-hit is repetition. I am at Number 1 this week in the official Legacy chart on 365 Radio. 'Melodrama' is a collaboration between me and Vangelis Polydorou who I met on The Voice. It's camp, it's cool, it's catchy but so was 'Agadoo', 'Remember You're a Womble' and 'Saturday Night' by Whigfield. You might not consider something cool, but it doesn't stop it being catchy. Why you prefer 'Purple Rain' to 'Agadoo' has nothing to do with the process but everything to do with the pose.

'Melodrama' (out now) is my second Number 1 on the Legacy chart. The last one was 'Underwater' which the listeners also voted to Number 1. In the end it's about getting your bag of rice on the shelf. People can't like something if they never hear it. The Legacy chart is a small but important thing because it proves the powers that be completely wrong.

People think being cancelled is a new thing, but BBC Radio have been doing it for fucking years. They decide when an artist has reached their sell by date, and they claim it's the listeners who decide. Forgive me but I'm not happy that my old songs get played on nostalgia radio. I am a vibrant, productive artist who writes songs every day. I don't have to wait twenty years like The Rolling Stones to do what comes easily and naturally. So please understand that when you tell me someone or something is genius and I pull a face it's because I'm not baffled by how it's done. How come BBC Radio did not play 'Padam Padam' by Kylie if it's the public that decides? Commerce and creativity are not the same thing, but creativity still lives happily without commerce. I realise that not every artist can make it to the playlist but don't pretend there is some intellectual process involved. You are a bunch of c***s.

Dolly Parton is adorable, but I have never heard otherwise. She sang on a Culture Club track 'Your Kisses Are Charity' and she was super gracious and undemanding. All she wanted was a limo to the studio and a thousand pounds. I would have paid more. We performed the song on the National Lottery Show in 1998 and I took her to Retsina, a Greek restaurant in Belsize Park. She ate nothing but said the food was amazing. What a beautiful person she is. When I first met her at the studio I arrived in my civvies, and she said, 'You go out like that?' I laughed and she quickly caught herself. 'I'd be terrified the paparazzi would jump out and snap me.' I often say I should be more like Dolly Parton when it comes to my appearance. My day look is a disaster. She said she loved my song writing and we talked about writing together. I would still love to do that.

If I like your music, I really don't care what you are like. Courtney Love was like Kaa, the snake from *Jungle Book,* but I love her Hole album, *Live Through This* and that's the end of it. I bumped into her at the Grammys afterparty just after saying hello to Billy Corgan from The Smashing Pumpkins, another one my favourite bands. I love nineties rock and nineties R&B.

I told Courtney I loved her album, yawn, I know people care less when you compliment their music. I'm the same. I don't really care and why would I? It's not like any other musician is doing anything different. It's just words and noise. We talked for a while and then she looked at me with those big eyes and said, 'I was in another conversation so would you mind.' I walked off and said 'trrruuust me', to Amanda Ghost who was with me.

Minutes later I was chatting to Marilyn Manson who was with his parents. His ass was on show and his mum said, 'Hasn't he got a great ass.' I didn't answer but I had seen Marilyn's performance earlier and it was electrifying. Twiggy was still on bass and Marilyn Manson threw a bottle of water that hit Tony Bennett. Manson later said, 'It was a moment for me.' A provocative statement for sure because how could anyone not love Tony Bennett? Manson said he was thinking of covering 'Church of The Poisoned Mind' and I said I would pay him to do it.

Morrissey was cold when I had tea with him in France in the mid-eighties. He called me 'overbearing' which I was at the time. I had no off button in those days and even less self-awareness. I had to go to prison before Morrissey was cool with me. I think I just talked relentlessly when I met him and even though we are both Geminis he has that Scorpio moon and I guess I was too soon is now. I love Morrissey as an artist, and I don't need him to dance with me through the meadow.

I wrote an article for the *Sunday Express* for whom I did a weekly column for a couple of years. It was about how you can overlook a dislike of someone if you enjoy their work. I listed journalist and author Tony Parsons and Morrissey. I loved Parson's book, *Man and Boy* despite a scathing article he wrote about me and George Michael. In it he called me disgusting and camp and not fit to walk alongside George Michael who was a dignified homosexual. They were friends for fourteen years but then Parsons wrote that a journalist and a pop star could never be friends. Why not? When Parsons attacked me for being a hideous caricature of a homosexual they were still speaking. Which by the way I have never been but what the fuck if I am? Being camp is not a crime. Just another way of crawling across this rock we live on. I said I liked his book even though he was unkind to me.

I also wrote about Morrissey and said how much I loved the album *Maladjusted* which was critically panned. It was like a great Bowie album and full of gorgeous pop songs like 'Alma Matters' and 'Trouble Loves Me'. Me and Mike Nicholls played it relentlessly and would often stalk the house in a low-cut blouse. I wrote about our meeting in the eighties and said I still loved Morrissey despite everything. I must write that song. Morrissey left a message on my answerphone saying 'we should talk' but the message was garbled, and I couldn't make out the number he left in LA. I met him again backstage at Alexandra Palace when he played and he said '*Maladjusted*? Really?' I said, 'Yes. Really!'

The ability to write a great song doesn't make you a good or better person. We live in hope that our heroes are special but somehow ordinary. It can take years to learn how to be yourself in public and those first impressions can ruin a legacy. Just like the wrong earrings can topple a fashion empire.

Fashion for me is about changing the story of who I am, visually, not spiritually. I'm not dressing up to make a point about my sexuality. I wish it wasn't considered to be either male or female or anything in between. My friend's son is five and he's cross-dressing and we were talking about how it's a shame that it's not discussed in terms of shapes and colours and sounds and the feel and the whoosh of the fabric. When you start to weigh up the consequences of what you say and you realise words are an energy, you realise that not having an opinion doesn't make you cowardly, it can make you smart. Exhibitionism comes with a responsibility. I used to run down the road dressed as a nun thinking, 'Why is everyone staring at me?' Even if the freaks are only there to remind you you are normal, that's a good thing, surely you should be happy. But read the room you might peak too soon, the mad cow in high heels jumped over the moon, listen to me I am a psychedelic loon

As a teenager I bought into the hype but now I have been through the hype and can see it for what it is. I want a degree of mystery, but I also need to be as ordinary as I can. Anyone can dress and pose like a rock star these days, but David Bowie and Marc Bolan set impossible standards for us glitter dandies. When you see Ziggy Stardust at eleven it's hard to be impressed by anything else. I know all rock and roll is a pose and all fashion is a joke. That doesn't mean I don't love it or want to throw myself into the pose but please don't tell me anything is new. Every song is written, and every outfit has been designed. Only idiots say, 'I did it first'. I didn't start anything but me. I am responsible for creating the Boy George Circus and nothing else.

I have never considered myself beautiful, but I know how to make myself look pretty. Luckily, I am photogenic, but I work with an awful lot of illusion. My catwalk is the gutter not the gallery of perfection. I work with stylists, but I'm not worked on by stylists. I have worn designer clothes by Gaultier who is one of my fashion heroes, but I know I have also inspired his work. I see it all as a relentless sharing of ideas. Ideas that already exist. Ideas that you reshape with your imagination. Fashion is more pretentious than rock and roll, and Anna Wintour is a brilliant hoax.

Philip and I have always considered Vivienne Westwood to be a fashion goddess. Hilarious, irreverent and barking up the right tree. Very few people have changed the face of fashion the way she did. I was and always will be a fan. I wore a replica pair of bondage trousers that Mum had knocked up and she inspected them and said, 'Tell your mum she did a brilliant job'. Of course, Vivienne just made clothes, but she had a unique way of seeing the world and it shone through her creations. Alexander McQueen and Galliano are both Vivienne's children and they also make me scream. I love fashion but I do not take it as seriously as many people do. I would rather make and create my own looks and I take inspiration from everything and everyone. Expensive designer clothes, handbags and shoes are just bank notes on bodies. How insecure must you be to spend £40,000 on a handbag?

I don't think you need to be queer or female to wear make-up or a dress. Male peacocks have existed throughout history. Men during the eighteenth century make Harry and me look butch. In the end it's the intention that matters and what point you are trying to make. Read the room and look in the mirror. Fashion has a symmetry that should be respected. Clothes are designed to make us look stylish not desperate but desperate done well is okay.

I have never understood why people get so uptight about fabric and make-up. I think RuPaul hit the nail on head when she said, 'We are all born naked and everything is drag'. Maybe we need animosity to feel alive? It feels like there always must be someone to hate. Atheists spend too much time thinking about God and homophobes think too much about queers.

There was a time you had to go to the wrong part of the city to see the freaks. Now we are all up in your face. The internet has terrified and overstimulated the masses. The conservative media sometimes creates drama just for sales. I think of the *Daily Mail* as my schizophrenic lover. One day, I'm an icon, the next I stink or I'm broke.

I hate being called woke because I hardly ever sleep. Like Maggie Thatcher I get about six hours and fix myself with hairspray. I am fascinated by Donald Trump. Sometimes he reminds me of myself but only if I grew up getting everything I wanted.

Seriously, when he kicks off it reminds me of my early days in Culture Club. I watched a documentary about him years ago and he seemed more open at one point. He had a sign in his golf club that read: 'If you are going to think today, you might as well think big'. On *The Apprentice* he asked contestant Clay Lee, 'Are you a homosexual?' Clay replied, 'Yes,'and said about the women on the show: 'They are beautiful, but they are just not for me.' Trump replied, 'That's why they have menus in restaurants. Some people like steak and others prefer spaghetti.' Where is that Trump now?

I don't need you to understand or tolerate me. Just get on with your own life. Why are straight people getting involved in gay rights or trans rights. What has it got to do with you? As Nina Simone sang, 'You don't have to live next to me, just give me my equality'.

My ism is social but don't call me a leftie or even suggest I have an agenda. I'm slender Brenda with no agenda. How I treat people is all I can control. I worry about where the world is going but I trust that there amazing people everywhere. Women are the creators, and they are beautiful and fierce and must be valued and protected. Not every man is a neanderthal thug, you know. Not every man is out to fight or control women or start wars. There are good men. Good straight men, good gay men, good trans men. I am pro-choice because I believe that women must have absolute control over those decisions. No one gets a termination on a whim. It's huge. It leaves impossible scars that can never be erased but it's sometimes the only option. Why don't people care about little babies and children starving around the world or being bombed in war zones? Why is the concern so selective?

It's taken me most of my career to realise that words are everything. I have often started with the song title before writing a song. If you write a song called 'Karma Chameleon' it will never be written by anyone else. 'Because I Love You' is a more accessible sentiment but I dig deeper into the word bag because of Bowie, Bolan, Dylan and Morrissey. I could never leave out Leonard Cohen or Joni Mitchell who once said to me over lunch, 'It's OK for you, no one ever called you a genius'. At the time I was deeply offended but she had just told me that 'Dylan was a plagiarist' and the 'The Beatles were okay but at least had a good sense of melody'.

I no longer consider anyone a genius. Okay, Einstein and anyone who creates something impossible that changes the world; scientists, doctors and surgeons with steady hands. Musicians can seem genius if you never leave the house, but we are just observers and narrators of our own experiences. Every word we use already exists unless you make up new ones like Shakespeare and melody is just pitch and rhythm. Everyone has the ability to tap into their own genius but it is always subjective. I'm always being told someone is a genius, but radio and records sales do not make you genius. For me, how an artist sees the world is what makes them stand out but genius is mostly overstated.

Being young, angry or fame hungry can bring out the best in some people but ambition can turn some of us into fools. As Bowie once said, 'Fame puts you there where things are hollow'. As a songwriter, you need to listen to everything from Bessie Smith to K-Pop and read, read, read. Reading books has sharpened my lyrics but eavesdropping is just as essential. Some of my favourite opening lines have come from other people's mouths. I ask myself constantly, 'Is this a conversation or a song?'

I can turn most things I hear into a hook and people say 'Wow, how do you do that?' Hello, it's what everyone does. I am surprised that people can keep writing new songs because even when it seems everything has been written you can just start again.

At sixty-two, I am more cynical yet still as optimistic as ever. I see that music is a grid and that every guitar twang is the cousin of another guitar twang. When I'm channelling Smokey Robinson or Bowie I know I'm doing it but I also consider who they were channelling. How you put it together is what makes it genius or unique. In 'the words of Jim Jarmusch, 'Nothing is original. Steal from anywhere that resonates with inspiration or fuels your imagination.'

Trying to be original is what gets in your way. I have sat in so many writing sessions with artists as they try to find inspiration and it's painful. To be inspired you have to be inspiring. When I'm stuck I just play my favourite songs backwards or google a word or a sentence. Who said 'You're so much stronger than your excuses'. Look it up. If I had writers block, I would probably write a song about it.

# 18

# SATELLITE OF LOVE

I'm just home to London after nine weeks on tour, give or take a day. It's weird being back in London, but I got really into the tour in the end and could have kept going. We lost Roxy Yarnold and Carl Hudson from the band for the last date that was snuck in by PK, a last-minute non-paying gig for stinking rich people in Aspen. The event is called 'The Weekend' and it's attended by CEOs, leaders, politicians, music business types and movie directors.

I met director Ron Howard who I know from *Happy Days* and has become a hugely credible director. What a nice man with a humble energy. I actually found everyone to be really lovely, but Elon Musk walked out right in the middle of our opening song. We opened with 'Sympathy for the Devil', which is not significant but if a mix of Boy George and The Rolling Stones won't float your satellite, what would?

It's very easy, as a gay man, to jump to conclusions and assume Elon hates queers, perhaps incorrectly, but if I was at his Ted talk and walked out during the opening monologue it would be noticeable. I think it would be considered rude. So, I consider it rude. Being one of the most famous people on the planet comes with a responsibility. Let me remove your tick!

You are expected to bomb at these events, but I go to corporate shindigs prepared. Confidence is key and a lot of self-talk. I tap my body anywhere, a soft continuing karate chop followed by the mantra 'I am confident, I am charismatic, I am calm'. I believe I can always do better when trying to make a connection with the audience. Corporate or otherwise I tend to use the same methods. If it's a male heavy crowd, I seek out the ladies. Thankfully the ladies came to the front and danced. Some of my favorite CNN anchors: Dana Bash, Clarissa Ward, Kaitlin Collins. There were lovely guys too, but I hardly know who anyone is. I sang 'Do You Really Want to Hurt Me' directly at Bryan Cranston who looks like a friend and acts like one. I met a couple of people who had more security than Beyonce, but I didn't know who they were.

After the show, I was told by my agent that everyone normally struggles at this event, but we killed it.

'I have watched Elvis Costello and Dave Grohl bomb on that stage. Trust me you did great'.

My mind goes straight away to the responsibility of the audience. All that wisdom in the room and you can't embrace a legend for 30 mins? Wrap your arms and hearts around Elvis Costello and those who have fallen before him. If you are smart you know how important music is.

You've got to play your hits at these events, well, that's what they say but, again, you would think a smart crowd could think a little wider. Maybe they can but someone always puts themselves between the artist and the audience. I like to think on my feet and not be told to do what I know how to do better than anyone in the room. Be Boy George. What if Rick Ruben is right when he says the audience doesn't know what it wants or needs sometimes. It's usually the agent or the party planner that tries to dictate the setlist. If this approach works every time, then why would any artist struggle? I'm not putting it all on the audience but it's hard to be a bird that flies when someone has chopped off your wings.

Anyway, I'm not going to start walking backwards up a hill in loose Manolo Blahniks. We kick off with 'Sympathy for The Devil' which is one of many Stones' songs I have sung live. I also do 'You Can't Always Get What You Want' and have done 'Little Red Rooster'. I love the Stones and I want to be Mick Jagger when I grow up. Come on. Jagger is the go-to front man for any wannabe rock star and many of those who have made it. Jagger is in there for me, with the stance of Bowie, the arms of Siouxsie, Ian Curtis and Jim Kerr from Simple Minds.

Everyone is stealing a move from someone and adding something of themselves but only the best choreographers get to invent new moves. I hate choreography but only for myself. The way some people dance, blows my mind, but I rarely feel moved by much of the dancing pop stars I see. They always look a bit self-conscious. Michael Jackson pulled it off, James Brown, Prince and of course Beyonce and Tina Turner. God bless her. I have no idea why she could not warm to me. Hip Hop people seem to do the same moves, so it was a gasp of gorgeousness when Missy Elliot turned up. There are others but I'm not into aggressive messiah complex dancing or performance. You worship who you worship, I will love what I love. But why am I talking about dancing? I have moves but they are feral, and I'm happy to steal a bit of Mick or Joaquin Cortes. Most of my choreography is facial anyway.

When you walk on stage the entire world changes, and you can carefully lose control of the moment if you get into your own head. Look nervous and you make the crowd nervous. Dither and they get restless. There will always be someone who says, 'You didn't sing this or that,' and I am moving closer and closer to the idea of never singing this or that again. Fucking smile, even if the sound sucks and try and deal with those sound issues calmly. I used to throw mic packs in frustration. You want everything to be perfect and on stage is the worst place to lose it. A big smile even through gritted teeth can help.

Thank God for Keith the Teeth, my new gnashers that light up the universe. They even made it into a song: 'Fixed my teeth and now I smile'. Two songs: 'I'm smiling more these days, even in pictures.' I have had comments like, 'fake ass teeth' and funnily enough that got into a lyric: 'With my fake ass teeth and my filtered eek, I'll be the last man standing that looks like me'. The term 'eek' is gay slang for face.

We did a paying corporate gig in Phoenix for Cox Communication a few days before Aspen, and I was told, 'No Cox jokes' so I did them all in the room before hitting the stage. We had Roxy on backing vocals but she's more than just backing. I call her my secret weapon and Carl Hudson on keyboards is a bundle of jazzy light. This is no diss to anyone else as we have brilliant musicians with us on the road. Jermaine Whyte, who replaced Joan Moist on the drums, is incredible – his solid playing keeps us from swaying. Kevan Frost is our Musical Director and plays additional guitar, percussion and sings while controlling the computer. Everyone uses technology and tracking these days. Some people only use technology. Our mix of the two feels modern without losing the soul.

We have Vangelis on backing vocals and I would have more if I could. Vangelis is the other gay boy, and his outfits are a constant red flag for Roy to calm down. I met him on my first and only season of *The Voice* in the UK. His voice is beautiful and strong, and he can hit some ridiculous notes and I say, 'You need to be able to do that in those shoes'.

There is an uptightness in the world right now and as a gay performer, is that what I am? You need to read the room and have fun with the issue without saying the wrong thing. I'm lucky that my sexuality is not a big deal to me. PK says you need to own the LGBTQI+ movement but I already jump-started the bus years ago. I was queer when it was just as bad as having a big nose and bad shoes.

We all went to see Sam Smith, talk about reading the room. I wasn't shocked and I loved some of the outfits more than others. He's brave getting his tits out. His voice is beautiful, and he did my favorite song 'Latch' with Discloser. It was great to go out with a bunch of people from the band, me, Roxy, Jermaine and Sadie, who doesn't play anything but works for us on the road and runs my art business alongside Dean Stockings.

Back to Elon. Nothing I say about Elon will change his life or his mind, he has far too much Cancer in his chart. Like Amanda Ghost, he would tell me I was shit to my face and after I cry say it again. Do we want a world where no one has an opinion, and everyone is terrified of getting cancelled? This conversation I am having with myself has inspired a new song 'I was a punk'. You can turn adversity into art. It's what I have always done but I think I do it better now. Wait, I can hear a chopper over my house. Let's all just say nothing and we can fester in our own brain fog or run the risk of appearing obsessive and bitter. No, you lot are obsessed, and I was bitterly disappointed by my Elon moment. It's over. Move on.

I will watch *Breaking Bad* now I'm emotionally invested. I will watch Ron Howard movies with more intent. I can hate a band but dig its music, but when humanity is involved I'm all in. Same for everything. I met Tom Hardy without my hat, and he found me see-through but he's a dish. If he kissed me, I'd buy the calendar. Is there one?

'Be honest', everyone tells you until you are and then no one has your back. What about the truth? I find it elastic. These situations give me tons to write about. I write without having the answers because my songs are questions asked out loud. It's hard to be in the world with so many lies and not say anything. I have my own lies and things I'd rather not talk about. Do I want to go into detail about why I went to prison. Probably not because who will it help? I wonder sometimes when is it that we get to say something helpful? Am I finally allowed to say what I feel without the filter of Piers Morgan? Is it safe to say what I know in my heart is true? It's a strange world that allows Jimmy Savile and others to roam free while others are persecuted for not being biologically female. You may shudder at the comparison.

I'm not being general because many things are unforgivable but when they are, and we know they are let's give our energy to real suffering. If you are truly bad, you will get found out. If you are seriously bad, you need help. When recovery from drugs isn't helpful then you are probably out of excuses. It's funny what you remember in these heightened states of self-doubt. At the Brits in 2011, which I had struggled to get a ticket for, Ceelo Green got an award and said something sweet like, 'Oh, I just met Boy George'. The weak, hardly reaction was a sign of the moment I was in. It was too soon to cheer a criminal and the music industry will turn its back on you quicker than a Grinder hook-up. I only get invited to The Brits to give out awards these days. So let me say it right away: Fuck the music business because music is my business. Now I operate outside of the business I helped to create. When Culture Club had its first hit, I saw the Virgin offices move from people's living rooms in Denmark to proper office blocks. Country by European country, we watched the buildings rise alongside Richard Branson's empire. There were people from the clubs who diverted like Diana Ross seeing Marilyn when they saw me in daylight. I was like that song lyric, 'You can bring Rose with the turned-up nose but don't bring Lulu'. Yet, here I was helping to build an empire with its own boats and planes. I didn't think about it at the time, but I do now because I'm writing a book. Back then Jon Moss was my only obsession and what a waste of obsession. It wasn't just Culture Club that helped Richard, but we opened a queer can of worms. We were and are much more than a band, just like Bowie was more than a pop star or an alien.

I got famous so quickly that going out was a nightmare. I had no idea how to enjoy being famous. I should have been like Marilyn on the bus with a can of Elnett but fame made me more uptight. I could give lessons on how to be famous these days but the fame I experienced just doesn't exist now. Back then the press hounded you and photographers hid in trees. When I went out, I got driven mad by everyone and I didn't know how to handle it.

I can switch it off now and I know I could have back then, if I had the thinking skills I have now. At F1 in Singapore recently I was pursued relentlessly for selfies. I must have done 600 at least and my team were like, 'Sit there and we can stop people'. Whoopie Goldberg say's when she leaves the house, she remembers she is Whoopie Goldberg which isn't supposed to be arrogant. Twenty-fourhour recognition is the price you pay for fame. Do it with a smile, disarm people and tell yourself to remember what you get from all of this.

I had an incident with a punter backstage at our Hollywood Bowl concert. I had come off stage and had a strong Margarita. The guy wanted to tell me a long story and I guess I drifted off. PK may have been exaggerating by saying the guy said, 'Never meet your idols'. Lord, it's too easy to upset people these days like the guy who asked me to play some Faithless in my DJ set in Singapore. 'I don't have it', I said and it was true, but he walked away fuming. I should be firm like Fat Tony when I DJ. No requests.

I mentioned that I was drinking. It's true. I drink a little now, removing myself from the notion that I am forever an addict. I am surrounded by people in recovery, so I have safety rails in place. I must be who I am right now. Right now, is all there is.

I am not interested in my laurels or the past, except to scream about a song I loved that only three other people know about. I'm not interested in staying in the space that your minds think I occupy. I am not 'you were' but I am 'you are'. They sign you to a record deal because you are brilliantly original and then stamp on your creativity with their commercial instincts. It's an old familiar lament called 'Working Class Hero' penned by John Lennon:

'As soon as you're born they make you feel small'.

I don't want to sound bitter because I'm not. Cynical, sure, I am as cynical as fuck but always prepared to change my mind. What is a TERF and why do I get shouted down every time I say something positive about the 'Trans' community? I saw my friend India Willoughby on *Question Time* battling some real hostility. If you're so uptight that you need to destroy the confidence of another person, then who are you helping? No one made JK Rowling's the gender headmaster but let her say what she likes. She is a brilliant writer and I love Harry Potter, which is full of creations that pull on the imagination. Medical science is way beyond us and yes, anyone can identify as anything they want.

It's just not as simple as putting on a dress and pretending. It's deeper than even JK's imagination. I know Trans people and, while I'm not privy to every complication, I know most just want to get from A to B without getting attacked. There is no one type of Trans person or any other person, or surely every biological woman would be on the streets. Some women have a real issue, but they confuse blokes in drag at stag parties with the Trans community. Is 'safe spaces for everyone' as controversial as 'all lives matter'? Everyone matters and we must share this space whether we like it or not. Let's find solutions to remove the fear on all sides.

It's weird when men like Ben Shapiro or Matt Walsh talk about safe spaces for women but don't make space on their podcasts or social media for any of the people they are discussing. If you're talking about women or Trans people, they must be part of the discourse. Intelligent debate is a safe space for all of us. I don't know much about anything, but I know what it's like to feel outside. Feeling outside has also brought me many advantages. Not everyone can join a band or hop into the theatre. Some people are forced to live in the real world where people do and say rotten things.

I probably sound like Jack Nicholson if I say 'Why can't we all just get along?' but, seriously, why? I feel like we are all over stimulated. It's the internet, it's Elon Musk's satellites. It's everything in front of us all the time. Naomi Campbell can insist, 'I never touched my dress' and double down even when there's video; Donald Trump says anything and even if you hear it you're told he meant something else.

Life is like an annoying song right now that is played over and over. But hearing things over and over can make you believe them. Just like the stuff we tell ourselves about ourselves. These visions of Tran's activists rubbing their hands with glee as young kids are given puberty blockers. Is it real or is it the ogre over the hill, the sound of the gossip tree being shaken. Please show me some actual evidence.

I think if I wanted to change my gender it would be very emotional and very painful. I don't imagine any doctor is giving out puberty blockers on a whim or that any parent choses this route for their child without serious advice. I have friends who are mothers to Trans children, and I know how they struggle to do the right thing. A stranger with an axe to grind on the internet cannot be the deciding voice.

What you've read about me isn't the whole truth but I've been guilty of letting myself down. In Narcotics Anonymous, the first question they ask is, 'What you are going to do about your problem?'. Like the Joni lyric, 'It all comes down to you'.

# EPILOGUE

I decided **to do acting lessons about four**
years ago after a live show where I thought I was a bit
disconnected. I was looking for a confidence coach or
someone who could help me work on my stage presence.
I had two choices and luckily chose Charlie Walker-Wise
from RADA. Charlie has taught me acting methods and
because acting is about finding the truth it has turned
into therapy. I started reading Shakespeare and *The
Homecoming* by Harold Pinter. We did practices involving
breathwork, meditation and just getting out of my physical
comfort zone.

The sessions always start with a chat about what is going
on in my personal life and then get very involved. I call it
theatrical therapy because it has also helped me to deal with
my communication with Roy and Mikey. More Roy, because

we tend to bang heads over every decision in the band. Through my work with Charlie, I was able to understand that the way I think about Roy and Mikey is sometimes unhelpful. Even worse is the way I express my frustration, which is still no easier at times. I went into rehearsal one day and before going inside I removed my metaphorical cloak of disappointment.

Roy says I force things on him without warning, but I have become accustomed to his face pulling because I know that he doesn't like performing songs he was not involved with. PK says I can do what I want, but bullying people into performing something just doesn't work. I talked to Roy on a flight about it and we both promised to communicate better, but at Mikey's recently we were trying to write and I felt those feelings again. Sometimes you just can't change certain relationships. I need to decide what I perform on stage, and I want to transcend the nostalgia racket. I have hundreds of beautiful, catchy songs that will eventually piss on 'I'll Tumble 4 Ya', which I am no longer interested in singing. Everyone, it seems, is an expert on what the audience will accept. I argue that the audience should never dictate the art form.

Working with Charlie has helped with communication and while it's not perfect it is greatly improved. He gave me amazing advice about being on stage and how to expand the moment. Instead of focusing on my singing and worrying about the notes he suggested to take everything in. The rest of the band, the venue, the lights and of course the audience. Expand the moment and remember to always look forward. An audience responds best to confidence and through thinking differently I have become more at ease on stage. I joke, 'I feel like I'm in my living room but better dressed.' I look at the audience now and talk to them and make them laugh. I'm sometimes a bit of a stand-up comedian.

In the past I would always be wound up and anxious before a show but now I'm chanting, meeting friends, stretching, doing yoga and getting loose. I mix my EFT tapping with stretching and I tell myself, 'Tonight will be amazing, I am connected.'

Bringing mindfulness to performing has been so powerful. I try to bring it to everything I do. Even making a cup of coffee. Just like my spiritual hero Eckhart Tolle who has helped me conquer meditation. I sit, close my eyes, breath slowly and every time my mind wanders, I ask myself. 'I wonder what my next thought will be.' It's a brilliant way to clear your thoughts. I listen to guided meditations by Alan Watts who is genius, and Ram Dass.

I was hoping to work with Charlie before doing *Peter Pan* at Christmas 2023 and *Moulin Rouge* on Broadway in 2024. Lots of people are snobby about pantomime and I was until I was approached and offered a small fortune. The last few years I have not turned down any well-paid work and I know that I can bring some proper fun to the role of Captain Hook. I never do anything solely for the money but it's a good incentive and I like to make sure no one is disappointed. I love what I do. I don't really think of it as a job but I try to be professional when I'm being well-paid.

I will be a bit Leigh Bowery and a bit Alan Rickman. Plus, there might be another book. I like to take myself out of my comfort zone and I know it's a cliché, but my motto is always, 'Enough moments and you have a life.' I'm afraid the impact the court case had on my finances has meant making different decisions, but I always commit to what I do and suck every bit of joy out of it. I aim to be the best pirate ever. Captain Off the Hook. I'm supposed to be doing it with Dorit, but right now who knows if she will turn up. Dorit in Blackpool would be a hoot.

It was actually while I was working with Charlie that I came across The Three Principles, which I've spoken about a lot throughout this book. It's really just another way of looking at how you think. Mikey Craig's beautiful Italian wife Liliana teaches The Three Principles, and I heard her discussing it at dinner. 'I want in,' I said, 'Can we do a session,' and not long after we sat in my garden for two hours and I listened. In all I did about six two-hours sessions and I think I got it quickly. Of course, I am guilty of overthinking the principles which are 'Mind, Thought and Consciousness' but I can truly say that it has transformed the way I live. The practice was summoned by a man called Sydney Banks who was a welder. He challenged traditional psychology and therapy and insisted there are easier ways to look at and think about everything. Turns out he was right, and I found myself going back to Eckhart Tolle's wonderful book *The Power of Now* and realised I had missed so much.

I'm not the ideal person to explain the principles but it works on the basis that most of what you insist is real, you are making up. Your regular thinking can be like a hornet's nest with thoughts flying around incessantly but you can pull it down to somewhere lower like your gut and you might find a different perspective. Pausing before you respond is key and carrying rage around with you is counterproductive. It's why I can say for sure that I do not hate Jon or anyone. Even Awful Cauldron or McKinky knickers. Hate is a headache, and it gives you crow's feet. If I had been able to access this practice maybe I would have never fallen out with Jon.

I had started my sessions with Lili shortly before the mediation with Jon and his army of lawyers. I sadly lost my temper and was devastated. I called Lili to say, 'I fucked up' but she said, 'Give it a few days and you will feel very different'. In the end, I did feel different.

In the end it was down to a lack of communication like most things are. Because of my close relationship with PK and Dorit, I have watched the way shows like *The Real*

*Housewives of Beverly Hills* swallow each housewife and spit them out. It wrecks marriages and drives people to booze and pills. It's very *Valley of the Dolls* pretending to be *Little House on the Prairie*. Look at Kanye and Kim or Kim and everyone. You can appear to have everything, but joy cannot be bought at Cartier or Vuitton. The true joy of life is in the mundane. The smile of a stranger, even better, the smile of a handsome stranger but you can get happier. There's nothing wrong with stuff, stuff is great if you can afford it but question if the stuff you crave is the stuff you really need. To laugh with those you love and not have to explain yourself. To sit in silence or to gossip but know what gossip is. Talking about others is a great way of not looking at yourself. I hope I have done both.

Love you, Big Nose.

# ACKNOWLEDGEMENTS

Much like putting on a show, writing an autobiography takes many people working away behind the scenes, without whom it simply could not happen.

So thank you to my team – PK, Tiffany, Christine, Sadie, Dean, Mykey O, Hamilton, Benny D, Shoshanna and Ben; to my bandmates, Roy and Mikey; to Lili and Charli; to my friends and all of my fans; to Spencer, my co-writer, and to Bonnier, my publishers.

I feel very fortunate to have some wonderful people in my life, far too many to name here. You know who you are!

Love, G x

Spencer Bright is the co-writer of *Karma*. He also co-wrote Boy George's first autobiography, *Take It Like a Man*. He worked in Fleet Street for many years writing for multiple publications, notably as a staff writer on the *Evening Standard* and feature writer and rock critic for the *Daily Mail*. He is the author of books on music, Soho and the Holocaust.

Bright's acknowledgments are: to Theresa McLoughlin for riding to childcare rescue; my transcribers Hilary Bright and Sue Banks, and also Hilary for holding the fort; Georgina Bright for life support and techno rescue; my editor, Ciara Lloyd for her guidance and all-hours unflappability; Tiffany Austin for her calming presence and keeping the dots joined up; and to my everything, Gráinne, and darling sons, Dáithí and Fionn.